Wunderkind:
The Reputation of Carson McCullers, 1940–1990

Judith Giblin James

Wunderkind

The Reputation of Carson McCullers, 1940–1990

CAMDEN HOUSE

Copyright © 1995 by
CAMDEN HOUSE, INC.

Published by Camden House, Inc.
Drawer 2025
Columbia, SC 29202 USA

Printed on acid-free paper.
Binding materials are chosen for strength and
durability.

ISBN:1–879751–88–7

Library of Congress Cataloging-in-Publication Data

James, Judith Giblin, 1945–
    Wunderkind : the reputation of Carson McCullers, 1940-1990 /
Judith Giblin James.
        p.   cm. -- (Studies in English & American literature,
linguistics, and culture. Literary criticism in perspective)
    Includes bibliographical references and index.
    ISBN 1-879751-88-7 (alk. paper)
    1. McCullers, Carson, 1917-1967--Criticism and interpretation-
-History.   2. Women and literature--Southern States--History--20th
century.   3. Criticism--United States--History--20th century.
4. Southern States--In literature.   I. Title.   II. Series: Studies
in English and American literature, linguistics, and culture
(Unnumbered).   Literary criticism in perspective.
PS3525.A1772Z69   1995
813' .52--dc20   95-23464
                                                              CIP

For Faye Giblin

Contents

Acknowledgments

I am pleased to acknowledge the intelligent and conscientious efforts of graduate research assistants Paul Price, who helped launch this book, and Diane Russo, who helped finish it. Patricia Armstrong's graciousness and reliability gave me the gift of time in its final stages. I am also grateful to Ben Franklin and Jim Hardin for editorial and collegial support and to friends and family for their encouragement, most especially that of Mary Crawford, Nancy Thompson, Shannon and Olivia James, and their father, Glenn, who shares everything. This book is dedicated with love and gratitude to my mother.

Preface

CARSON MCCULLERS'S REPUTATION both confirms and defies the cherished label with which she began her career in her first published work, "Wunderkind" (1936). Enthusiasm for *The Heart Is a Lonely Hunter* and its youthful author, barely three months past her twenty-third birthday when it was published in 1940, seemed to confirm her family's estimate of McCullers as a prodigy. The five novels that comprise her major fiction were conceived by age twenty-five and all but one published before she was thirty. Then, the decline. The careers of wunderkinder are expected to plummet from the peak of "acute limited excellence" that F. Scott Fitzgerald described, and understandably so. In McCullers's case, crippling illness and the relative financial security derived from her successful Broadway adaptation of *The Member of the Wedding* (1950, published in 1951) diminished her creative energies and delayed further publication for almost a decade. Her second play, *The Square Root of Wonderful* (1957, published in 1958), and her final novel, *Clock Without Hands* (1961), were disappointments, if not failures. Both have been out of print for almost thirty years.

Sustained popular interest in her other works has been bolstered by the perennial success of *The Member of the Wedding* as both a film (1951) and a play in community theaters, as well as by film adaptations of *Reflections in a Golden Eye* (1967), *The Heart Is a Lonely Hunter* (1968), and *The Ballad of the Sad Café* (1992). The publication of previously uncollected work in *The Mortgaged Heart* (1971), her collected stories (1987), and Virginia Spencer Carr's revealingly detailed biography *The Lonely Hunter* (1975) provided occasions for public recollection of her life and career.

Critical interest, however, has fluctuated with the times, rising or falling in response to cultural forces and following the ascent or decline of particular methods of literary inquiry. My account of McCullers's reputation among scholars and literary critics inside and outside the academy will, I hope, usefully demonstrate the dynamic tension between texts and their audiences over a relatively short period. Fifty years of McCullers criticism, viewed minutely and whole, provides a testament to the richness and power of her best work and shows the diversity of aesthetic response within this time.

Such a view of McCullers criticism does not accord with earlier assessments which complain of an "unfortunate consensus" in discussions of

her work (Carr and Millichap 1983, 319). One of the first students of her
reputation observes, "The loneliness of McCullers' characters and her
tragic view of love are commonplaces argued again and again in the critical literature, and her tendency to use music symbolically and freaks rep-
resentatively has been noted with wearying repetitiveness" (Kiernan 1976,
98). These accounts reflect the temporary but important dominance in the
study of McCullers of New Critical methodology that was already in decline by the mid-1970s. Although the New Critical "consensus" continues
to exert an influence on the direction of McCullers scholarship, other
methods of examining and valuing literature – methods which helped
shape McCullers's aims as a writer in the 1930s and 1940s – have re-
emerged in recent decades and have been applied with considerable success to her fiction.

Like other volumes in the Literary Criticism in Perspective series, this
study traces McCullers's literary reputation by recording chronologically
the trends and prominent issues in commentary on her work and by examining the critical assumptions which support them. My purpose has
been to illuminate, where possible, the origin of such assumptions in social
history and in literary and intellectual politics. The first chapter gives an
overview of the crosscurrents at work in shaping McCullers's reputation,
in establishing and modifying the New Critical consensus. The next traces
the shifts in critical opinion about her first novel against the changes, decade by decade, in the makeup and politics of the professoriate as well as
against the conditions of postwar life in the larger culture. The second
chapter, then, describes in detail the origins and decline and, occasionally,
resurgence of the several critical paradigms by which readers have understood her works. Subsequent chapters draw on arguments elaborated in
the first two in treating the history of responses to each of the remaining
novels in chronological order. Her plays and her short fiction are treated
in two composite chapters, and a concluding chapter forecasts trends in
McCullers criticism based on the response to her work since 1990.

A list of works cited, arranged chronologically from 1940 to 1994, is
divided into three parts: (1) a primary bibliography of the works treated
in this study; (2) a list of secondary works, from newspaper reviews to
book-length studies, that discuss McCullers and her writing; and (3) a list
of secondary works that pertain to the history and theory of literary criticism or reception studies but do not discuss McCullers. An index rounds
out the volume.

Readers should note that editorial policy for this series mandates silent
changes in quoted passages – e.g., in the adapting of initial capitals or
lowercase letters to fit syntactical context – and does not indicate where

quotations have been entered or ended in midsentence. Typographical errors within quotations have been corrected except where the errors themselves are relevant to the history of a work's interpretation or bear on the overall reliability of the critic quoted. Italicized words or phrases within quotations occur in the source text unless otherwise noted.

1: The Shaping of Carson McCullers's Reputation

PUBLICITY PHOTOGRAPHS OF Carson McCullers in the 1940s help explain, and may have encouraged, the protective enthusiasm of her earliest critics. The wary young face on the dust jacket of *The Heart Is a Lonely Hunter* (1940), the round-cheeked mischievous smile in a famous book-signing portrait for that novel, and the fragile reticence in a tuck-chinned photograph of the same period, but printed on the dust jacket of *The Member of the Wedding* in 1946, suggest the youth and vulnerability her first readers found compelling. In each portrait she wears limp, bowl-cut bangs and a man's oversized white shirt, which became her trademark in New York literary circles. She is iconographically the wunderkind, like a colt, both confident and cautious. In only one of the photographs does she appear lighthearted.

The reviews of her first novels focused on her youth and the relative magnitude of her achievement. The *New York Times Book Review* headline pronounces *Hunter* "A Remarkable First Novel of Lonely Lives" (Feld 1940); the *New Yorker* says, "Pretty Good for Twenty-Two," her age at the time it was written (Fadiman 1940); and *Time* lauds *Reflections in a Golden Eye* (1941) as a "Masterpiece at 24." The reviews of *Hunter* brought McCullers immediately to the attention of New York writers and intellectuals, and, having moved from the South to a Greenwich Village apartment shortly after its publication, she was on hand to reap the personal and professional benefits.

Within two months she had established a connection with *Harper's Bazaar* that would prove formative. Her friendship with the magazine's literary editor, George Davis, resulted in the timely serialization of *Reflections* in its October and November issues prior to its publication as a book the next February, on Valentine's Day in 1941. Davis also introduced her to an array of influential friends and installed her as the centerpiece of a talented assemblage with whom he shared the house he rented at 7 Middagh Street in Brooklyn. The occupants of and visitors to this house – among them W. H. Auden, Louis MacNeice, Janet Flanner, Klaus Mann, Richard Wright, Denis de Rougemont, Jane and Paul Bowles – provided entrée to several eccentric and influential coteries, out of which at various points over the next two decades would come helpful allegiances. Moreover, the mutually beneficial association with *Harper's Bazaar* continued with the publication of *The Ballad of the Sad Café* (1948), part 1 of *The Member of the Wedding* (1946), and the arresting story "A Tree. A Rock. A Cloud." (1942). A similarly sustaining relationship developed after 1942 with *Mademoiselle,* where Davis had relocated, although McCullers published less significant pieces there. Her sister, Margarita Gachet Smith, became assistant fiction editor of the magazine in 1944.

McCullers's identification with *Harper's Bazaar, Mademoiselle,* and, to a lesser extent, *Vogue* (in which she published two essays in the 1940s) and the *New Yorker* (where three stories appeared) served to boost her popular reputation but may have damaged her standing with critics because it linked her with a suspect bohemian elite. Leslie Fiedler describes the *Harper's Bazaar* circle and a group associated with the *Partisan Review* as "competing 'academies'" of writers who profitably devoted themselves to specialized audiences rather than maturely commanding the mainstream. Fiedler, himself a *Partisan Review* writer, ascribes to the competing group "a new sort of sensibility, defined by a taste for *haute couture,* classical ballet, baroque opera, the rites and vestments of Catholicism – and above all for a kind of literature at once elegantly delicate and bitterly grotesque" (1955, 201). Fiedler identifies McCullers as the "most important writer of this group" and Truman Capote as "the most typical," connecting them with a "kind of fiction often merely chic behind its pretense of being subtle and advanced" and complaining of the apolitical, or antipolitical, cast they brought to bohemia (202).

Fiedler's remarks rely on crucially negative assumptions about a predominantly female audience: "*Harper's Bazaar* is, of course, not primarily a literary magazine at all, but an elegant fashion magazine for women, read not only by those who can afford the goods it advertises but by many who cannot and who participate vicariously in its world of values, picking it up on the table of a beauty-parlor waiting room." Fiedler was also the first publicly to voice a further association between an apolitical female elite and a degraded sexuality, by calling this new sensibility "quite frankly a homosexual one [that] appeals profoundly to certain rich American women with cultural aspirations" (201). He was, of course, correct in identifying the explicit and implicit homosexual content of McCullers's fiction, and he was, significantly, one of only a few early critics to do so, making a contribution that will be taken up shortly. However, his categories rely on and perpetuate unfortunate associations of women, homosexuality, and "delicate," apolitical fiction with childishness. The reader hardly has to wonder where the *Harper's Bazaar* writers will register on the scale Fiedler constructs in the essay's title, "Adolescence and Maturity in the American Novel."

McCullers's identification with a narrow range of concerns, limited subject matter, a single theme, arose in part from the defining conditions of gender, region, and sexuality. Because she was female, southern, and – in her photographs and her fiction – at least mildly defiant of heterosexual norms, McCullers fell prey to the prejudgment that such conditions, automatically precluding scope and relevance, fatally restrict her worth. Another factor in the constellation which influenced the early shape of her reputation was the erosion of consciously ideological criticism in this period and the rise of formalist aesthetics. McCullers wrote four novels in which the politics of small societies – southern towns, an army base – reflect and comment on the larger world of the United States at midcentury. The first and last, *Hunter* and *Clock Without Hands* (1961), are dramatic commentaries on race and class persecution, these large injustices counterpointed with the tragic impotence and isolation of individual lives. In the other two, *Reflections* and *The Member of the Wedding,* restrictive social hierarchies provide the oppressive background against which trapped individuals rebel. Only *The Ballad of the Sad Café* fails to gesture toward the problems of the world at large. Yet even in it, poverty and wage slavery undergird the questions of power in individual relationships.

The social content of McCullers's work has been little or only sporadically noticed. The treatment of her first and last novels will serve to illustrate a pattern of response dictated in large measure by a changing climate of critical expectations. It is true that McCullers's focus is principally on the crippling existential and spiritual conditions which create human unhappiness and only secondarily – or, as a consequence – on the causes of social discord. But climactic moments in both novels – labor agitation leading to a race riot in *Hunter* and a racially motivated bombing in *Clock* – seem to require explanation in political terms. In 1940, after disillusionment over the 1939 nonaggression and trade pacts between the Soviet Union and Germany had diminished the intellectual force of American Marxist criticism, reviewers spent little time analyzing the societal implications of *Hunter,* even though in an interview less than a month after its publication McCullers had called the work "an ironic parable of fascism" (Paterson 1940, 11). Only a few commentators touched on the political dimensions of the novel, and then typically dismissively or punitively, averring that any novel conceived in 1936 would be bound to carry a proletarian taint or suggesting that her picture of mill-town miseries "conform[s] entirely to a tired formula" she would do well to abandon (Putzel 1940, 61). One of the most perceptive reviewers was Richard Wright, whose *Native Son* was published in the same year as *Hunter* and who would the following year become a friend and housemate of McCullers in George Davis's home in Brooklyn Heights. In an August 1940 issue of the *New Republic,* Wright says the novel's "picture of loneliness, death, accident, insanity, fear, mob violence and terror is perhaps the most desolate that has so far come from the South." He is struck, moreover, by "the astonishing humanity that enables a white writer, for the first time in Southern fiction, to handle Negro characters with as much ease and justice as those of her own race" (195). But Wright's recognition of the novel's social content recedes before his admiration of its formal properties. For Wright, McCullers follows in the modernist tradition of stylistic experimentation, and he recognizes in her work as well a mythic dimension.

For most of three decades discussion of *Hunter* bowed to the aesthetic orthodoxies to which John Crowe Ransom's *The New Criticism* (1941) gave its name. Concern with the novel's unity and its complex ironies took precedence over the issue of its social realism until Joseph R. Millichap in 1971, fresh from a revisionary dissertation on McCullers, revived Wright's implicit question about the importance of the work's naturalistic elements. McCullers's description of the novel as a "parable of fascism" was not explored in detail until Nancy B. Rich's 1977 rereading of it against the background of world conflict between democracy and totalitarianism in the 1930s.

The long-awaited *Clock Without Hands* appeared in September 1961, four months after the civil rights demonstrators known as Freedom Riders sustained bloody attacks by white vigilantes in Alabama. The novel ends with a southern judge's senile rage on the day in 1954 the Supreme Court mandated school integration. The most plentifully reviewed of McCullers's novels, it was – surprisingly, given the climate – frequently described in phrases interchangeable with those applied to *Ballad* a decade earlier: "Carson McCullers Tells Parable of Loneliness" (Sherman 1961, 6); "Loneliness Continues to Intrigue Southern Writer" (Cheney 1961, 23), according to the headlines. Even former Marxist critic Granville Hicks, writing for the *Saturday Review,* focuses on the work's "familiar themes . . . identity, the meaning of life, the nature of love" (1961, 14). Although he acknowledges that "In an important sense this is a novel about the race problem" and that McCullers "hates the casual brutality that prejudice engenders," Hicks emphasizes that "her real concern is with subtler kinds of corruption," by which he means "the mysterious [because often 'unsuitable'] operations of love" (15).

Other reviewers did make more of McCullers's treatment of racism. Nick Aaron Ford, surveying for *Phylon* "Significant Belles-Lettres by and about Negroes Published in 1961," calls *Clock* "the most significant novel of the year concerning race relations" (1962, 130), but his praise was atypical. More often reviewers discussed racial themes in oblique terms or — as with reviews of *Hunter* — with the wish that McCullers had not strayed into "social comment that is very close to propaganda — which truth doesn't need and neither does art" (Sullivan 1961, 56). Meanwhile, after an early effort to read *Clock* in familiar terms as a "baffled search for an identifiable Self" (Emerson 1962, 15), academic criticism tended to ignore this rich but uneven novel as a topic worth serious independent discussion, though it continued to be treated, and most often dismissed, in the comprehensive critical assessments of McCullers that began to proliferate in the 1960s. Of these, only one of the most recent devotes proportional attention to the role of social criticism in the work (McDowell 1980).

The question of why McCullers's concern with social conflict and repression has been so sparsely or belatedly recognized may be answered in two ways. The first is to assert that McCullers does subordinate realism to symbolism. To marvel that in *Reflections,* for instance, "not even the horse is normal" (Evans 1965a, 80) is to acknowledge that a symbolic layer of character distortion calculated for its extremity takes precedence over realistic evocations of place or social interaction. Individuals are always more important in McCullers's fiction than institutions. Therefore, it is possible to argue that, in the main, the critical response to her work accurately reflects this emphasis. But it is hard to think so. The general and longstanding failure to explore the connection she establishes between individual and institutionalized cruelties is a product of a tendency to see what we want to see or, more precisely, only what a complex combination of cultural forces makes us capable of seeing. McCullers consistently articulated an intricate fusion of psychological and social determinism in an era in retreat from literary naturalism. Her theories about love, even when stated most pessimistically, were read for most of three decades (and often continue to be read) as Platonic truisms of universal scope and significance. We can only wonder what might have been made of her fiction — in many respects the product of the Depression decade — had it been published prior to 1939. Or we might wonder as well about the reception of *Clock* had it stood free of the expectations developed by two decades of reading McCullers as an apolitical Gothicist.

McCullers's treatment of adolescence provides another gauge of the evolution of critical opinion. Three of her novels directly examine adolescence as a fertile period of creativity and confusion in the lives of Mick Kelly of *Hunter,* Frankie Addams of *Member,* and Jester Clane and Sherman Pew of *Clock.* Adolescence, in fact, may be said to constitute her principal subject from first to last, especially if we are willing to acknowledge the overgrown children of *Reflections* (Ellgee Williams and Anacleto) and *Ballad* (Miss Amelia and Cousin Lymon) as well as those of many of the stories.

If adolescence was invented in this country after the Civil War, it began to figure prominently in our literature after World War I and was discovered by literary critics after World War II. A cluster of critical works announced and dissected "the cult of adolescence" in the 1950s and 1960s. Distinctive among them are essays by Leslie A. Fiedler and Ihab H. Hassan, who reach opposite conclusions. Fiedler implicates McCullers in the pattern of disguised biracial homosexuality he finds throughout American literature. Frankie Addams and Berenice Sadie Brown reproduce the relationship between Huck and Jim: "This time the Father-Slave-Beloved is converted into the figure of a Mother-Sweetheart-Servant, but remains still, of course, satisfactorily black" (1955, 149). Furthermore, he condemns the "homosexual-gothic" impulses of writers he identifies as "the McCullers school" or the *"Harper's Bazaar* Faulknerians" whose characters, like Mick Kelly and Frankie Addams, unconsciously "project the invert's exclusion from the family" and a fear of heterosexuality that is "easily translated into the child's bafflement before weddings or honeymoons or copulation itself" (1958, 26–27). To Fiedler, for whom literature and culture are virtually synonymous, the adolescent flight from adulthood is cultural suicide.

Although Hassan shares many of Fiedler's assumptions, he sees the emergent emphasis on adolescence in literature as progressive rather than regressive, a shift of interest from innocence to the threshold of experience. McCullers and other novelists as diverse as Saul Bellow, James Purdy, and J. D. Salinger use adolescent characters as registers of radical protest against midcentury mass society. The adolescent provides a likely guise for the "rebel-victim," whom Hassan calls "the central and controlling image of recent fiction" (1962, 3). McCullers's portraits of adolescents as grotesques (another version of the rebel-victim) increase her representative value for Hassan. That Mick Kelly and Frankie Addams are female, unlike most other adolescent protagonists Hassan treats, makes little difference to him or to others who focused on the trend. James William Johnson, in delineating characteristics of fictional adolescents, does notice that the trait of sexual confusion is more often to be found "when the protagonist is a girl" (1959, 6), but he resists analyzing why this might be so.

Not until the 1980s, after a decade of social debate over the roles of women in private and public life, did critics focus on McCullers's adolescents as female, rather than as deviants or as extensions (and then fre-

quently of an inferior sort) of universalized male experience. Barbara A.
White (1985) views "conflict over gender identity" as the principal theme
in novels of female adolescence (20). McCullers's heroines are victims less
of spiritual isolation than of social exclusion; they rebel – consciously and
unconsciously – at the diminished state their growth to womanhood por-
tends. In this reading, the meaning of Frankie Addams's distress at growing into a too-tall freak is not an undifferentiated fear of isolation but
rather "the horror of being an *ugly woman*" (93), a paradoxical revulsion at
yet fear of failing in the feminine role.

Gendered readings such as White's and the more elaborate efforts of
Louise Westling (1980, 1982, 1985) altered our understanding of McCullers's use of the grotesque and her place in southern literature. Westling
identifies a distinctly female tradition in the works of McCullers, Eudora
Welty, and Flannery O'Connor that defies Fiedler's invidious description
of them as a group of "distaff Faulknerians" who have emasculated the
purer and more powerful southern literary lineage. For Westling and
Linda Huf (1983), Mick Kelly and Frankie Addams represent talented artists in revolt against the necessity of growing up female. This view made
possible a radical rereading of each novel's final chapter in which the protagonists seem to conform to prescribed gender behavior. To see Mick's
and Frankie's final feminine concessions as tragic capitulation rather than
acceptance or affirmation revealed for the first time a sustained and darkly
unified vision in these novels.

A similarly widened view of McCullers's male adolescents has occurred in the twenty-five years since the publication of *Clock,* when Sherman Pew and Jester Clane were seen uncomplexly as southern
stereotypes. Margaret B. McDowell (1980) demonstrates the intricate
bonds between the seventeen year olds, both mocked and exploited by
Judge Clane and the racist abuses he represents. However, a full-fledged
analysis of the two youths as rebels against their gender, as well as the
strictures of race and class, remains to be done.

The influence of New Criticism abetted several formative tendencies
in McCullers studies. The first is the desire to see her writing as apolitical,
timeless, universal. New Criticism might as easily have been called
"ontological criticism," as Malcolm Cowley has suggested (1954, 12).
Ethical, moral, and social dimensions of literature were subordinated to
formal properties and patterns under its influence. The concept of theme
was most typically confined to statements of derivable ironies or paradox
rather than framed in an older fashion as meaning arising from patterns of
dramatic conflict. A second tendency is the emphasis on the poetic features of McCullers's fiction. Because New Critical analysis grew out of

and functions most memorably as a response to poetry, it encouraged the recognition of poetic elements in fiction. That stylistic excellence is the proper gauge of greatness in the American novel is expressed as a tenet of faith in Mark Schorer's influential essay "Technique as Discovery" (1948). Discussions of her style as poetic or lyrical appeared in abundance during the first three decades of McCullers criticism but have been less numerous in the last twenty years, as a consequence, we may presume, of a shift in critical categories and interests.

A third tendency is the increased interest in McCullers's work as a species of southern literature, an interest driven in part by New Critics' ties to the South and especially by their investment in William Faulkner. If Faulkner's ascendancy – particularly his elevation over Hemingway – was culturally motivated by the cold war "need to find an important American *nationalist* writer" (Schwartz 1988, 39, emphasis added), McCullers's reputation may have been diminished by the same forces. Critics in the 1940s often ranked McCullers above Faulkner in talent and interest, but after he received the 1950 Nobel Prize for literature, to do so would have seemed absurd. Leslie Fiedler's frequent jibes in *Partisan Review* and elsewhere at *"Harper's Bazaar* Faulknerians," "distaff Faulknerians," and even "epicene Faulknerians" may have been less outrageous as a critical gesture than, at base, a rather banal and predictable consequence of advocating one writer's preeminence at the expense of all others.

Carson McCullers's reputation offers particularly fertile ground for an inquiry into the fluctuation of critical fashion over five decades. This is so because of the adventitious conjunction of three facts about her life and work. The first is her gender, the second is her regional affiliation, and the third is a point of chronology. The publication of her first novel in 1940 and her last in 1961 positioned her on either side of the international catastrophe that encourages us to divide considerations of the American novel into pre- and postwar eras. McCullers, as a result, draws approval or disapproval in proportion as she satisfies critical generalizations about these eras. Is her vision social or intensely private? In what proportions does she mix realism, determinism, existentialism?

She has been read as the last proletarian, a modernist, and a proto-postmodernist. And if the praise for her work has fallen somewhat from the pinnacle on which the wunderkind initially found herself, it is also true that the quality and variety of critical methods her work has invited have not diminished in recent decades and have, if anything, been beneficially expanded. Whatever its flaws, the current critical climate has produced wise and richly considered responses to McCullers's works.

2: *The Heart Is a Lonely Hunter* (1940)

> *Genius is ageless — and here one faces nothing less.*
>
> (Edward D. McDonald 1940)

MCCULLERS'S STUNNING FIRST novel is characteristic of wunderkinder among literary artists. Such works are frequently autobiographical, rich and overreaching in their display of talent, and difficult to repeat. Had she written *The Member of the Wedding* first, Carson McCullers would fit this pattern. The novel she did write was in many respects all the more remarkable for its relative lack of autobiographical resonance. The adolescent Mick Kelly is one of six well-crafted major characters and an assortment of effectively drawn minor ones, all, apart from Mick, adults of some psychological complexity and challenge.

Developed from a series of preliminary sketches, vestiges of which can be traced in the posthumously published stories in *The Mortgaged Heart* (1971), *The Heart Is a Lonely Hunter* explores the relationships of a thirteen-year-old tomboy, an itinerant labor agitator, a respected Negro physician, and the proprietor of an all-night café with each other and with the focal character, John Singer, a deaf-mute whose only emotional tie is to another mute, Antonapoulos, who has been consigned to an asylum after episodes of degeneracy. One by one Mick Kelly, Jake Blount, Dr. Benedict Mady Copeland, and, to a lesser extent, Biff Brannon believe they have found in Singer the source of what they need: someone who understands Mick's passion for music; an enlightened sympathizer with Jake's radical doctrines; a wise and noble friend of the Negro race; and a fascinating human puzzle for Biff to contemplate. As their investment in Singer builds, he smiles and nods accommodatingly, and writes to Antonapoulos that he endures their talk but does not understand it. "I write to you," he says, "because I think you will understand." The design of these relationships occurs to Singer in a dream. Antonapoulos kneels naked at the top of a pyramid, gazing at an object he holds in his hands. Singer kneels behind him; below Singer are the other four and behind them the townspeople. The pyramid collapses. Singer awakes, terrified. When he learns on a visit to the asylum that Antonapoulos has died, Singer shoots himself, fatally. In the final of three parts, the characters are shown a month after Singer's death. Dr. Copeland, dying of tuberculosis, is taken in by his wife's relatives, his dream of racial justice, the strong, true purpose of his life, bitterly extinguished. In an explosive and fatal race riot, Jake Blount fights viciously, unleashing against both blacks and whites the fury he more customarily turns against himself; at fourteen, a school dropout, a clerk at Woolworth's, Mick feels cheated of her dreams and can barely muster hope that it all must have been "some good"; alone at his counter, Biff the observer experiences a visionary moment that opens his spirit and quiets his fears – until he realizes he is staring at his own face in the glass.

Edward D. McDonald's enthusiasm for McCullers's genius was shared by the majority of initial reviewers. The rush to praise the twenty-three-year-old writer included paeans to her novel's intensity, compassion, and originality in pioneering a "new American spiritual country" (Fadiman 1940, 69). She was compared favorably to Ernest Hemingway, John Steinbeck, and Thomas Wolfe and called greater than Erskine Caldwell and Faulkner. Rose Feld, in a highly influential assessment in the *New York Times Book Review,* also notes the young author's surprising force and poise: McCullers "writes with a sweep and certainty that are overwhelming. From the opening page, brilliant in its establishment of mood, character and suspense, the book takes hold of the reader" (1940, 6). Not all reviewers, however, thought the novel equal to its author's promise. Lewis Gannett calls it "a strange and uneven book" (1940, 13); Robert Littell suggests its thematic focus is too narrow (1940, x); but, surely, the reviewer for *Time* had occasion to regret the breezy dismissal of McCullers as a writer "never in one glint verbally original" ("First Novel" 1940, 90).

The English reviews were frequently sharper in both praise and blame. With a skepticism that proved typical of its treatment of McCullers, the *Times Literary Supplement* said that *Hunter* lacks "any real imaginative power or distinction" ("In the Deep South" 1943, 153). Other London reviews were strongly favorable. The *Sunday Times* pronounced it "remarkable" (Straus 1943, 3); the *Observer* called McCullers "a writer to watch" (Pryce-Jones 1943, 3); the *New Statesman and Nation* said that she "writes with a bitter compassion which gives deep humanity to her characters" (Toynbee 1943, 292). More often than their American counterparts, the English reviews took notice of the social world of the novel, its "industrial underpaid workers, and slum houses and mean cafés" (Spring 1943, 2).

A notable exception among U.S. reviews of *Hunter* in this respect is Richard Wright's perceptive tribute in the *New Republic.* But he is less intent on praising the accuracy of McCullers's portrait of the Depression-era South than in setting the novel within the modernist tradition. He identifies the novel's mythic dimension; praises its narrative technique, especially the intimate third-person sections for each character (the technique Wright used to stunning effect with *Native Son's* Bigger Thomas); and gauges her stature among the Moderns he sees as her forebears: "Miss McCullers' picture of loneliness, death, accident, insanity, fear, mob violence and terror is perhaps the most desolate that has so far come from the South. Her quality of despair is unique and individual; and it seems to me more natural and authentic than that of Faulkner. Her groping characters live in a world more completely lost than any Sherwood Anderson ever dreamed of. And she recounts incidents of death and attitudes of stoicism in sentences whose neutrality makes Hemingway's terse prose seem warm and partisan by comparison" (1940, 195). Despite their verisimilitude, "the naturalistic incidents of which the book is compounded seem to be of no importance; one has the feeling that any string of typical actions would have served the author's purpose as well, for the value of such writing lies not so much in what is said as in the angle of vision from which life is seen." In his most quoted observation, Wright praises "the astonishing humanity that enables a white writer, for the first time in Southern fiction, to handle Negro characters with as much ease and justice as those of her own race. This cannot be accounted for stylistically or politically; it seems to stem from an attitude toward life which enables Miss McCullers to rise above the pressures of her environment and embrace white and black humanity in one sweep of apprehension and tenderness." He concludes, "In the conventional sense, this is not so much a novel as a projected mood, *a state of mind poetically objectified in words,* . . . devoid of pettiness and sentimentality" (195, italics added).

Wright could not have registered the prevailing critical discourse more precisely than in the allusion to T. S. Eliot's concept of an objective correlative, locus of the New Critics' verbal icon and an article of faith among the academic critics who began to take notice of McCullers after a decade of extraordinary productivity and high visibility on the part of the young writer. For good or ill, the pinnacle of McCullers's success in the early 1950s coincided with the postwar expansion of the professoriate, the emergence of the first generation of critics educated under the GI Bill, and the full flowering of the age of criticism begun by the, by then, old New Critics of the 1940s. What Virginia Spencer Carr and Joseph R. Millichap (1983, 319) call the "unfortunate consensus" in McCullers criticism was shaped in this era by an interpretive paradigm which yokes the technical strategies of high modernism (irony, paradox, multivalent symbolism, structural complexity) with the conservative ideologies of southern agrarianism (veneration of the past and moral uniformity, a preference for allusiveness, abstraction, universality, and sameness above anomaly, particularity, idiosyncracy, and difference). Repeatedly, *Hunter* is described in the "epitomizing language" that Carol and Richard Ohmann have demonstrated "takes [a] novel quite out of real history and makes it an eternal story" (1976, 27). Wright's suggestion that McCullers transcends culturally specific experience and embraces a universal – and undifferentiated – "white and black humanity" qualifies as "epitomizing language" by that definition. More objectionable examples of inflated and pointless abstraction are not hard to find: "The inclusion of a pair of mutes in the novel is not morbidity on the part of the author, as has been frequently charged; it is instead a brilliant symbolization of man's condition" (Phillips 1964c, 61); or "In a sense the theme of her novels is violation – the ravaging of the spirit by a cruel universe" (62). This last is a strangely inadequate formulation, given the near rapes, the stalkings, the threatened and completed suicides, the attempted castrations, the deaths by gunshot, etc., that occur across her fiction.

The "epitomizing" impulse was challenged in its own time, twenty years before the Ohmanns took up the cause. Writing of the "Higher and Higher Criticism," Maxwell Geismar indicts New Critical formalism:

> What strikes one finally about this whole critical tendency is how completely it reflects, in the spiritual area, the worst aspects of the American society it has repudiated.
>
> It *is* that society – with its emphasis on abstraction and techniques, rather than human values; with its conspicuous consumption of scholarship and learning; with its mass-minded and "other-directed" stress on aesthetic concepts and laws; with its yearning for refinement and "culture" in art, at the expense of all vitality and life . . . . While the crucial and revolutionary issues of our time are being fought out in the dark, and the human race may be getting ready to be atomized, it almost seems that the real function of the New Criticism is to keep our best young intellectuals absorbed with their playthings, no matter what happens to the nation or the world. (1956; rpt. Geismar 1958, 32–33)

The paradigm that combines epitomizing high-mindedness with explications of style and structure prevailed at the moment when the first serious academic criticism of *Hunter* began. Occasioned by the stage success of *The Member of the Wedding* (1950) and Houghton Mifflin's consequent publication of an omnibus edition of McCullers's fiction, Dayton Kohler's "Carson McCullers: Variations on a Theme" (1951) offers the first sustained critical discussion of McCullers's work, focusing on the admirable stylistic and thematic unity of *Hunter* and her other novels, with the exception of *The Ballad of the Sad Café*. In assertions that correspond almost point-by-point to Wright's views a decade earlier, Kohler places McCullers in the company of Nathaniel Hawthorne, Herman Melville, and Sherwood Anderson, though her symbolism is more mythical than allegorical. She "has created a world of tragic reality, as violent as Dostoevski's, as richly symbolic as Kafka's, though unmistakably her own." Her imagination operates at once "on two levels – one real and dramatic, the other poetic and symbolic" (3). Kohler believes he is the first to identify "the thematic structure" of *Hunter,* using the phrase as it derives from musical composition: "Themes and character motifs appear early in the novel, only to be dropped and later resumed, so that the structure becomes one of introduction, repetition, variation, dissonances, unresolved harmonies. The design of the novel alone should have indicated to her first reviewers how far she had progressed beyond realistic reporting" (6). This last statement fixes the contrast between the initial reviews, wherein the novel's ties to a finite social world were at least acknowledged, and the prevailing critical strategies of the 1950s and 1960s that focused on overarching symbolic and structural patterns. Kohler consciously distances himself from the previous decade's concern with social realism, standing thereby in the forefront of a majority view that ignores, qualifies, or dismisses the novel's 1930s political context.

In an unrelentingly lyrical analysis, Jane Hart (1957) advances the consensus account of "the constant theme of human loneliness" in McCullers's fiction. Hart finds that the novelist's intricate and compassionate rendering of this theme elevates her above others in "the Gothic School of Southern writers unconsciously established by William Faulkner" (56, 53). "If she has used the grotesque it is because the loneliest of all human souls is found in the abnormal and deformed, the outward and manifest symbol of human separateness" (54). McCullers permits the lovers among her characters radiant moments of freedom from isolation: "They find truth, a moment of pure love, a sudden illumination" (58). But of the mutes Singer is the only lover. "Antonapoulos is obese, sensual, separate in his own fleshy, faraway world, a complacent Buddha-figure sublimely indifferent to all of Singer's impassioned and spiritual love" (55).

Frank Durham (1957) calls *Hunter* "an iconoclastic religious novel, ambitious, sensitive, vivid, and underlaid with the rebellion against tradition not unexpected in a precocious young woman of twenty-two" (499). Focusing on Singer's dream of a sacrificial pyramid, Durham describes the relationships among the principal characters as "an ironic religious allegory employed to reinforce the author's concept of the discreteness of human beings, not just from each other, but from God Himself" (494). Durham sees the retarded Greek deaf-mute Antonapoulos and John

Singer, the ascetic deaf-mute with a "Jewish face," as emblematic of pagan and Christian deities, each incapable of understanding, much less fulfilling those who idolize them. In adducing "an ironic religious allegory," Durham refocuses McCullers's troubling remark that she had intended "an ironic parable of fascism . . . presenting the spiritual rather than the political side of the phenomenon." Much of the criticism of this period can be measured by the extent to which it takes her statement seriously.

A high point of New Critical analysis of *Hunter* in the 1950s is Frank Baldanza's "Plato in Dixie" (1958), which propounds an influential thesis about a school of southern fiction noted for Platonic "parables on the nature of love." Carson McCullers and Truman Capote are the chief practitioners, writing novels and stories marked by the loneliness and "imperfection" of their characters, microcosmic settings, a bent toward fantasy and allegory, and "the theme of love as an absolute, abstract force that overrides all barriers of age, sex, time, and distance and that manifests itself in an endless variety of ways" (156). The influence of a "natural" Platonism explains "that curious tone of purely and absolutely spiritual love which grows out of a diffused and circumambient atmosphere of sexuality that never clearly manifests itself" (151). The grotesque deformity of many of their characters, in Baldanza's scheme, symbolically emphasizes "the worthlessness of the material realm" (154). The waste of love is a central proposition of *Hunter:* "Biff's nearly motherly devotion to Mick remains entirely repressed; on Antonapoulos' death, Mr. Singer shoots himself; but the most frantically frustrated are Dr. Copeland and Jake Blount, both of whom are constantly rejected and reviled for their burning need to help others on a large social scale. Blount, in fact, is a kind of debased Socrates" (157). Baldanza's case for McCullers's Platonism derives from her overtly philosophical propositions about love in "A Tree. A Rock. A Cloud." (1942) and *The Ballad of the Sad Café* (1943). His is the first of numerous claims that McCullers's fiction is explicable by these propositions. *Hunter,* however, proves resistant to Baldanza's best efforts because, as he acknowledges, "the 'timely,' realistic tradition of naturalism" will not disappear or, for his purposes, be reconciled with the Platonic parable (157).

Ihab H. Hassan (1959b), in advancing a thesis about the redemptive role of the victim in American literature, describes McCullers as a central figure among contemporary writers who identify loneliness as "a major symptom of evil" and the "stigma of all victims." Loneliness is "the absence of love" (143). Other writers examined include Paul Bowles, Truman Capote, James Purdy, Flannery O'Connor, Saul Bellow, and J. D. Salinger. McCullers is linked especially to Tennessee Williams, and is in fact his heir in portraying isolated characters as scapegoats and redeemers. Describing John Singer as "a disconsolate and somewhat tawdry Christ figure," Hassan says McCullers's "doctrine of love comes close to defining evil in Christian terms." The victim suggests "ultimate human isolation and reveals, at the same time, an inescapable social indictment. The idea acquires a religious significance when the victim is conceived both as scapegoat and redeemer." Singer suffers both "the demands made upon him by his frenzied fellowmen" and "the unrequited love he bears for another deaf-mute" (144). Tying this contemporary figure of victim to classical and biblical fools, clowns, Alazons, and scapegoats, and to Christ as the hero-victim archetype, Hassan gives McCullers considerable prominence as the bearer in a rather pure form of this contemporary version of ancient myth. He justifies in this way the appeal of her fiction and validates for an academic audience her right to the popular reputation she had by this point gained.

Hassan's appeal to a world outside the text constitutes a challenge to the formalists' insistence on the poem, novel, or story as a complex verbal structure to be judged by its success in unifying its internal contradictions. Myth criticism entered the academy largely through the efforts of a generation of former enlisted men in the postwar boom in higher education. Although Hassan does not fit this profile, he resembles other challengers to New Critical orthodoxy in his status as an outsider critic. I use the term to designate those whose entry into the academy broadens our concept of who can know and define knowledge for others, or who can be a graduate student or university professor of literature. The influx of young veterans of World War II brought into a largely WASP enclave the sons of immigrants, ethnic minorities, laborers, and midwestern provincials. Their impact on the study of literature began to make itself felt at precisely this period in the late 1950s. Their attraction to myth criticism may have been a consequence, a benefit, of immigrant upbringings, Talmudic training, or simply the characteristic perspectives of outsiders marked by attentiveness to cultural difference. In its incipient stages myth criticism resembled formalist criticism in almost every respect except for its concern with an ultimate source of meaning or narrative structure external to the text, whether extant in culture, racial memory, or a collective unconscious.

Myth criticism, moreover, is one of several strong legacies of Freudian and Jungian theories that flourished at midcentury in popular culture as well as among the intelligentsia. The magnitude of interest in the influence of Freud on the creation and criticism of literature can be suggested by a partial list (cited in Peden 1964, 88n) of studies published in the

1950s and 1960s: Daniel E. Schneider's *The Psychoanalyst and the Artist* (1950); Frederick J. Hoffman's *Freudianism and the Literary Mind* (2nd ed., 1957); Simon O. Lesser's *Fiction and the Unconscious* (1957); and Louis B. Fraiberg's *Psychoanalysis and American Literary Criticism* (1960). Alongside such specialized applications of psychology we must also count the widespread infiltration into mass-market social science of the ideas of David Riesman, Erich Fromm, and Vance Packard about the alienated individual, the lonely crowd, and the organization man. Although echoes of such theories are to be found everywhere in the thematics of postwar literary criticism, they resonate with particular strength in the writing of myth critics, who view themselves as divers into the wreck of civilization in search of atavistic knowledge to redeem a world of organization men and suburban sameness.

As a consequence, even strongly New Critical interpretations begin to reflect, if only in an incidental way, the vocabulary of psycho-social analysis. John B. Vickery (1960) provides a surface map of the function of love in McCullers's fiction. She is "primarily interested in the drama that is enacted within the soul of the lover and which finds its source in the painful discovery of the self as a sharply defined and limited ego" (13). In *Hunter* McCullers is concerned with fraternal love or "love as understanding" (16). Only in Biff Brannon is the desire to understand stronger than the desire to be understood, but the others do not turn to him. From the abandoned quests of the others, Brannon is said to learn "that fulfillment comes not only through the assertion of one's own individuality but through the recognition of the individuality of others" (18).

In a gracefully written analysis, virtually a classic in the New Critical engagement with modernism, Horace Taylor (1960) suggests a parallel between *Hunter*'s themes and the controlling myth of *The Waste Land*. Biff Brannon's observation that Singer is "a home-made God" implies that society, through its lonely individuals, suffers from a spiritual malaise. "The psycho-religious bond of community has been lost and only the empty forms of communal existence remain." Despite the violent reactions against this "death in life," each of the principal characters is "a solipsist, completely bound up within himself" (160). On the way to this conclusion, Taylor makes some interesting points about the relationship between psychological turmoil and social injustice: Copeland and Blount are "frustrated idealists who cling to their visions with all the crazed fanaticism of those who are driven to the brink of insane despair by ridicule and indifference"; psychological isolation, the loss of communal attachments, and the failure of families are implicated in the individual failures as "even those who would normally bear the closest of relations – husband and wife, father and children – are psychological strangers" (158); and when "the normative bonds of a society die, its sensitive individuals are left in spiritual isolation and they are denied social release. Thus . . . . Jake and Dr. Copeland never once suspect that their passionate championing of economic and social justice is but a psychological revolt against the death clasp of society. They are excellent illustrations of why social crusaders so often fail. One cannot correct the abuses of a society by agitation for social reform when that society is dead or dying" (159–60). The echoes of *The Waste Land* may derive less from McCullers than from Taylor's willingness to equate social ills with crippled personalities that admit of healing only in the abstract realm of faith: "Ultimately, the problem of both the society and its individuals is a religious one" (160). Given this tenet of high-church agrarianism, half-measures like economic and racial justice are distractions from a nobler aim.

In advancing such a thesis and in treating *Hunter* as a southern novel illustrative of it, Taylor's essay contributes to the movement to establish southern writing and southern history generally as enclaves within the study of American culture. In this effort the 1960s were generative, if not peaceful. Among the first to oppose the invidious treatment of southern women writers as all of a piece, a piece cut from the hem of Faulkner, Ruth M. Vande Kieft (1962) says that a school of southern writing "never existed; and it could scarcely have taken its inspiration directly from Faulkner or anyone else; nor could it have 'found,' full-blown, its supreme introspective artists in Carson McCullers and the weighty Robert Penn Warren, by a line of descent which leaps across the ocean and back, ultimately, to James and Hawthorne" (168). Vande Kieft's point about the distorting effect of such sweeping genealogies on women writers derives from her study of the career of Eudora Welty.

Of the six novelists Irving Malin treats in defining the *New American Gothic* (1962), three southerners – McCullers, O'Connor, and Capote – close ranks with James Purdy, John Hawkes, and J. D. Salinger. Demonstrating the deep roots of the genre in the history of the American novel since Charles Brockden Brown, and setting the new Gothic in opposition to social fiction, Malin explains that the genre "depends to a great extent on image, not idea. Because it deals with limitations of personality and wars in the family, it seeks not to be expansive but intensive. It presents a vertical world," one that is best approached as *"poetry* of disorder" (12–13). Among the insights this adaptation of New Critical analysis brings to *Hunter* is a precise delineation of patterns of imagery and symbolism, especially those associated with the "compulsive narcissism" Malin says is definitive of the genre. He notices, for example, that McCullers makes speech, or human communication, the symbolic measure of solitary self-absorption: "John Singer cannot sing because he is a mute; although articulate, Doctor Copeland often moans; Jake Blount screams with drunken fury; and Mick wishes that there was some 'place where she could go to hum [music] out loud'" (19–20). Likewise, the carousel Blount tends is the image of the solipsistic orbits, "compulsive circles" in which the characters move. With the exception of Singer, the major characters are narcissists. Blount uses "Marxism to assert his superior intelligence [and thereby] fights anxiety" about his deficiencies. Copeland "is a compulsive follower of his strong true purpose because it helps him to refrain from questioning what he has done to himself and his children" (21). As an adolescent preoccupied with self, Mick Kelly also fits the pattern. The four narcissists cannot see what they have in common, but, individually, they project their narcissism onto Singer. "Singer is like Moby Dick. His muteness is 'white.' People read meanings into both nonreflecting images" (22). "Singer's final act is narcissistic. By suicide, he asserts that he loves himself so much that he can destroy this love. He wills himself to power. In this respect he becomes a false Christ" (23).

Compulsive narcissism extends into the family for practitioners of the new Gothic. In *Hunter* "almost every family tie is broken" (54). Mick and her father fail to communicate; she finds a surrogate parent in Singer. The Copeland family is irretrievably broken, and the maternal affection of Biff for Mick carries a taint of "muted incest" (56). In the neo-Gothic setting, "rooms are also haunted by self-love" (83): Mick's inside room, Brannon's rooms above the café, and the "focal point of the novel," Singer's rented room (84). Voyages also characterize the genre: from Singer's visits to Antonapoulos, their walks around town, and Blount's travels, to Mick's desire to escape into the larger world. "McCullers uses the polarities of room and voyage to suggest suspension between imprisonment and violent movement; there is no 'firm nexus' because these characters have no resting place, no ordered, flexible pattern" (113). "The writers of the new American Gothic *view reality itself as deceptive* – hostility masquerades as peace; self-love masquerades as love; children masquerade as adults (or vice versa). New American Gothic uses the reflection – the mirror in which reality is double, cracked, or wavy; only one image is constant – the beloved self" (127). Malin claims to be a formalist critic, but his approach, the method, and the goal of his close reading are one and the same: psychological insight. He is therefore among the ranks of the outsider critics of the 1950s and 1960s who imported extrinsic considerations into what he calls the "vertical world," the closed synchronic temple of the verbal object. His outsider status could not be more clearly, and strategically, proclaimed than in his dedication of the *New American Gothic* to "my father and grandmother who cannot read this."

John M. Bradbury (1963), in one of the histories of southern literature that began to appear in this decade, treats McCullers as a writer, like Faulkner and Robert Penn Warren, adept at "weaving together large patterns of experience into meaningful designs. Like Faulkner, she exhibits a partiality for grotesques, but her concern for the lonely and loveless, with failures of communication and self-betrayal ally her more firmly with her feminine compatriots," though she lacks the "mastery of short forms" exhibited by Katherine Anne Porter and Eudora Welty (110). Of *Hunter*, Bradbury says, "the ironically named Singer seems to sum up all the finally unsatisfactory recourses of modern man in his heart's loneliness: religion, psychiatry, political or social expedients." Apart from the symbolic mutes, the other characters are treated "realistically and sympathetically" (111). McCullers "never suggests the agape of universal brotherhood [as a remedy for social ills] – Blount the labor organizer and the idealistic Negro doctor . . . implicitly deny such a possibility since they fight each other on being left alone without Singer." Biff Brannon's "suspension 'between the two worlds' of love and terror" is the figure not of the paralysis of a social philosopher or potential healer but of "the artist's withdrawal" (112).

Klaus Lubbers (1963), a German critic of southern literature, revalues "the interrelation of themes and artistic organization" in McCullers's major fiction against standards set by Faulkner and judges her harshly for her lack of interest in "basic Faulknerian themes" such as the burden of the past and reverence for the land. *Hunter* is her "most puzzling novel," giving "the impression of being made up of loosely juxtaposed elements which are parts of a barely coherent whole" (187–88). Lubbers dismisses the two prominent structural patterns that the novel can hardly be said to disguise – the image of Singer as the hub of a wheel, whose spokes are the other characters, and the dream vision that arrays Singer and the rest in a hierarchy leading to Antonapoulos at the pinnacle of a pyramid. "The wheel image, then, together with the mute's vision, groups the persons in a way consistent not with actuality, but with an imagined and hoped-for order. The wheel, if it did exist, would give meaning to the lives of Biff, Mick, Jake and Copeland, but not to Singer's life." The pyramid, likewise, "falls apart with only the idiot content, at peace with himself and the world because he alone has no need for human sympathy and communication" (190). In their place Lubbers argues that formal unity is gained by what he calls the "technique of side-by-side action, of parallel movement," principally in the ordering of chapters (189). An understanding of this structure makes possible a more accurate perception of the novel's theme: it is "not the social problem nor is it primarily that of human isolation. It is rather the question of truth and illusion (or, disillusionment). Each of the four characters around Singer is in his own way concerned with distinguishing truth from illusion" (191). One would think it might be difficult to discover a theme more "epitomizing" than the one Lubbers attempts to set aside; but he may in fact be said to have found it in the venerable but often meaningless formulation of truth-versus-illusion. "The meaning which the book finally adds up to is this: Christ's gospel is dead for the protagonists. The substituted truths they embrace are private truths, not comprehensive enough to include others. The most acceptable truth is Biff's (which, by the way, comes closest to the biblical doctrine). It is Christ's message of love in a secular form which Brannon has arrived at by constantly attempting to solve the riddle of Singer's life, the hard path toward unrequited human sympathy in an exacting world heading into darkness" (194).

Chester E. Eisinger (1963) borrows a definition from John Crowe Ransom to describe McCullers as

> governed by the aesthetics of the primitive. This means that her overview is essentially antirealistic. She has cut herself off from the world of ordinary experience and ordinary human beings who might entertain ordinary ideas. Her people are bizarre, freakish, lonely, hermaphroditic. This aesthetic dictates an intense concentration on man's most urgent emotional needs: a communion of dialogue and love. For her, further, the truth of the fable is the truth of the heart. It is not concerned with abstractions about the structure of society or with ideological conflicts in the contemporary world. She has banished these sociological and intellectual matters from her fiction, narrowing its range, perhaps to its detriment, in favor of memory and mood, and above all, feeling. This aesthetic demands a poetic prose and a style which, in Mrs. McCullers' case, often appears childlike. (243–44)

Although Eisinger is willing to engage McCullers's comment about an "ironic parable of fascism," his use of the critical model derived from Ransom allows him to dismiss it as unimportant: the phrase "makes sense only if we assume that the economics of capitalism and the racial practices of the South suggest to her the barbarism of fascism. But these matters are hardly at the heart of the novel . . . . Isolation is of the soul, not of the small southern town. The failure of love is the failure of communion, not of labor unions or Negro-white relations" (251). Invoking the spiritual ideal described by Martin Buber as "the meeting of *ich und du,* joined in a mystical reciprocity" (244), Eisinger says that, "with magisterial firmness,

[McCullers] condemns her characters to failure .... They have stubbornly embarked upon a monologue in the mistaken notion that they have established the reciprocity necessary for dialogue" (246). Instead of according Singer a Christ- or God-likeness, Eisinger views the mute "as the figure of the Virgin Mother and the Son," as the others derive maternal comfort and grace akin to the sacrament of communion from him. "If Singer is conceived as hermaphroditic, incorporating in one body the male and female principles, then in him is the potential for universal balm." Of course, he turns out to be "the false Virgin and the false Son" (247). Antonapoulos is "a symbol for vacuity": "He is the reduction to the abysmal zero of the human hope for communion" (248). Eisinger approaches an important insight about Mick Kelly in the observation that "the adolescent girl, in Mrs. McCullers' fiction, has the problem not only of sex awareness but of sex determination. It is not the responsibility of womanhood that she reluctantly must take up but the decision to be a woman at all that she must make .... In Brannon and in Singer, the sexes seem to achieve a beneficent union. In Mick they make for a chaotic confusion." That her sexual initiation is "more redolent of surrender than of glory" is further evidence of "life's blasted promise," the failure of dialogue (250–51).

Wayne D. Dodd (1963) surveys the bleakness of McCullers's metaphysical themes through the symbolism that advances them. He characterizes such symbolism as "suggestive and developmental," designed to emphasize "the discreteness of individuals from each other and from God himself" (206). McCullers's portrayal of Singer as God-like culminates in the dream of the pyramid: "The violent upheaval suggests, of course, the collapsing structure of the lives of the characters when the top link snaps, when Antonapoulos dies .... The implication is that this is an unending process: one is not in communication with one omnipotent god, but rather with an infinite series of limited gods, each of whom is as dependent on another as those who worship him" (207). Furthermore, "Singer, a god to many, is a deaf-mute, and . . . Antonapoulos, a god to Singer, is a moron. The effect is to suggest that God is somehow deformed or abnormal. And when one recalls that this is God the Creator of the world, one begins to perceive the value of the less obvious, but equally effective and suggestive, symbolic analogue to God the Creator that is provided in the child-as-artist (creator) motif that runs through all the novels," in this instance, through Mick's paintings of an airplane crash, a sinking ocean liner, a sea gull broken by the force of a storm, and crowds, fire, and carnage on the streets of her town. That the products of such creativity "are always grotesque suggests that each one renders the world according to his vision, which, isolated as it is, must of necessity seem grotesque to others" (209). Another motif is the need to preserve one's sanctum or private world. The unconscious motive for the characters who confide their dreams to Singer is that "each instinctively knows that the deaf-mute will not understand and that he will not, therefore, be a threat to the hidden, uncommunicative inner self. The reason why there can be no complete commitment to love is that each person must guard jealously his personal sovereignty against the imposition of an alien will" (212).

Walter Allen's influential study *The Modern Novel in Britain and the United States* (1964) gave an important boost to McCullers's reputation. Allen lauds her as, "Faulkner apart, the most remarkable novelist the South has produced" (132). Allen's treatment of *Hunter* is strictly conventional for the period: the novel is "a parable of the human condition, of human isolation, of the craving to communicate and of the impossibility of communication; and also, perhaps, of the inescapable delusions attendant upon the inescapable human need to love" (133). The value of his analysis lies in the attention he gives to the impression of "a grave, sad beauty, a diffused poetic pity," that results from the "nature of Carson McCullers's prose, which is not in any obvious sense poetic or heightened and which looks plainer than in fact it is. It is actually a very cunning style, ever so slightly removed from the contemporary" (134). Her "genius is at least as strange as Faulkner's, but expressed with lucidity and precision, a classical simplicity. However tortured her vision may seem, there is nothing tortured or odd in the texture of her prose; and the raw material of her art is the world as commonly observed" (132).

Louis Auchincloss (1965) makes a more qualified case for her genius. *Hunter* is "extraordinary enough for a first novel, but it is prodigious for an author of twenty-two. Mrs. McCullers, understandably, had not yet learned the tight control of her art that was to make her next book so memorable" (161–62). In an unusual assessment, he regards Mick Kelly as the least successful of the characters, merely "an advance study" for Frankie Addams but without "the brilliant sensitivity of the latter" (162).

Jack B. Moore (1965) is more approving of Mick and the portrayal of her "poignant loss of virginity" through a mixture of verisimilitude and mythmaking (76). A detailed analysis of Mick's sexual initiation against the stages of the initiation myth as described by Joseph Campbell and illustrated in such American classics as "Rip Van Winkle" and "Young Goodman Brown" leads Moore to the conclusion that "Mick Kelly is then a real girl in a real Southern town, a fairytale princess, and a hero. She learns about sex, experiences a transcendent and temporarily beautiful awakening, and faces her difficult entrance into the adult, real world heroically. The world she enters – as woman or princess or hero – is a strange and terrifying one, yet it is to be hoped an occasionally satisfying new world with its own wonders" (80–81). Apart from the deficiencies of the hero archetype as a pattern for female experience, Moore fails to notice the pervasive tone of disgust associated with Mick's first sexual experience.

In the first full-length study of McCullers, a critical biography prepared largely from personal interviews with the author (and, as a result, more reliable as criticism than biography), Oliver Evans (1965a) points to McCullers's allegorical and ironic treatment of characters: Singer is venerated because he cannot sing, or disagree; he is "a projection of [others'] desires" (38). Although Singer is the focus of the other characters, Antonapoulos is the true center of the book, being the projection of Singer's needs. To the extent that McCullers intended "an ironic parable of fascism" in *Hunter,* it amounts to a statement consistent with the work's religious symbolism: "it is possible if we think of Singer and Antonapoulos as leaders, blindly invested by others with attributes in which they are only too conspicuously . . . lacking, for us to see the terrifying meaning of the parable: in this absurdly grim game of follow-the-leader, the ultimate leader, the power beyond the power, is a lunatic" (43). Moreover, "any practical attempt at communication between individuals must end in failure." Love is destined to be thwarted. However, "of all the lovers and would-be lovers in the book the most passionate – and the most successful – is Singer. It is in this sense that, although a mute, he is the most eloquent of all the characters: the language of the heart does not require a tongue and may even be the more eloquent for lacking one . . . . The deaf-mute is indeed a *singer,* and his song – like that of the shepherd on the Grecian urn – is all the sweeter for its silence" (44). Singer's muteness is consistent with a pattern of symbolic physical deformity or freakishness by which McCullers conveys human "loneliness and incompletion" (51). There are as well Jake Blount's outsized hands and misshapen mouth; Dr. Copeland's tuberculosis; Mick's tomboyishness; and Biff Brannon's private assumption of a feminine persona after the death of his wife.

Evans deserves credit for calling attention to the degree to which McCullers integrates themes and images across two stylistic modes, symbolism and the social realism "without which almost no writer in the Thirties would have dared to offer a first novel – especially one with a Southern setting – to a reputable publisher" (48). Evans makes an even more important contribution to the study of *Hunter* by printing "Author's Outline of THE MUTE," a lengthy and revealing prospectus for the novel that secured McCullers a contract with Houghton Mifflin in 1938.

Criticism based on the analysis of this document soon began to revise interpretations produced under the influence of New Critical methods.

A study of violence in contemporary southern fiction led Louise Y. Gossett (1965) to the observation that "the sickening sweep into the oblivion of complete isolation is one of the constituents of violence which Mrs. McCullers portrays with special effectiveness. The consequences of a broken trust may be violent enough to change the personality of a character" (162–63). Mick's disciplining of Bubber has this effect. "His wounding Baby Wilson was less a shock than was the willingness of Mick to turn his violence and fear into a weapon against him" (163). Singer's suicide suggests that "the violence which dwells with loneliness is finally the absence of any real god" (164). "It is significant that Mrs. McCullers does not involve Jake in a strike at the mills, for the violence which interests her is that of the individual personality rather than that of economic and social systems . . . . In this respect her treatment of violence in relation to social criticism in Southern fiction is a transitional step between the more nearly doctrinaire approach of a writer like Caldwell and the indirectness of William Goyen" (171). Given her thesis, Gossett does not do justice to the racial violence and brutality in the novel. The tendency to see social and political struggle as peripheral to McCullers's concern with spiritual isolation is, as we have seen through the first fifteen years of academic criticism of *Hunter,* a rejection of the radicalism that shaped an alliance between art and social idealism in the United States for the first three decades of the twentieth century.

In the year of McCullers's death, the prolific English novelist and critic Anthony Burgess went a short way toward asserting the representative value of her ventures into social realism. Burgess observes "that most post-war American fiction — and not just that of the Negroes and Jews — is about the cry of the minority." *Hunter* captures this cry in portraits of "a child or adolescent, bearing a half-realized innocence through the dirty world, or else a freak who is really a saint" (1967, 203). Why this should be so, he does not explain. He is, however, original in suggesting that the rebel-victim-saint identified by Hassan and others might manifest not so much a statement about the human condition as a specific cultural desire for toleration and acceptance. Just as the youth rebellions of the 1960s and 1970s would prompt us, in retrospect, to see James Dean's teenage "rebel without a cause" as symptomatic of more than merely the existential angst with which we were already familiar, McCullers's tortured and occasionally rebellious characters seem increasingly to bear out Burgess's sense that specific injustices rather than loneliness or alienation lie behind the fear and violence she depicts.

But that was not the view of southern novelist and critic David Madden in 1967 or subsequently in 1972, when he remarked that *"Hunter"* is the most pessimistic book ever written" (155). However, on both occasions he insisted that psychological patterns rather than social institutions are McCullers's subject. His 1967 essay in *Literature and Psychology* proposes that all of the central characters are neurotic. Even Mick Kelly and Biff Brannon, the least neurotic, are psychologically damaged. Mick, though "a unique, individual adolescent . . . will be a neurotic, bitter woman" (134). Psychological debilities ranging from latent homosexuality (Singer, Antonapoulos, Brannon) to monomania (Blount, Copeland) outweigh social injustice in the scale of importance. *Hunter* "is not a realistic novel about the modern South, nor is it, despite certain critics or whatever McCullers' original intention may have been, a political polemic against capitalism and racism." The social world of the novel is "a hovering, insidious menace," but it is not McCullers's focus. The novel "persuades us that extreme poverty powerfully effected in Jake Blount certain anti-social, pro-martyr compulsions; that southern cruelty against Negroes and the Negro's own ignorance compelled Copeland to become a doctor and a Marxist; that Singer's childhood in an institution for deaf-mutes impeded his ability to move smoothly among the unafflicted; that his early love for and dependence upon his mother has caused Biff Brannon to fail sexually; and that poverty, living in a large family, and being born at an awkward time contributed much to directing Mick along certain channels of maladjustment. But the novel is not only *not* an indictment of environment (no social institutions are directly vilified . . .); it is not an indictment of anything" (128). Oblivious to the link between the economic and psychological determinism he has just described and the tradition of naturalism in favor when McCullers began her career, Madden insists that social conflicts in her work are "primarily objective correlatives to spiritual and emotional struggles" (1972, 152). His investment in the vocabulary of formalism is more beneficially reflected in his statement of the paradox that "everyone hungers for human understanding while simultaneously desiring an inviolable privacy." It is for this reason that each of the five main characters desires the solace of a single listener, whose own deficiencies virtually insure the temporary resolution of the paradox – the illusion of understanding that is no threat to privacy (1967, 132).

In a retrospective essay written in 1967, though not published until 1969, A. S. Knowles, Jr., observes that John Huston's film of *Reflections in a Golden Eye* was, ironically, arousing new interest in her work amid news of her death: "The writer perishes, the reputation is nourished" (87). Knowles looks specifically at McCullers's reputation in the 1940s when preparations for war and holdover feelings from the Depression fostered concern for social justice and a faith in the decency and courage of common people. Such beliefs "were given sentimental encouragement in the literature of the period," as, for example, in the novels of Steinbeck and William Saroyan. McCullers's first novel belongs in this category only to a limited extent. It is true that all her "characters are little people, their lives rescued from oblivion only by the author's concern. There are no great events in the novel, only events that mark, almost silently, a few obscure lives." To the extent that McCullers "felt distress at injustice" and brought an activist stance to her portrayal of "the economic and social oppression of the white workers and, especially, of the Negro," she is unique among writers of the period in "her realization of the degree to which the white worker was a victim of his own apathy, and the 'Negro problem' a function of the Negro's inability to develop a consistent idea of himself and his goals" (89–90). Remarkably prescient, even prophetic at age twenty-two, McCullers "saw, in 1940, the precise nature of the present Negro movement, what would cause it to arise, where it would try to go, and the agony it would produce." The angry confrontation between Blount and Copeland, ending in accusation and rupture, is a "prefiguring of our present anguish . . . . It would, in fact, come to this" (90–91).

Knowles also identifies in *Hunter* another, perhaps lesser, preoccupation. The portraits of Singer, Mick, and Biff suggest a pattern in which "artistic sensitivity – indeed, sensitivity of almost any kind – will be linked with either sexual neutrality or transformation" and with spirituality (92). Calling this pattern a measure of the wunderkind's naïveté, Knowles says it marks her talent as adolescent: "The basic assumption is that in order to be sensitive one also has to be 'different,' a little freakish, perhaps, a little fey. The corollary, of course, is that if one isn't 'different,' he also isn't sensitive, and all sorts of related propositions cluster around these: that talent and eccentricity are inextricably related; that the sensitive must always [be] martyred; and that, in general, the world can be divided into the sensitive few and the insensitive many. There is reason enough to suspect that there is some truth in all these attitudes, but when they are used as a basic rationale one is entitled to suspect that a measure of adolescent self-pity or, at least, preciousness is really behind it all" (93–94).

Knowles concludes that, despite her talent and courage, McCullers is overestimated. "She now seems less important than she once did, and we may hope to be forgiven for observing, without malice, how greatly her reputation was enhanced by the time in which she wrote and by her regional associations." Although he is correct in acknowledging that she

profited from the academic (and popular) interest in southern literature
that seems to have followed swiftly in the wake of Faulkner's Nobel Prize
for literature in 1950, he is less convincing in his assertion that, "in dealing with Carson McCullers we are dealing with a writer who was favored
by a self-supporting coterie that held sway over American letters for a
decade. If we should now decide that she was essentially a minor writer,
however, this is only to suggest that her vision was often limited and special" (97–98). Knowles refers to 1940s-era New Critics, largely southerners, many of them poets and critics allied with the Vanderbilt Fugitives –
Allen Tate, Robert Penn Warren, John Crowe Ransom, Cleanth Brooks,
to name the most prominent among them. A look at the bibliography for
this period, however, will demonstrate how rarely she was noticed by any
of the mainline New Critics or treated in their journals. To believe her the
darling of the New Criticism, Knowles must overlook the extent to which
her work was distorted, or prematurely ossified, by its methods. It may be
that the attention paid to southern literature helped her boat to rise along
with others, but she was a phenomenon before Faulkner's elevation and
was actually demoted in the clamor to lift him up. McCullers did, of
course, profit from the New Criticism to some extent. It is not that New
Critics dismissed her or did not read her. It is rather that they mistook her
as mired in their intellectual preoccupations, largely dismissing her root-
edness in the rich soil of social conflict.

To understand what the ideology of New Criticism caused readers to
overlook, we may consult the estimate of Soviet expert on American literature Inna M. Levidova. In an article first published in Moscow in 1966
but translated into English only in 1972, Levidova offers a reading of
Hunter informed by socialist realism and acute intelligence. *Hunter* is "an
imperfect book, perhaps somewhat too overloaded, here and there com-
positionally weak – but a work which truly caught one up in its stern
penetrating lyricism, power, and the precision of the author's psychological imagination, her ability to depict everyday life in all its concrete, tangi-
ble details – without weakening the unity of conception." In the southern
town, "the Depression has put its dirty-gray mark on the life of the inhabitants of the suburbs, on the workers, on the factory hands, on the poverty
of the Negroes. A war is on in Europe; and though few of the ordinary
people give any special thought to it, a dull menace hangs over the town.
Unrelenting social enmity softly bubbles under the surface, occasionally
breaking loose in ugly bloody encounters. All this is not background of
the book, but its essence, its atmosphere; but the heart of the novel lies in
something else" (90).

> Like all of McCullers' novels it exists in two organically united planes —
> psychological and social realism, and allegory, fable. The allegoricalness
> of the book is underlined by a whole series of devices; it was the "oral"
> repetitions, the role of numbers, and the intentional "roundedness" of
> plot situations that provided material for the numerous interpretations of
> the novel — religious, mythic, Freudian, political. Apparently closest to
> the truth is a *moral* interpretation . . . . Man tries to save himself from
> loneliness by love. But love is not simply blind, it is almost always di-
> rected at an object which by its nature cannot give the lover happiness
> and harmony. Love does not pierce the wall, but by its very presence it
> helps the personality find itself and feel even if only for a short while,
> genuine fullness of being. The bitterest irony is in the fact that the
> lonely, lost, and despairing ones go with the burden of their sufferings
> and thoughts to the deaf, the dumb, and the *indifferent*. Even more ironic
> is the fact that this chosen one who seems clairvoyant and compassion-
> ate to them has devoted himself completely to a fictitious creature, the
> product of his own loneliness, and who is in reality quite simply a repul-
> sive idiot. Chaos reigns in the world, and the same kind of chaos rules in
> human souls as well. (91–92)

What is striking about Levidova's account and, certainly, contrary to expectation, is its poise and relative freedom from ideological judgment.
Levidova is under no obligation to resolve a paradox of contradictory
purposes because she does not see the social/psychological and the alle-
gorical/fabulistic as paradoxical. Instead, they are "organically united
planes" needing only a tolerance for ambiguity which can entertain the
possibility of affirmation amid, not in spite of, chaos. Levidova continues,

> Contrary to everything, over a world which is ominous, depressingly
> banal, absurd, which is choking in the grip of its age-old misunderstand-
> ing and fatal alienation, rises the eternal and irreplaceable power of
> goodness — love, self-sacrifice, the striving for beauty, the striving to get
> closer, even if only for a single instant, to the comprehension of the
> meaning of human existence. McCullers is able to tell about this with the
> amazing charm of conviction, without a bit of sentimentality or rhetoric.
> That is why although much has changed since then in the spiritual
> make-up of America, her first book lives on even now; that is why it did
> not end in the vast heap of "black" novels and plays which asserted the
> universal absurdity of being. (91–92)

Nearly thirty years after *Hunter*'s publication, and shortly after McCullers's death in 1967, critics were still in thrall to the wunderkind. A brief
study by Dale Edmonds for a Southern Writers Series (1969) presents, on
the whole, an appreciative analysis. Edmonds calls *Hunter* perhaps McCullers's "most perplexing work" (9). In "epitomizing language" of an ex-

treme sort, he says, "The pyramidal relationship of the principal characters . . . may represent the boundless eternal human quest for wholeness.
Some critics see the 'unknown thing' that Antonapoulos holds above him
as the cross he wears around his neck, but a strict religious meaning is not
necessarily intended. Rather, the object Antonapoulos holds before him
symbolizes that fulfillment, by whatever name, which all men seek. In
terms of the dream, then, the quest itself may be seen as a source of suste-
nance; frail, collapsible, idealistic, it is nonetheless inspirational and meaningful." Edmonds concludes, "The richness of the novel is both the source
of its continuing appeal and its basic weakness: the ultimate effect is that
of a profusion that cannot be contained. This does not alter the fact that
The Heart Is a Lonely Hunter is a powerful, original work and certainly one
of the most ambitious first novels on record" (14).

In an otherwise not entirely sympathetic study, published in the same
year as Edmonds's pamphlet, Lawrence Graver (1969) says, "For a
twenty-two-year-old girl to probe at such length the passionate idealism of
a half-dozen adult characters was an astonishing act of imaginative sympathy" (6–7). "From the opening pages . . . one is aware that this strange
and absorbing story is designed to be read both as a realistic tale of a half-
dozen displaced southerners and as a generalized parable on the nature of
human illusion and love" (12). Graver, unlike Levidova, believes "that
contemporary reality and legendary story are one" only for "the first one
hundred pages" (13). Thereafter, he acquires reservations – about the
portrait of Biff Brannon (Is he a *"raisonneur,* the one person to make objective sense of the action," or not?); about the relationship between a character's faith in Singer and the fate of that character after Singer's suicide
(Is Mick's fate or Copeland's causally related to the absence of Singer in
their lives?); about episodes that strike him as irrelevant (What is the
point of the shooting of Baby Wilson, the race riot at the carousel, the appearance of "the crazed evangelist"?). "There is a growing sense, toward
the close of the novel, that the death of God is anticlimactic, or perhaps
even beside the point. The dreamers would have been doomed to frustration had the mute never lived" (14–15). Some problems are those of a first
novel, and one written by someone so young. "But the failures on the
level of fable are more troublesome because they point to an ambivalence
that was a permanent feature of Mrs. McCullers' sensibility." Graver follows the New Critical consensus in the desire to make ambiguities, ultimately, cohere. He notes as a flaw the "continuing conflict between her
nearer and her further vision, between her desire to document the world
and a desire to give it evocative poetic significance" (15–16). However, all
in all, "the original design is brilliant enough not to be wholly dimmed by

the failure of the performance. If the inflated myth finally collapses, the sense of small-town meanness holds up. Few books of the 1930's communicate as well the stagnancy of life in a depressed textile community and the inevitable frustration for those who try to stir free from it." But the novel is not shrouded in an altogether oppressive atmosphere. Graver is one of the few who have appreciated McCullers's considerable wit. She "reveals an affectionate gaiety that provides wholesome leavening for the pessimism so pervasive in this first novel" (18).

Alice Hamilton (1970) explores the tension between allegory and realism in another way, framing it as a distinction between the inner world of dreams where the dream-image of a beloved is conceived and "the outer world of people" (215). One is associated with radiance, the other with chaos. "What Mrs. McCullers is offering . . . is a strange variant of neo-Platonism. In classical neo-Platonism beautiful soul cries out in longing to beautiful soul, finding its happiness in a union beyond the flesh as it reaches out to the bliss of the Transcendent Good. Mrs. McCullers' affirmation is that a Creator has formed an incomplete humanity, one that can only trust that there is sense in creation. Some good, rather than total good, is the meaning available for man" (216). Jake Blount's "outer life is Marxist. His inner dream is tied to Christ's miraculous feeding of the thousands, and the promise of peace to those who bring their burdens to Him. Jake would be God" (220). Mick, on finding herself shut out of the inner dream of music, questions the purpose of dreams and abandons "the idea of total good and of a 'divine plan' for the individual. To survive in the 'outside' room you have to be mean and tough, and she intends to develop these characteristics in her baby brother Ralph and in the seven-year-old Bubber." Her verbal abuse of Bubber is severe, but "in her hard young heart she speaks the truth as she knows it." The dream vision of the pyramid may betoken a philosophy: "Since man is less than perfect, his god is a freak with some part of the total Good missing" (221). Ignoring "the pettiness, nastiness, envy, and anger" of Antonapoulos, Singer worships his friend's "pagan delight in elemental variety compounded of gentleness, abundance, growth, colour, and love unchecked by will . . . . In a disorganized society, so Mrs. McCullers has pointed out, the 'individual Gods or principles' are very likely to be fantastic and chimerical." Biff's vision, however, leads to affirmation: "Riddles do work out, otherwise everything is a planned, ugly joke. Biff had done crosswords for years, and he affirms that there is order and the possibility of solution for problems . . . . The intelligent mind can ask questions and expect to find a fitting answer. Tranquillity is found in this trust" (222). Hamilton's essay points backward to Frank Baldanza's discussion of Platonic themes and forward to the relationship between microcosm and macrocosm that occupies Joseph R. Millichap.

Millichap (1971) follows Graver and others into the debate on the perceived imbalance of the novel's symbolism and its realism. His conclusions provide a new interpretation, similar to Levidova's but not indebted to it. In challenging the prevailing opinion that the novel is more Gothic romance or allegory than social realism, Millichap lays out a patient analysis of the novel's structure toward the claim that McCullers's complex narrative strategies establish a "fundamental tension between the personal and the social worlds" and thereby stress the relationship between social problems and individual personality (12).

In this revisionary essay, Millichap may be said to inaugurate the criticism of the 1970s or, at least, the distinctive trends of that criticism. Although they did not emerge with force until midway into the period, the concerns of a majority of 1970s critics with interpretations sensitive to race and class became, by the end of the decade, prominent even in essays ostensibly devoted to purer purposes, like demonstrating the role of music as a structural device. One sign of the increased concern with McCullers as a social critic is the growing interest in characters more strongly associated with the critique of racism and class prejudice than the mutes or Biff Brannon or, for some, Mick Kelly. Increased attention to Jake Blount and Benedict Mady Copeland profitably expanded our grasp of the dense social, intellectual, and emotional milieu in which each moves. Even the assessments of southern literature as a distinct subdiscipline begin to register a shift in how and for what purposes the grotesque functions in McCullers's novel, defining it less in terms of a symbolic connection with loneliness than as an barometer of moral or ethical coherence. The decade's attention to social and political themes reflects the diminishing influence of formalist methods and a growing interest in the academy as a site of political activism. For better or worse, the resurgence of dissent on a variety of fronts – most notably in the campaigns against war and for civil rights – developed among students of literature a sense of urgent purpose and consequent quickness to fault abstraction, evasion, and perceived lack of relevance.

Millichap develops his argument about the inescapable interplay of macro- and micropolitics by demonstrating that McCullers, not satisfied simply to examine the mill town society in which her central characters move, gestures meaningfully toward impending global conflict. "The microcosmic social world of the mill-city erupts in the unbridled hatred of a race riot, while the larger world, the macrocosm, teeters perilously on the brink of total war" (12). Among the structural devices that negotiate be-

tween the personal and the political, Millichap points to the lack of a single protagonist ("The action of the novel . . . is not centered on any one
individual; it involves the social group, both the central characters and the
whole mill-city society" [12]); a combination of a distanced, legendary
narrative voice, which pronounces on the larger, even timeless, movements of the plot, and close third-person narration angled to reflect the
particular voice of each of the four characters who attach themselves to
Singer (a structure that reminds Millichap of *The Grapes of Wrath* and
*Winesburg, Ohio); and the pointed manipulation of character, setting, and
symbol. Set in western Georgia, the mill town "is a symbolic type of the
culture produced by industrialization – a world of decay, deprivation, and
loneliness." The ironically named Sunny Dixie Show, home of a broken-
down merry-go-round and site of the climactic race riot, "becomes the
major example of setting used symbolically. A tawdry place of entertain-
ment and escape appropriate to this world, the show is a combination of
an urban wasteland and a mechanical nightmare"; it "symbolizes the
meaningless and oppressive round of mechanical activities associated with
modern urban civilization" (15). Like the setting, action, and narrative
technique, even the minor characters "connect . . . the society of the mill-
city and . . . the larger world outside." The Jewishness of Harry Minowitz
"amplifies both the religious and social themes of the novel. His presence
also raises the issue of Fascism, bringing the macrocosm of the world
situation of 1939 into focus with the microcosm of the mill-city." The
young man's "reaction to Fascist anti-semitism creates a personal chaos.
His very hatred of Hitler causes him to desire to live within a militaristic
society which would fight Nazism. His own physical desires lead him into
the sexual exploitation of the younger Mick," from which he flees in fear
and remorse. In explaining McCullers's claim that the novel is "an ironic
parable of fascism," however, Millichap's surefootedness fails him. "The
novelist undoubtedly uses both terms [*parable* and *fascism*] in a very broad
sense, meaning by the second any social system which bases its order on
hatred, aggression, and human exploitation. These are the bases of the social structure in Nazi Germany and in the mill-city, and thus the 'parable'
is ironic. Fascism in this sense can be present in any social organization
because its seeds – hate, greed, and fear – are constants of the human
situation" (16). Minowitz's temporary attraction to fascism is offered as
evidence. Millichap also falters in his analysis of Singer's dream pyramid.
"Singer plays John the Baptist to Antonapoulos's Christ," while Antonapoulos venerates the cross on a necklace given to him by Singer. Millichap
concludes that "this pyramid of stupid devotion indicates that religion has

little relevance for modern society, a favorite theme in Proletarian fiction" (13–14).

The question of McCullers's achievement was addressed in a retrospective review of her career by novelist Nadine Gordimer (1972), who, in comparing *Hunter* to the "Author's Outline," remarks that both are juvenilia:

> Here was a writer who published at 22 a first novel that was as structurally complex as it was fresh, as controlled as it was brilliant, and that stands up to repeated re-readings. Since she was a slow writer, it is reasonable to suppose she must have begun *The Heart Is a Lonely Hunter* not later than the age of 19. Any writer will recognize in the outline a truly extraordinary accomplishment of another order: the rare ability to stand outside one's own conception and analyse it in terms of its own methodology — and this from a young girl who became what one thinks of as the most instinctual and least cerebral of writers. This outline reveals another aspect of her genius (perhaps the key one) by demonstrating the skill with which she concealed the wires of cerebration, carrying the societal ideas of her work, in the living subconscious of her characters, transmuted into totally implicit actions and words. (134–35)

Gordimer, furthermore, probes McCullers's treatment of race:

> When one thinks back broadly on her novels, it is not what they have to say about black and white that seems to matter at all . . . . Yet if one returns to her work one sees that the reason why her blacks don't stand out of the page is because they are not "observed" from without, but are simply people presented, apparently, from the same level of knowledge from which she presents whites. It's easy to say she was too fine a writer, etc.; of course, she was, but the shameful "problem" was there, and one of its senseless tragedies is there, acted out, in her first novel, in the person of Doctor Copeland, an astonishingly prophetic portrait of the kind of educated black of the 'thirties to whom present-day black thinkers point as the emasculated man.

But in her work as in Faulkner's "the brutality of white Southerners towards black, and the degradation of black and white through this has — I'm afraid — been brought to life more devastatingly than by any black writer so far" (136–37).

Sam Bluefarb (1972) in a chapter devoted to Jake Blount calls him "an escaper . . . in the tradition of Melville's isolato" (115). Blount is a perpetual wanderer, a would-be rabble-rouser, labor organizer, and street-corner preacher and philosopher; however, he has no gift for understanding or making himself understood by the downtrodden he aspires to save. When violence erupts, he fights only for himself, lashing out at black and white indiscriminately. This escape, like the ones before it, is "neither resurrective nor initiatory: [escapes] are the chronic condition of his life" (121). The motif, it must be said, is an ill fit with Bluefarb's nebulous thesis that would connect Jake Blount's escapism with the American Dream.

In a chapter entitled "The Secret of the South," Alfred Kazin (1973) writes, "There is a place for the artist willing to be alone with the South that only certain women have been able to fill" (50). McCullers and Flannery O'Connor are among these women, who, by virtue of their gender, are quintessential outsiders inside. Despite a promising thesis, Kazin mixes arresting insight with blindness: "Each in her way was doomed from an early age and knew it; each was dependent on her family for the sparse numbers of characters in her fiction; each was a woman novelist in a South that excited her by its brooding violence, but by its insistent conventions made her feel that she was a freak" (51). Neither woman, of course, was dependent on her family for characters or helpless before the conventions of her region. "Carson McCullers was a greater myth-maker than she was a novelist. Her theme was the utter dislocation of love 'in our time' and 'in our town.'" (How easily in such phrases Kazin inscribes a modernist male ethos onto hers.) "Her extreme sense of human separateness took form in deaf-mutes who were also Greek foreigners in the Southern town in which they inexplicably found themselves, Negro doctors maddened by their intellectual isolation, fathers always widowers, and above all a young tomboy who, whether she is too young for sexual love or too odd for it, attributes her own unusedness to everyone else, then projects this 'loneliness' against the political terror of the Hitler period and the excessiveness, vacancy, and stillness of summer in the town." (Masochism may start in desire, but not for passive "usedness" in any sense. McCullers's female adolescents assume a creative power and subjectivity, even when the world demonstrates that it should be otherwise for them.) "The world is so bleak that it is always just about to be transformed. *The Heart Is a Lonely Hunter* astonishingly comes alive still not only as a virtuoso performance dramatically engaging so many hard solitudes, but also as a novel of the depressed Thirties haunted by the powerlessness of people and the ferocious powers of governments" (51–52).

Delma Eugene Presley (1974) also explores McCullers's relationship with her native region, advancing the view that she disdained the South but wrote less well after she left it: "Her early success and her ultimate failure . . . can be attributed in large measure to this pattern of struggle in her relationship to the South" (19). The struggle is reflected in the autobiographical portions of her fiction. "Mick Kelly's destiny as a clerk in Woolworth's is the author's projection of her future in the South, had she not escaped" (20). Like Frankie Addams in *The Member of the Wedding,* Mick "verbalizes a deep sense of betrayal" at the end of the work (26). "These adolescents discover excruciating pain – the result of their having been placed on an arid spiritual desert where youthful dreams and tender sentiments evaporate with the dawning of adulthood." *Hunter,* more than her other works, "is the most artful instance of how she appropriated her perception of life in the South. In this novel she transmuted her own feelings of frustration into a shrunken cosmos in which even the most fundamental moral efforts, the most basic attempts at communication, are fruitless. In this extraordinary first novel, Mrs. McCullers elaborated her bleak metaphors and cast doubt on man's ethical potential" (27). *Hunter* is her only novel written in the South and the "only novel which approaches a serious exploration of the moral dimension of her characters." *Hunter* "does rest upon a solid foundation of place. Furthermore, it elaborates a correlation between the emotional estrangement of the adolescent Mick and the anomie of those around her – the only instance of a successful correlation of this sort in her works" (31).

Presley's influential essay has behind it an unsympathetic view of McCullers based on more than her attitude toward the region of which they are both natives. As described more fully below, Presley and others pilloried McCullers on personal grounds in an era of biographical revelations during the 1970s. Sympathy for Reeves McCullers occasionally lies behind the increased tendency to see Carson McCullers and her characters as deviant and selfish. Presley may in fact have devoted more time in this stage of his scholarly career to the study of McCullers's husband than to her (see Presley 1973).

English critic Rosalind Miles (1974) contributes to the decade's widening interest in McCullers's social criticism. The political theme in *Hunter* is "handled with characteristic use of resonant allusion and luminous detail. In the McCullers universe, politics provide yet another arena in which human ideals and aspirations are pitifully measured against human weakness and wickedness." Dr. Copeland "embodies a series of paradoxes – he is a healer, yet dying of tuberculosis; he is intensely proud yet forced to endure the routine contempt of every white man; he is a committed father, yet estranged from his children. His politics naturally fit in with this pattern of longing and disappointment. His passionate vision of socialism denies the true (and the social) nature of his own race; his christening his son Karl Marx signifies his ideal, but shows too how he unknowingly undermines it by his determination to Westernise his people at all costs, even at the price of their ethnic identity" (133). Blount's socialism fails; he is unable "to mobilise, or even to get on with, his fellows." The mad evangelist is "a ludicrous and unregarded prophet of primitive Christianity. In this crushing association we are given a glimpse by the author of how Jake appears to the millions who have no time or use for his 'message'" (133–34).

Charlene Kerne Clark (1975a) explores McCullers's use of tragicomedy against the tradition of southern literary humor, but ultimately sees her creation of comic horror as a political strategy. The combination of horror and humor often derives from McCullers's "injection of child characters into roles and situations normally reserved for adults. The result is the diminution of the tragic effect by the heightening of the comic effect." In Bubber's "near-tragic shooting of Baby Wilson, the talented toddler," Clark finds "a parody of the impassioned lover who tries to do away with the indifferent beloved. The tragedy is undercut by the proliferation of petty details and material concerns. As Baby lies sprawled and bloody on the sidewalk, she clutches in her fist her candy box prize, an apt reminder of her material aspirations for stardom. Her mother's overriding concerns are for adequate and just compensation for the cost of the toddler's ruined soirée costume and her new permanent wave, and she is quick to express her outrage over the irreparable damage done to Baby's promising career as a second Shirley Temple. A special touch of comic horror is added to the scene by Mick Kelly's admonition to her brother . . . that in the state prison there are little electric chairs perfect for 'frying' small-fry criminals like himself" (164). Perhaps the most characteristic source of tragicomic effects is the incongruous pair. With the first words of her first novel, McCullers signals the pattern: "In the town there were two mutes and they were always together." Clark says the two mutes are "an interesting variation of the male pair that dominates American fiction and film, and . . . assumes the popular form of the 'straight' man with his comic sidekick. In appearance and personality, Singer and Antonapoulos resemble Laurel and Hardy" (165). McCullers's essay on "The Russian Realists and Southern Literature" (1941) appeared shortly after *Hunter* and illuminates for Clark the writer's belief that "a mixed vision of life is inherent within Southern culture itself; consequently, the Southern literary imagination seizes upon the juxtaposition of the idyllic aspect of life with the barbaric – the sentimental attachment for the black mammy with the inhumanity of racism itself" (166).

Richard M. Cook's sensible and balanced critical monograph (1975) emphasizes that Mick's story is the novel's "most representative. Her initiatory confrontations with the adult world, her failures to adjust, her limited successes, shed light on how the other characters came to be the way they are. At the same time the pathetic fate of the others stands as a terrible warning of what may happen to her in the end – gifted and determined as she is" (28). "In sacrificing her talent, her plans, her vitality, to the dehumanizing monotony of clerking in Woolworth's for as far as she can see, Mick creates that impression of tragic waste – not the less tragic for its being contemporary and familiar. One feels that Mick, once a fascinating, bright youngster, will grow up an unhappy, neurotic woman, and that the loss involved in such a growing up is tragic" (31). Mick's story and those of the other characters are rooted in time and place and reveal a real-world landscape. From this perspective, Cook takes issue with critics in the previous decade, particularly David Madden (1968) and Horace Taylor (1960), who dismiss Jake Blount and Dr. Copeland as "monomaniacal egotists" whose socialist politics are not to be taken seriously. Allying himself with the myth critics against the formalists, Cook quotes Ihab Hassan on McCullers's deep concern with issues of society as well as "issues of the soul." Cook argues that "one of the achievements of the book is Mrs. McCullers's success in grounding the problems of the soul in the actualities of time and place." To discount "Copeland's anguishing over the poverty and the disease of the Negroes [as] a 'pretext' or a 'sublimation'" constitutes its own brand of injustice. "The Doctor, who has had a son tortured and maimed in prison and who has been beaten and jailed for simply trying to see a judge, knows racism to be a real, not a 'convenient,' evil. Mrs. McCullers sees a great deal that is mysterious and strange in the heart of man, but she also sees and records the very real pressures – economic, racial, sexual – that make the extraordinary behavior of her characters in part at least understandable" (34–35).

In one of the most fascinating interpretations of *Hunter,* tucked too obscurely in a festschrift, Edgar E. MacDonald (1976) says the novel's symbolic unity encompasses multiple forms of symmetry: Christian hagiography, Jewish theosophy, Gnostic philosophy, and mystical numerology, which McCullers deploys with precision. The essay is a catalog of occult patterns which "throb beneath" the surface of the novel – particularly, allusions within character names (Biff-Bartholomew, Jake-Jacob, Mick-Michael, Benedict-St. Benedict) and repetitions and combinations of the numbers four, twelve, and three. The tripartite plot divisions concern "the establishing of Singer's godhood, the suffering of his priesthood . . . and [its] dissolution . . . with the emergence of the new god" (171). In this reading, the novel explores the "nature of godhead itself and presents an historical overview of those traits that Western man looked for in his gods" (178). Antonapoulos (twelve letters to his name) is the pagan eastern god; Singer (six letters) is the Christ, a "sorrowful wanderer at the age of thirty-two," whose ministry ends in death at the age of thirty-three; and

Biff Brannon is the modern synthesis. The novel's final scene in the New York Café, Brannon's "altar for the lonely, the lost, the heavy laden," on the portentous night of August 21, 1939, on the eve of world war, offers revelation and reason for optimism. Where others see polarities and incompatibilities – "radiance and darkness," "bitter irony and faith" – MacDonald sees fusion: Biff "could say with Apollo in Keats's *Hyperion,* 'Knowledge enormous makes a god of me.' To the Christian virtues of Faith, Hope, and Love, Biff will add the fourth sacrament – human understanding based on knowledge. Mick as Faith ('Maybe she would get a chance soon,'), Jake as Hope ('There was hope in him . . . . '), and Copeland as Charity ('His heart turned with his angry, restless love') may realize their aspiration in some problematic future, but Biff Brannon as the sympathetic man-god of understanding will watch with them through the dark night of the spirit. The vision of suffering humanity appalled him, but in the final lines of the novel 'he composed himself soberly to await the morning sun'" (81–82). Although McCullers "wrote at a time when the world seemed to be plunging again into elemental darkness, . . . her symbolism makes clear her belief that despite the anguish inherent in man's experience, the purified being could glimpse a transcendental vision, a flash of comprehension illuminating the struggle. In its rise from darkness to light, from the 'black, sultry night' of the opening action to the 'morning sun' of the final words, in its movement from incomprehension to knowledge, Mrs. McCullers created a Divine Comedy whose symbolic architecture and symmetry are everywhere in harmony and which reveals a profound sense of form and artistic completion" (185). One result of MacDonald's perspective is that Mick is displaced from the central position many readers give her and which, in terms of space devoted to her, McCullers gives her as well.

Sylvia Jenkins Cook (1976), writing of the Depression decade, says,

> a strange dichotomy was perpetuated in depression literature between those worthy and victimized poor whites who, somehow, deserved revolutionary change and those cunning and servile poor whites who, somehow, deserved to go on living in poverty, contempt, and neglect. At the very end of the decade, Carson McCullers came close to observing this tendency in . . . *The Heart Is a Lonely Hunter.* Here the author's sympathy for both the black and white poor of a southern mill town does not distort a devastating and despairing portrait of the traditional vices and shortcomings generally associated with the two groups. The blacks have a model leader and hero in Dr. Benedict Copeland, who attempts to instill in them pride of race, personal dignity, and a sense of justice; they respond with abject acquiescence in their mistreatment and look only to

heaven for relief, where "straightway us will be white as cotton." The poor white mill workers are even harsher and more hostile in their response to Jake Blount, a self-appointed apostle of revolution.

Cook assumes McCullers's political engagement and leftward social philosophy, but the novelist "presents a bleak future for political and social radicals in the South; they are so utterly estranged from their community's mores that they become like the grotesque characters in Sherwood Anderson's Winesburg – the truths to which they are committed distort their possessors because they must be so fanatically preserved in an alien environment . . . . If McCullers's novel does not absolutely close out hope for reform in the South, it certainly appears to be a bitter and accurate recognition of the pitfalls before any idealist with a scheme for saving or radicalizing the poor there" (156–57).

Alan Henry Rose (1976) analyzes "elements of the old demonic imagery . . . evoked by the vision of racial disorder" in McCullers's portrait of Dr. Copeland. "Doctor Copeland's frustrations result in 'a black, terrible, Negro feeling.' At times he drank strong liquor and beat his head against the floor. In his heart there was a savage violence' . . . . But when Copeland feels 'as though he had swelled up to the size of a giant . . . ' the narrative suddenly offers a curious internal vision of its central black man. Copeland opens his own medical history [including x-rays] . . . . In this photograph the mechanics of the 'dynamo' in the Negro's chest are laid bare. The once flashing images of light associated with demonic energy have atrophied; within Copeland there is 'a calcified star.' It is an indication not of power, but of disease" (121). Rose makes the point that such an image, an x-ray of "the soul of a black man," perpetuates rather than meliorates a tradition in southern writing of demonizing black characters by their association with violence and disease (121–22). "It is as if this photograph, plumbing to the soul of the black man in a way that extends the meaning of the photographic metaphor of dissolution seen in the case of . . . Joe Christmas, indicates by its very form the doubtful 'Prognosis' of the dying demonic tradition" (121–22).

Joan S. Korenman (1976) offers a sustained analysis of the novel's investment in the economic determinism of Marxist aesthetics and the 1930s-style proletarian novel. "The poverty, sickness, and violence bred by capitalism gone awry . . . serves as the background for *The Heart Is a Lonely Hunter*. But economic and social concerns are not merely a backdrop, the obligatory props of the era. Such concerns figure significantly in the lives of nearly all the major characters" (8). Citing lengthy passages of Marxist doctrine and invective against the class stratification of the South that McCullers puts in the mouths of Blount and Copeland, Korenman

reveals the considerable extent of the novel's critique of capitalism and especially its role in race and class oppression. One example from Blount
may suffice to show the indictment of class difference: "There are corpo-
rations worth billions of dollars – and hundreds of thousands of people
who don't get to eat. And here in these thirteen states the exploitation of
human beings is so that – that it's a thing you got to take in with your
own eyes . . . . At least one third of all Southerners live and die no better
off than the lowest peasant in any European Fascist state" (qtd. 9). The
economic fate of Mick Kelly and her family serves as well "to illustrate the
destructiveness of a materialistic society" (11). Precarious from the start,
the family's security is endangered by their liability for Baby Wilson's ex-
pensive hospital room and private nurses and the loss of Etta's income
when she requires an operation. Mick is trapped behind a Woolworth's
counter because of her family's economic vulnerability. "Mick's situation
exemplifies some of the criticisms levelled by Jake and Dr. Copeland.
Blount assails a capitalist system that keeps the masses in such poverty
and suffering that 'something dies in them' [and] Dr. Copeland feels that
the one injustice more bitter than to suffer from real need is 'to be denied
the right to work according to one's ability. To labor a lifetime use-
lessly' . . . . He has in mind his fellow Blacks whose talents are wasted in
menial jobs, but what he says holds true also for Mick's writing sales receipts instead of symphonies" (11).

Korenman makes a convincing case for McCullers's consciousness of
the "political vision" the novel contains. The "Author's Outline" for the
novel (in Evans 1965a and in the posthumous *The Mortgaged Heart* [1971])
shows that McCullers initially projected a scene in which Copeland and
Blount come together as "spiritual brothers" to end their "lifetime of isolation." They talk late into the night and, exhausted, fall asleep in the same
bed. "The scene has the effect of elevating the two Marxists above the
novel's other characters. The two men experience a moment of mutual
closeness and understanding unmatched even in the blissful relationship
between Singer and Antonapoulos" (12). In the published novel, the scene
appears "radically altered" as the two men refuse to understand each
other and the evening ends with shouted insults. "The very different version of their relationship in the novel suggests that, as she wrote, the
author backed away from her earlier enthusiasm for Marxism. But why?
The relatively little that has been published about McCullers does not
provide adequate explanation" (13). Korenman's analysis never engages
the question of why McCullers referred to the novel as an "ironic parable
of fascism," but in documenting the novelist's "political vision," it goes
some distance toward implying a reasonable answer.

Nancy B. Rich (1977), in a highly uneven analysis, scrutinizes McCullers's remark about the novel and fascism. Using statements from McCullers's outline as well as biographical information about the writer's politics, Rich adduces "considerable evidence . . . that politics was a motivating factor in the genesis of the novel and that the parable is a key not only to broader implications in the theme but also to the tight construction McCullers claimed" (108). "The parable's theme is an affirmation of the democratic process, but its implications are the universal problems of illusion versus reality and the nature of man himself" (109). Rich must ignore the existence of Roosevelt's New Deal to argue that governmental restraint or inaction during the Depression produced a Fascist denial of liberty by default – that is, by inaction and silence. Choosing to define fascism in this way, Rich finds that Singer represents democratic government in the parable and that "the instrument of [that government's] oppression is the sound of silence" (110). The overdetermined allegory of this reading is visible in such a pronouncement as, "Thus as the figure of Singer gradually fades into the background, the parable shows that for all practical purposes government has become defunct" (111). Other examples are not hard to come by. Antonapoulos's confusion at chess, because "he does not understand the female figures and prefers whites over blacks, [is] an analogy to the historical confusion of how these minority figures should be treated in a free democratic society" (112). In the dream pyramid, the object Antonapoulos holds above him is "the Constitution of the United States" (113).

The main contribution of Rich's analysis is the elevation of Biff Brannon to "the most important character in the parable, for its central question is concerned with the survival of freedom under a democratic political system" (118). Biff is a representative of the divine average in a democracy. To see him this way, Rich feels compelled to defend his heterosexuality, his normalcy as a middle-class man with "many . . . quite manly qualities" (she cites an "iron jaw" and "dark hairy armpits") and a wife who is a Sunday school teacher. Rich reads Biff's experience at the end of the novel as affirmative: A persevering and sensible man, Brannon will "unite with others like himself to put a new image of government before the people, just as surely as he puts fresh flowers in his display" (122). To secure Biff Brannon's importance as the emerging hero of the parable, Rich finds it necessary not merely to displace Mick Kelly but to discredit her. She is "a negative force – a 'silent' majority" (114); "she represents public apathy; its causes, which appear to be immaturity, immorality and irrationality, are manifest in her behavior" (115). "Judged by her actions, Mick is selfish, dishonest and prejudiced" (116). She is guilty of lying, stealing, and defacing private property. Furthermore, she self-ishly exploits Harry Minowitz, using him "to satisfy her own need to ex-periment with sex (it was her idea to swim naked)" (116). "Intellectually and morally, Mick never matures"; she "never grows up; she only grows tall" (117). The essay's sole value lies in taking McCullers at her word and thereby revealing the extent to which McCullers's stated intentions in the "Author's Outline" hint at a political purpose. Rich does not provide a believable analysis of what that purpose is.

Few students of McCullers's reputation have been more insistent on her minor status than has Richard Gray (1977). In his assessment of postwar southern literature, designed to counter enthusiasm for technical and thematic virtuosity apart from fiction's social and historical context, Gray argues that, "because her work represents a perfect adaptation of means to ends," she was overestimated by New Critics (272). To a con-siderable extent Gray, like the critics he faults, errs in dismissing or vastly underreading McCullers's concern with the dynamic interplay of individ-ual and environment.

> The very perfection of McCullers's work depends, after all, upon her own level-headed acceptance of her limitations. She knows that she can describe, quite subtly, one particular dilemma or area of life and she concentrates almost her entire resources on that. There is no place in her fiction, really, for the rich "over-plus" of experience – by which I mean any aspects of behavior that cannot be included under the heading of theme, or any dimensions of feeling that cannot be reconciled with the major effect of pathos. And recognizing this she demonstrates little inter-est in such matters as the historical and social context, and no commit-ment either to the idea of a developing consciousness. Her people walk around and around within the circle of their own personalities, their in-ner world of thought and desire hardly engaging with the outer world at all. They seldom change, except physically, they never reflect more than one aspect of our experience (admittedly, it is a significant one); and to inflate them, their world, or indeed their creator to a major status – to suppose, in fact, that McCullers's novels and short stories are any more important to the tradition that they genuinely are – is . . . to smother a quiet but effective talent by heaping upon it unearned and patently un-acceptable praise. (272–73)

History, Gray says, "function[s] as an *absent presence* in her fiction. It seems to be not so much omitted from her writing as concealed, made to disap-pear, and in such a way that the disappearance itself, like the disappear-ance of the religious perspective from later Victorian fiction, encourages our active comment" (273). Plainly, there is no paradox here. By showing the intimate operations of history in a novel like *Hunter* – that is, the ways the legacy of slavery, class prejudice, war, economic uncertainty (to mention only the most obvious) impinge on individual lives – McCullers does, in fact, evince a considerable interest in the outside world. Gray makes a mistake equivalent to the one in which he catches the New Critics: his focus on figure eclipses the ground.

Joseph R. Millichap (1977), in his second important contribution to McCullers criticism in this decade, works toward an accommodation between social realism and modernist aesthetics, the site of which is the structural disjunctiveness of the grotesque. Millichap links *Hunter* with *The Sound and the Fury* and *Winesburg, Ohio* to argue that the literature of the grotesque as practiced in these works and others is a peculiarly modernist genre. To counter the critical perception that the grotesque has more to do with subject or theme than with the aesthetic form emphasized in discussions of modernism, he suggests that the two converge in a subgenre marked by distorted matter and disjunctive form. In the example of *Hunter,* "disjunctive structure . . . perfectly elicits the themes of loneliness and fragmentation from the Grotesque materials of mill town life" (345–46). In its four short chapters, the third and final section of the novel, especially, shows the failure of Mick, Biff, Blount, and Copeland "to regain their psychological equilibrium after Singer's funeral." The four "have become, through the disintegrative forces of their exploitive social setting and through their own personal incompletions, too distorted to function in life . . . . McCullers's social setting is heavy with grotesquerie, but it is her disjunctive narrative structure which fully realizes the Modernist vision of personal fragmentation and alienation in the modern industrial town" (346). The work of the three modernist writers cited "exhibits a definite similarity of grotesque subject matter – abnormal characters, bizarre events, wasteland setting; more importantly, they also are similar in disjunctive form – multiple narrators, isolated chapters, disjoined levels and sequences of narration" (347).

The most important contribution to an analysis of the novel's structure during the decade was C. Michael Smith's demonstration (1979) of how the polyphonic pattern of the fugue, especially its elements of imitation and inversion of voices, provides the structural model for McCullers's management of voice and theme. Autobiographical notes at the Humanities Research Center contain a comparison of *Hunter* to a Bach fugue, "and her notes for a Ford Foundation grant application in the late 1950s refer to the fugue pattern of her first novel and the musical form of her later fiction" (259n). These documents and McCullers's statement about the novel's musical structure in her "Author's Outline" establish the value of the detailed examination of polyphony that Smith undertakes.

The conventional elements of a fugue, as he presents them, could serve as a rough sketch for the novel's organization:

> Imitation is the simplest pattern; it is a repetition of one theme by another voice. Inversion is a form of repetition that reverses the progress of the theme producing a mirror image of the original voice. Whether repeated through imitation or inversion, the initial theme in a fugue is developed in a three-part structure. In the exposition, or first part, the theme is introduced. Characteristically, one voice sounds the theme, then a second voice is introduced, then a third. The fugue then proceeds with the second part, the development, consisting of a series of episodes in which the separate voices are interwoven. A final section, the return, then follows. It is a partial restatement of the theme, sometimes emphasized through stretto, the relatively rapid entrance of one voice after another. (259)

Singer introduces the theme in his selfish attraction to Antonapoulos, using the retarded mute to create "a dream world of imagined communication." Ironically, "Singer . . . sings for no one but himself." Associations of Singer with Christ imagery "are ironic, reflecting the illusions others have about him rather than the reality of his character." The ironic pattern developed in the portrait of Singer is "repeated through imitation" in the characterization of Blount and Copeland, who, "like Singer, seem on the surface to sacrifice themselves for others" (260). By comparison of the novel with the outline, Smith observes, as did Korenman (1976), that McCullers altered the characterization of Blount and Copeland to prevent their mutual understanding. Their shouting match reveals that "they have become too concerned with themselves, their own inner worlds, their own doctrines, and their racial identities to recognize their commonality with others. Blount has even come to hate the mill workers whose cause he would champion, while Copeland is misunderstood by his people and resents his own children. It is not surprising, then, that these failed social reformers, like Singer, are associated with ironic Christ images" (261).

As Blount and Copeland imitate the ironic theme associated with Singer. Mick and Brannon "extend the fugue pattern through inversion." They "underscore the ironic self-deception of the other major characters by reversing their movement toward illusion and isolation." Mick Kelly's "progression from childhood to adulthood, from self-deception to reality, stands in counterpoint to the stories of Singer, Blount, and Copeland" (261). Smith interprets Mick's inner room negatively, as "the world of her imagination in which illusion and self-deception rule. This world contains her desire for isolation, her dreams of escape, and her romantic fascination with music." Her sexual initiation is the "turning point": "her initiation into the social world" of family responsibility and work behind a Woolworth's counter. "The objective world, however, is the best option open to her. Life may not be very sympathetic or appealing, the author seems to suggest, but it is better to have the courage to thrust oneself entirely into the everyday world than to try to cling to a past dream world that is, like the worlds of Singer, Blount, and Copeland, based on illusions and self-deception" (262).

The third section features the return of the voices "in a rapid succession as in a stretto." Copeland "has become more like a child . . . . His movement out of town signifies his separation from reality and his increasing dependence on others." (This is a point of inconsistency worth noting. Smith wants to have it both ways in formulating dependence on others as akin to unreality in this instance and, before, as in the example of Mick, equating isolation from others with unreality.) Smith notes that Blount abandons "his manifesto on 'The Affinity between Our Democracy and Fascism'" (262). At the end, Brannon "grasps his own position, suspended between the extremes of 'bitter irony and faith' that define all the action in the novel. Committed to the reality of day-to-day existence, he emerges as a 'sensible man.' He raises the awning outside his shop, as though lifting the curtain of illusion, and awaits 'the morning sun'" (263).

One of the oddest features of Smith's essay is his interpretation of McCullers's theme as an endorsement of conventional "adult" behavior. Give up your illusions and be sensible – that's all. In this respect, his analysis has the shape that defines most New Critical readings: a demonstration of the complex innerworkings of structure or other aspect of technique, paired with (or, rather, resolved into) a conservative and uncomplex formulation of universal theme – in this case, the admonition to grow up, applied moralistically in his discussion of Mick Kelly.

Smith concludes that "recognition of this musical pattern should lead not only to a better understanding of McCullers' first novel but to a reevaluation of the structure of her other novels as well." *Clock Without Hands* "clearly duplicates some aspects of the fugue pattern" in *Hunter; The Ballad of the Sad Café* "has a musical form replete with a coda"; *Reflections in a Golden Eye* and *The Member of the Wedding* "display traces of musical structure as well." McCullers "was a writer whose sense of form was strongly influenced by her early training in music. Certainly her first novel, though unconventional in form, is more carefully structured than critics who have ignored the musical pattern have recognized" (263). Given earlier, though less detailed treatments of the structural analogy between verbal and musical counterpoint by Barbara Nauer Folk (1962), Oliver Evans (1965a), and, in Spanish, by Alicia M. Cervantes Leal (1977), Smith somewhat overstates the originality of his analysis. He does, however, demonstrate with specificity what others have suggested in a more general way.

As the 1970s ended, a flurry of critical and popular interest in McCullers was stirred by the appearance of Virginia Spencer Carr's biography of *The Lonely Hunter* in 1975. A massive study, six hundred pages in length, the biography won praise for its thoroughness but disappointed readers who had hoped for a greater leaven of literary analysis within the compilation of life records. However, its contribution to literary studies and to the growth of McCullers's reputation has been immense. Gauged by the ratio of doctoral dissertations completed in the decade before and the decade after 1976, a twofold increase from fewer than ten in the earlier period to more than twenty in the later decade, Carr's detailed biography stimulated considerable new interest among young scholars. Veteran students of McCullers, however, occasionally recoiled at revelations of the wunderkind's adulterous bisexuality and self-destructive indulgences. Linda Huf (1983) has effectively cataloged the negative reaction, which centered less on the manifold evidence of neurosis than on McCullers's willingness to accept the alleged sacrifices of Reeves McCullers in furthering her career. National newsmagazines were at the forefront of the rush to condemn: "*Time* magazine called her 'monstrous' and hinted that it was her insensitivity that drove her long-abused husband to kill himself after sixteen years of marriage . . . . *Newsweek* even charged her with refusing to ship Reeves's body back home to America, after he had 'subordinated himself to her career' and tolerated her 'sexual vagaries.'" And veteran McCullers critic "Dale Edmonds, writing in the *Southern Quarterly,* went so far as to say that McCullers's life 'should never have been written,' because she was 'one of the most selfish and destructive literary figures who ever lived'" (106). The sexual betrayal of Reeves McCullers, if it was that, emerged as the focus of anti-McCullers opinion after Carr's revelations and was immediately read back into the fiction. Mick and Frankie's abnormality – the fact that "when they have to become women, as they must, they are, as characters, all but destroyed" – makes Louis D. Rubin, Jr., think of the boyish photographs of Carson McCullers "and of what she did to poor Reeves McCullers" (1977, 279). The signal revelation for Rubin, as we might suspect it was for Edmonds and others, is that "Mrs. McCullers was a lesbian." Such a condition explains in her case, as it does for Proust and his homosexuality, the "hunger for possession" (276) that pervades character, theme, and aesthetic sense. Rubin argues that "art was a way of possessing. It was the creative act of taking what she saw and molding it, transforming it beyond identifiable shape into the form of art, so that it represented her kind of world"(277). The identification of her writing with a presumed deviancy, a predatory sexuality, is complete in this critical judgment.

Reaction to the reversal of gender expectations within the McCullers marriage – read as benevolent self-sacrifice in the case of the husband and as unnatural and devouring selfishness on the part of the wife – galvanized a critique of McCullers's fictional portrayal of gender and sexuality that dominated discussions of her work in the 1980s. But the response to revelations in Carr's biography, while important, was not solely responsible for this shift in critical emphasis. It was, again, more than anything else, a product of changes in the culture of the academy. The influx of the male outsider in the 1950s, which challenged New Critical orthodoxy, was followed twenty years later by the more gradual infiltration of academic ranks by the female outsider. A numerical accounting reveals the trend dramatically. During the first three decades covered in this history, 1940–1970, U.S. women published only three essays on McCullers that appeared in academic literary journals of the period. In the decade 1970–1980 academic women in this country published eight such essays. In 1980–1990 women had become, numerically, the foremost academic critics of McCullers in the United States, responsible for thirty essays and the majority of dissertations on McCullers as well. National statistics show that the percentage of women in the professoriate and in graduate schools rose 58 and 83 percent respectively from 1960 to 1980 (Touchton and Davis 1991). The shift in critical methods in the 1980s, from the assumption of a male norm to an awareness that gender marks experience variably, is understandable in demographic terms. Only a small number of African American women are represented among the total number of academic women in the United States who have written on McCullers. The number of African American men writing on McCullers is even smaller. Continued gains in diversity can be expected to expand even further our understanding of the life and work of Carson McCullers. It should be noted that important women critics of McCullers have been visible from the first among reviewers for U.S. periodicals (Marguerite Young, Diana Trilling, and Joan Didion among them) and that women have been represented in approximately equal numbers with men among McCullers's international critics and reviewers.

The first notable feminist criticism of *Hunter* was Gayatri Chakravorty Spivak's deconstructive reading (1979/1980) focusing on the "failure of collectivity" and "the irreducible separation [that] is based on race-, class-, and sex-struggle" (16). Spivak, a formidable pioneer theorist of feminist, post-colonialist, and deconstructive projects, brings to McCullers criticism the philosophical, often highly technical vocabulary that began to characterize theoretically informed criticism in this period. Spivak observes that through a passion for music, indulged within her "inside room," Mick Kelly "hopes to transcend the subject-object dichotomy and time itself by way of a vicarious auto-eroticism." Spivak marks the opposition between Mick's "inside room" and "the real outside – the man's world, where the only viable female commodity is sex" (17). Sexual initiation for Mick, however, is merely a stage in the loss of her dreams. "It is not her sex-predicament but her class-predicament that finally defeats her. The book laments not so much her loss of innocence as her entry into the work force. Her dreams are the dreams of a classbound free spirit" (18).

Unlike most 1980s critics who focused on gender as an analytical category for responding to McCullers's fiction, Spivak is less interested in Mick than in the gendered meanings of two of the novel's key scenes. She identifies Singer's dream pyramid as central. The mysterious object Antonapoulos holds above his head is "an undisclosed phallus . . . the mysterious unifier of the book's world. The final exchange between [Singer and Antonapoulos in the asylum] shows us a childlike and idolized Antonapoulos who, indefinitely displaced through mutism, homosexuality, and idiocy, reveals the brutal image foreclosed by all the 'normally' objectified love-goddesses of the world" (19). At the heart, or apex, of the novel is the image of Antonapoulos, "the male homosexual as the institutionalized insane" (20).

Biff Brannon's failed epiphany at the end of the novel signals his impotence in fusing microstructural (personal) and macrostructural (collective) insights. It fails, in other words, to unite (i.e., to deconstruct the opposition between) the personal and the political. Brannon's vision is narcissistically short-circuited by the counterglass, which reflects his image back to him. Of this merely partial insight, Spivak says,

> This is the careful glance into history and the broad glance into the future; on another register, it is the relationship between theory (knowing) and practice (doing). In yet another register, not quite the same but a similar one, it must be recognized that both knowing and doing are undermined, yet made possible, by the micro-structural network of an ever-fractured sense of being. A politicized socialist and inter-racialist feminism will work at redefining the personal as the micro-structural network of being that undermines as it makes possible the production of both theory and practice. McCullers's book is unable to provide a coherent redefinition. But the kaleidoscope of the micro-structure "changes minute by minute," and its motives come from many places at once; indeed, a recognition of the micro-structure might disclose that a *coherent*

redefinition is impossible. *The Heart* at least dramatizes the incoherence: the simple story of an adolescent girl victimized by her class; the mysterious and secret story of the nature of sex as such and/or marginal sex; the political story of the lack of contact between race- and class-politics; the hopeless story of idolatry; the safe story of the recovery of reason. (24)

Spivak's critical stance grows out of a radicalized epistemology in which "pure reason" no longer deserves first place. Her reading of literature "within a feminist perspective" is a direct challenge to New Criticism and, therefore, to received interpretations of McCullers: "Dated noises that would call all mingling of the text of 'texts' and the text of 'life' naive and would recommend demystified investigations of the poem itself, leading surely to a mood of wise passiveness disguised as suspended ignorance can still be heard from mainstream literary criticism" (31). Spivak intends "to use and subvert the method of close reading bequeathed to us for the decoding of divinely moral or aesthetically neutral allegories" (24). And she reminds us that "how unorthodox a reading the text can *convincingly* be made to engender depends sometimes on the vested authority and power of the critic within the system of academic patronage" (20).

In a full-length study published in Twayne's United States Authors Series, Margaret B. McDowell (1980) offers a reading that displaces Biff Brannon as the focal figure at the end of *Hunter*. She looks instead to Portia Copeland and Mick Kelly, the "young black woman" and the white teenager who together bring "a qualified optimism" to the final sections of the novel. The two women "reach out with some hope to the future": "Mick's voice rings in the finale above the voices of the other three [acolytes of John Singer], who remain locked in their despair. Mick has a vision of a future for herself, even if the way to fulfillment will be arduous. Portia, whose rancor against her father has been supplanted by a vision of self-sacrifice for the welfare of her father, her husband, and her brother, and who dreams of a simple, pastoral existence, [attenuates] the strident negation of the other characters. The ending intermingles a fleeting vision of a brighter future with the bleakness dominating the characters who react most intensely to Singer's suicide" (32). By focusing on Portia Copeland, a character who remained submerged in most earlier critical discussion, and putting Mick's experience at the center of the novel's meaning, McDowell effects a revisionary reading typical of feminist practice.

No other character in *Hunter* has undergone so dramatic a shift in critical perception as has Mick Kelly. Recalling the distance between Jack B. Moore's assurance in 1965 that Mick grows heroically into adulthood following a "transcendent" sexual awakening and the view of Mick as exploited by both her family and her adolescent seducer gives some idea of how readers read their culture with each book. Like the proverbial fish who has to escape the water before knowing what water is, readers could identify Mick's struggle against womanhood only after leaving behind the era in which growing up female was supposed to consist of submission and self-sacrifice. Of Mick's sexual initiation, McDowell says the experience "merely baffles [Mick] in its suddenness and brevity, rather than producing psychic trauma. The impact of the experience is even more completely wiped out of her memory by greater violence when she returns home to discuss the event with Singer and discovers him dead. Harry, on the other hand, is shocked that he has violated a virgin – and has been himself defiled by contact with a gentile. He goes to another city to take a job there" (39). "At her best, Mick is heroic in offering to quit high school to support her family by working in the dime store . . . . Her defiant words . . . show that she is still above despair and that she will battle the society that demands of her so unfair a sacrifice" (39–40).

Mary Roberts (1980) brings a biographical perspective to her study of androgyny in McCullers's fiction. The novelist "was undoubtedly aware of that 'other-sexed' element in her personality which, despite her marriage to Reeves McCullers, drove her repeatedly to search for a love relationship with a woman" (74). The term *androgyny,* "derived· as it is from the Greek *andros* (male) and *gyne* (female), . . . expresses a union between the masculine and feminine principles within an individual" and implies psychic integration and wholeness. Roberts quotes Samuel Taylor Coleridge on its relevance to creativity: "The truth is, a great mind must be androgynous" (75). She furthermore credits McCullers with a perception of one of the first principles of modern feminism: "Carson McCullers' attitudes toward sex (biological maleness and femaleness) and gender (masculinity and femininity: expressed in psychological behavior) spring . . . from her conviction that sex and gender are by no means always closely related." Biff Brannon's thought that "by nature all people are of both sexes" is taken for McCullers's own: "And thus she is not interested in depicting relationships which have their dynamic in some kind of polarisation. Since she is haunted by the incongruities and contradictions of human existence, her world contains no true androgynes" – or persons in whom male and female qualities completely balance (76).

The term *androgyny* is much misunderstood and mistakenly taken as synonymous with bisexuality or homosexuality, hermaphroditism, or effeminacy in men. Roberts points out that the *Oxford English Dictionary* records only two historical references to women described as androgynous.

Implicit in this difficulty of definition for Roberts must be an awareness of the shifting fortunes of the word within modern feminism, where, circa 1970, it reached a peak that may be conveniently marked by the publication of Carolyn Heilbrun's *Toward Androgyny* (1973), but fell out of favor as liberal feminism was joined in the forum by more radical or separatist or essentialist views that questioned the word's historical ties to a model in which passive "female" merely supplemented or served active "male" in the concept. (See chapter 9 for a discussion of the concept in current youth culture and among "third wave" feminists.) Roberts evades the problem by conceiving of the androgyne as primarily characterized by "a psychic unity" (77). McCullers is concerned only with a figure Roberts calls "the *incomplete androgyne:* a person possessing an ambiguous sexuality, potentially but not actually androgynous, which produces a strangely asexual mode of being. Incarcerated within a dualistic nature (where the masculine and feminine, though strongly present, are fractured), he or she attempts in desperation or frustration to achieve an androgynous self by imagining a beloved who can make him or her whole. Love thus becomes a power-based phenomenon in which narcissism is the impetus" (77–78). McCullers's "concept of love implies a belief in Eros as 'the double-sexed god,' who 'knows no boundaries' and who does not 'willingly accept limitations, regardless of how energetically societies seek to impose them.' Moreover, if (as it has frequently been maintained) the bias of all religion is an androgynoid god-figure, then in a world where sexual polarisation has displaced the androgynous instinct, the loneliness of an incomplete God, a Father God or Mother Goddess without a mate, must be an expression of the human need for that which is unknown to him or her, the unconscious element in the psyche, namely, that which carries the potentiality for creation" (qtd. June Singer, Jungian analyst, Roberts 78).

Roberts quotes Aristophanes' definition of love as "the desire and pursuit of the whole" and his suggestion "that there were originally three spherical beings: male, female, and male-female (the androgyne). Zeus decided to humble their pride by splitting each into two; thus each unhappy nature, in seeking his or her original half, might yearn for someone of the same or the opposite sex. This myth, apart from granting equal validity to the heterosexual and the homosexual impulses, suggests that the symbol of the androgyne is as enduring a part of human consciousness as the symbols of the 'masculine' and the 'feminine'" (78–79).

Applied to *Hunter,* "the five central characters ... are extreme and quasi-allegorical examples of such loneliness: each is obsessed by a sense of incompleteness and alienation, each fails to unite with another in a reciprocal relationship; hence all except Singer are driven to create illusory gods. But there is no mutuality in love, for it is impossible that illusory gods should heal real anguish. Singer, the repository for others' fantasies of order and communication, is himself an incomplete androgyne: deprived of the companionship of Antonapoulos, he is confused and fragmented" (80). Mick Kelly is "potentially androgynous . . . . Her name . . . expresses her ambiguous sexual nature: a nature split by the psychic dualities of 'masculine' and 'feminine.' She is both envious of and irritated by the role-playing of the older girls, and her sister" (81). Her prom party is an attempt to create and to enter a world "where 'masculine' and 'feminine' roles are to be appropriately acted out in an effort to release her from her confusion" (81). But Mick's longing for "The Thing I Want, I Know Not What" is thwarted, both by the failure of the party and, more seriously, by the economic difficulties that require her to become a dime-store clerk. "Mick, in a poor and repressive environment, is compelled to adopt what seems a parodic female 'identity' which must crush any potential for androgyny" (82).

Biff Brannon is more fortunate in achieving androgyny. After the death of his wife "he becomes a less divided personality and his energies are directed towards psychic integration." Biff, therefore, "becomes able to effect within himself a kind of marriage between the male and female, and his direct sexual needs are sublimated into parental emotions" (83). "In his constant meditations on the 'why' of human life, he alone has any real awareness of his predicament and he alone realizes that because Singer is a mute – and cannot disturb their fundamental narcissism – his fellow creatures have made him a fount of wisdom and understanding. Biff has moved partially toward the state of Platonic love at its highest: the spiritual achievement of androgynous intuition; only partially, however, for as Mick grows older and her 'rough and childish ways' disappear, his love [for her] dies." *Hunter* "ends equivocally . . . . There can be no resolution, but the geography of alienation is skillfully mapped, the contours of the human dilemma lyrically exposed" (84).

Louise Westling (1980) provides a new reading of McCullers's tomboys, displacing the stereotype of lively and likable prepubescent girlhood by pinpointing its more troubling implications of sexual ambiguity and social constraint. "McCullers dramatizes the crisis of identity which faces ambitious girls as they leave childhood and stumble into an understanding of what the world expects them to become. The images McCullers associates with the crisis are the images of sexual freaks, supported by an ambience of androgynous longings, homosexuality, and transvestitism" (339). A girl's "ambitions are the psychological equivalents for the physical assertiveness of the tomboy, and again cultural emphasis on submissiveness and graceful restraint operates to discourage pursuit of professional, artistic, or political goals. These pressures exert themselves subtly, woven as they are throughout the texture of adolescent life. But they produce a fear that to be female and to dare to achieve is to venture into dangerous territory, to violate one's gender, to become a kind of freak. The girl who insists on following her ambitions almost inevitably pays the price of shame and guilt as an adult" (339–40). Westling sets McCullers's treatment of Mick Kelly and Frankie Addams in the larger context of proscriptions against women's achievement in public life. Women who strive to exceed the expectations associated with their gender have no legacy, no vocabulary for considering themselves both accomplished and female.

Of Mick, Westling says, "The images she projects for her future self waver from masculine to feminine, from evening suit to rhinestone-spangled dress, because there is no tradition of female composers upon which she can model her daydreams. In fact, Mick's sense of romantic heroism is entirely masculine." Responding to Beethoven's *Eroica,* Mick feels

> a masculine kind of assertion. Her response to the music is ecstasy and terrible pain. To alleviate this pain she resorts to a typically female kind of masochism, turning her frustration back upon herself. As she had done earlier in the story when driven frantic by an inner voice crying, "I want – I want – I want," . . . Mick pounds her thighs with her fists. Her response to the *Eroica* is shockingly violent. "The rocks under the bush were sharp. She grabbed a handful of them and began scraping them up and down on the same spot until her hand was bloody. Then she fell back to the ground and lay looking up at the night. With the fiery hurt in her leg she felt better." . . . Mick's reaction to the *Eroica* is clearly no voluptuous sublimation or misplaced pleasure but a frantic effort to release intense emotions which she must feel are forbidden. The circumstances of her musical life are fraught with guilt and the corresponding need for secrecy. Her musical pleasure is illicit, stolen in the darkness from wealthy people by a kind of voyeurism. (342)

Mick is not unaware of the dangers to which her femaleness exposes her. She understands that girls walking alone at night might invite a rapist who could "put his teapot in them like they were married," but "with a boyishly sturdy confidence she refuses to be intimidated." Yet, "despite her independence, Mick lives with profound anxiety." She paints disasters and has nightmares. "Mick's sleeping mind, at least, knows that the world will not allow her to succeed in realizing her dreams of independence and art" (343). As a new teenager and high school student, Mick makes her first attempt at a feminine appearance. "She emerges . . . as from a co-

coon, metamorphosed into the conventional female in an adult dress, a hairstyle with spit curls, high heels, and make-up. 'She didn't feel like herself at all'" (343). When her party dissolves into rowdy play, she finds herself "physically crippled by feminine clothes." Soon Mick finds herself "trapped in a narrow adult world which reduces her to little more than a machine . . . . She does not like the sensation [of sex], and McCullers's imagery [of decapitation] suggests why: sex destroys rational control and blots out the self. In a different way, Mick's job at the dime store shuts out her private world of music and stifles her fantasies. The long days of work leave her feeling exhausted, caged, and cheated, but she can find nothing and nobody to blame. At fourteen she is a grown woman whose life seems to have reached a dead end. There McCullers leaves her" (344).

Frances Freeman Paden (1982) finds autistic gestures characteristic of each of the five main characters. Using a definition whereby "autistic" appears to be synonymous with "inwardly motivated" or "self-absorbed," Paden focuses on repeated gestures involving hands – notably, Mick's beating her thighs with her fists, Brannon's pushing his nose with his thumb – that she reads as revealing "the alienation that they feel in their unsuccessful quests for love and acceptance" (454). Apart from contributing a new term to the lexicon of character psychology, Paden offers an unusually positive, and dubious, reading of the novel's last scene: "Upon recognizing his face in the glass, Brannon objectifies himself and comes to terms with his own paradoxes. What begins as an autistic gesture – finding one's face in a mirror – develops into an epiphanic moment. Brannon confronts his loneliness, and from the confrontation he gathers the courage to turn away, not from the world, as did Singer, nor from ideals, as did Blount, Copeland, and Kelly, but from his own reflection. In the novel's final gesture, Brannon seems willing to embrace experience as he steps out to raise the awning and 'to await the morning sun'" (463).

Taking seriously McCullers's statement in her outline about the depth of Mick's commitment to and talent for music, Linda Huf (1983) reads the novel as a story of tragic sacrifice. She castigates critics who see Mick Kelly's ambitions as fantasies or girlhood illusions (Evans 1965a; Moore 1965), and those who view Mick's fate as normal rather than tragic (Eisinger 1963; Knowles 1969; Moore 1965). However, Huf does not blame economic need or lurking sexism for thwarting Mick's dreams of a career as a composer. Instead Mick, like the other characters, is betrayed by her own need for love and recognition. Caught in what Huf calls the "compassion trap," the expectation of female self-sacrifice, "the adolescent tomboy who has struggled so fiercely against poverty, ignorance, and lack of space, at last succumbs to a craving for love. She throws everything away in an effort to help her family and thereby secure their affection and approval" (118). It is this capitulation to a prescribed role, rather than sexual intercourse with Harry Minowitz, that constitutes Mick's painful initiation into womanhood. Why would McCullers let Mick deprive herself of an artistic dream when McCullers's own pursuit of such a dream was succeeding? Perhaps, Huf suggests, she knew her audience: How much sympathy would accrue to Mick if she, like Tom Wingfield in *The Glass Menagerie,* were to desert her family to pursue her destiny?

Mary Jane Kinnebrew (1985) says that McCullers develops for each of the five characters in *Hunter* "not only a distinct dialect in direct dialogue, but also a distinct narrative voice to control specific sections of the novel" (76). Using concepts and terminology from M. M. Bakhtin, Kinnebrew calls McCullers's "contrapuntal voices" by the term "character zones" or "'hybrid' areas where a character's language influences narrative language and the authorial voice" (77). This scheme seems a useful model for examining the layered perspectives of the novel and what, in a broad Jamesian sense, has been loosely referred to as close third-person narrative through a focal character or angle of narration. Kinnebrew demonstrates that even Singer operates in a character zone, and she effectively analyzes the multiple linguistic layers in the letter Singer writes to Antonapoulos in which he imitates the language of other characters. Another scene illuminated by this method is Portia's rejection of her father's language (the language of the brain) for the language of ordinary black people (the language of the heart).

Constance M. Perry (1986) argues against the notion that Mick's job at Woolworth's thwarts her development as an artist, a widely accepted reading even among feminist critics as different as Huf and Spivak. Perry demonstrates that "another root cause of her artistic failure is Mick's devastating sexual initiation" (36). McCullers's own association of sexual feeling and love of music in her relationship with piano teacher Mary Tucker and the young writer's projection of that association onto the artistic failure of Frances in the story "Wunderkind" (1936) presage Mick's reaction to her first sexual intercourse: "After the intrusion of adult sexuality into her world, she also loses her identity and her artistic dreams." Mick's experience of being cheated is largely the experience of "what it means to be female and inferior in her culture" (43). Perry traces this pattern from the conjunction in part 1 of Mick's initials and sexual slang ("Mick's graffiti – 'PUSSY M.K.' – prophesies her ignominious fate in a culture where femaleness disqualifies genius" [40]), to her nightmares of mob violence and the self-mutilating response to the Beethoven symphony that "expresses her yearning for artistic power" (41) – a response Perry associates with Lancy Davis's attempt to castrate himself – to, ultimately, Mick's physical rejection of intercourse. Perry reads Mick's feeling of her head being broken off from her body not as orgasmic, but as an "image of decapitation [that] powerfully suggests her refusal to surrender emotionally to what is occurring" (42). The fear she experiences afterward is not the fear of pregnancy but rather "that in becoming an adult woman, she has somehow annihilated her artistic identity. Harry's guilty flight from sexual intimacy with Mick, and indeed from the town itself, forces Mick to realize that to be female is to be somehow shameful and obscene" (43).

Ann Carlton (1988) says, "McCullers' writing's unique quality is that it reflects the female's complex cultural position" (54). A "feminist cultural approach . . . moves Mick from the gothic and grotesque, 'a potential invert in jeans,' as she is labeled by Leslie Fiedler . . . , to the compellingly human and painfully real character coping with the female cultural role" (56). Carlton focuses in detail on the scene to which Perry alludes. Mick dresses Ralph and takes the infant and four-year-old Bubber for an outing in a child's wagon, which she pulls to the site of a house under construction. She abandons the mother-caretaker role to climb to the highest point of the roof and fantasizes fame for herself as a symphony conductor, her initials, M. K., blazoned everywhere. Having inscribed M. K. in the largest letters after having written "EDISON, DICK TRACY and MUSSOLINI" – models of power "from the dominant (male) culture," she writes "PUSSY" on the opposite wall, placing her initials below it. "Mick's culture has already given her the message that as a female she serves a sexual purpose, and that her life is limited by her sex" (57). Works such as *Hunter* are cultural products that show how women have been led to imagine themselves. "Indeed the [act of] naming has been a male prerogative – gothic, grotesque, freak, according to the critics, mostly male, and with male language. Mick senses the power of naming, but has no language, no image for naming except the male – Edison, Dick Tracy, Mussolini, and Pussy, and she names herself with the male language, M. K. But her music is her creative self, emanating from that inner self, that muted self, that finds 'expression through ritual and art'" (58).

Two interesting advancements in analyzing the novel's musical structure occurred late in the decade. Janice Fuller (1987/1988) covers much of the same territory as C. Michael Smith (1979) but examines as well "the conventions of counterpoint and the fugue that McCullers purposefully violates" (57). Convention calls for a balance of voices, but in the second part of the novel the balance among the five central characters is threatened as the "voice" of Mick Kelly begins to dominate . . . . If it were not for McCullers' comments in her outline, it would be easy to attribute this lack of balance to McCullers' unwitting and growing obsession with a character so much like herself . . . . [However,] Mick's dominance in Part Two . . . seems deliberate . . . . As the only "normal" central character in the novel, Mick is perhaps the character with whom most readers can identify since she has none of the barriers – blackness, muteness, effeminacy, drunkenness – that might prevent readers from identifying with the other central characters. Thus, McCullers seems to have chosen to violate the contrapuntal principle of balance temporarily . . . in order to engage the reader more fully in the novel . . . . [or she] may be attempting to mitigate the pessimism of her themes. (64–65)

The other violation of musical convention arises when McCullers eliminates one voice before the end – by Singer's death. "This unconventional shift in contrapuntal 'texture' is even more dramatic since the missing voice is the one that made the original 'statement' of the novel's theme or subject and since it is Singer and his relationship with Antonapoulos that the other 'voices' most consistently imitate in the course of the novel" (66).

The most important development in understanding the role of music in the novel's structure is Barbara A. Farrelly's persuasive demonstration that Beethoven's Third Symphony, the *Eroica,* inspired the novel and provided its "atypical structure and its thematic logic" (1988, 16). McCullers describes this symphony in part 2 of the novel, where it sounds to the enraptured Mick "like God strutting in the night." Napoleon proved so unworthy of the symphony's Promethean theme that Beethoven "scratched his hero's name from the dedication page"; McCullers's novel is likewise "about a hero with clay feet" (17). More striking are the structural parallels, which Farrelly diagrams with precision. They match not only Mick's perception of them but also stand up to formal analyses of the five themes that figure in the symphony's Exposition, Development, and Recapitulation. The only false note in Farrelly's argument is her wrenching of part 3 to accord with the triumph of freedom in the symphony's third movement. McCullers's characters do not win "their freedom with the death of John Singer" or proceed one by one in the final chapters to "face life on their own"; nor do they "all share the illumination with Biff Brannon when he sees 'a glimpse of human struggle and of valor. Of the endless fluid passage of humanity through endless time'" (20). Perhaps it is consonance enough that Brannon experiences this hopeful, if not liberating, vision.

Annette Runte (1988) explores *Hunter* in company with Truman Capote's *Other Voices, Other Rooms* as American novels with suppressed homosexual themes. Discussing McCullers's novel for a European audience (it is written in German) and from several critical perspectives, including postmodern social, political, and psychoanalytical theories, Runte likens the arrangement of voices to the montage experiments of John Dos Passos and describes the operation of a central narrative collage which functions structurally in the movement from one character to another and psychologically in the accretion of life fragments pieced together in various ways to allow for the layering of hindsight against, and simultaneously with, important events. Singer is idolized as "eine 'Superfigur' 'kreisen'" (57) just as he sublimates homosexual desire in idolatry of the sensual Antonapoulos, to whom he bears a variety of postures: maternal, ludic, supplicating, and erotic.

Kenneth D. Chamlee (1990), studying the prominence of cafés in McCullers's novels, examines Biff Brannon's New York Café through the preoccupations of its owner. "Brannon . . . does little *besides* intuit. Though he keeps the café open all night 'to receive the world and its riddles,' it is also 'to stifle his loneliness.' He is himself the most withdrawn of all the characters and is never able to engage any of the New York Café regulars on a level of genuine communication" (234).

Virginia Spencer Carr (1990) says that *Hunter* "remains, in the opinion of many critics, one of only a handful of truly distinguished first novels by major American writers of the twentieth century" (33). Carr, in a series monograph on understanding the fiction, says of the ending that "Brannon is not allowed a total vision." However, Brannon, rather than Singer, emerges as the Christ figure. "It is with Brannon in a tableau of affirmation that seems frozen in time that McCullers closes her novel" (32).

The fifty-year critical history of *Hunter* from first reviews to Carr's guide for students shows the novel's ability to repay multiple critical approaches. It has been examined for its formal unity, universal themes, psychological acuity, and archetypal resonance, as well as for its social and political ideology. The most recent approaches – those that take race, gender, sexuality, and class as central features of the human experience that literature portrays – have in some cases barely begun to illuminate this novel. If the current critical trends persist, we might expect to see an analysis that focuses on the intersection of these categories as they define the difference that the novel systematically punishes. Isolation is the penalty for deviating from the norm. We need also a fuller understanding of sexual ambiguity as constructed by and for readers in McCullers's time and our own. As the summary of the most recent criticism in chapter 9 suggests, McCullers's first novel continues to gain ground as a text that sustains close and intellectually aggressive reading.

3: *Reflections in a Golden Eye* (1940, 1941)

> *Reflections in a Golden Eye is one of the purest and most powerful of those works which are conceived in that Sense of The Awful which is the desperate black root of nearly all significant modern art.*
>
> (Tennessee Williams 1950)

MCCULLERS'S SECOND NOVEL was printed in two parts in *Harper's Bazaar* (October and November 1940) and published by Houghton Mifflin in 1941, fast on the heels of her glory-book, *The Heart Is a Lonely Hunter*. Contrary in aim and tone and sympathy to that critical and popular success, *Reflections* was bound to disappoint. The work McCullers had thought of as a "fairy tale" was read with utter seriousness and distaste by a majority of its initial reviewers. A story of voyeurism, jealousy, madness, mutilation, and murder on a southern army base, told with economy and detachment, *Reflections* inspired accusations of depravity and slavish Gothicism. According to the *Yale Review,* its "inversions and mutilations and nastiness stick in one's mind like burrs" (Littell 1941, xiv), and to the *Hartford Courant,* it is the kind of book "most persons wish to spew out of the mind as rapidly as possible" ("Book to Forget" 1941).

The plot focuses on two mismatched couples and their satellites. Capt. Weldon Penderton, a repressed homosexual, fatally shoots Pvt. Ellgee Williams, a worshipful intruder in the bedroom of Leonora Penderton, the captain's voluptuous wife. The Pendertons' neighbor, Alison Langdon, despondent over ill health, the death of her infant, and her husband's affair with Leonora Penderton, cuts off her nipples with garden shears, invests her affection in the misfits Anacleto and Lieutenant Weincheck, and dies from a heart attack a short time after witnessing Private Williams's invasion of the Pendertons' house. Leonora Penderton's stallion Firebird completes and complicates the relationships.

Among the novel's first reviewers, Hubert Creekmore, in *Accent,* describes the characters as clinical case histories "sealed in the pigeonholes of their neuroses" and says, "The whole thing has the atmosphere of snickering in a privy" (1941, 61). Basil Davenport, in the *Saturday Review,* calls it "a vipers'-knot of neurasthenic relationships among characters whom the author seems hardly to comprehend, and of whose perversions she can create nothing" (1941, 12). Charles Poore, in the *New York Times,* finds its plot "far too mechanically contrived" (1941, 13). Fred T. Marsh, in the *New York Times Book Review,* speculates wrongly that *Reflections,* so "vastly inferior" to *Hunter,* had been written first and hastily marketed to take advantage of the earlier success (1941, 6).

Marsh continues in a vein that became typical of U.S. reviews, expressing disappointment at the wunderkind's exploitation or mismanagement of her gift: "No one could say ... that Miss McCullers has not succeeded in making her genuine talent felt, a talent which is less of subtlety than of infant-terrible insight expressed with quite grown-up precision, as yet unmellowed and unhallowed" (6). Other reviewers advise the twenty-four-year-old writer to "give herself a humorous once-over" (Fadiman 1941, 68) or portray her as "an artist who has still a good deal to learn about reality" (Weeks 1941, viii) or good taste: "One is merely impressed with and offended by her arrogant and pitiless fearlessness which, besides giving an unpleasant effect, betrays her youth" (Feld 1941, 8). This last review, by Rose Feld in the *New York Herald Tribune,* however, does acknowledge the novel's tight stylistic control, and reviewers in the *New Republic* and the *New Statesman and Nation* call *Reflections* an artistic tour de force (Ferguson 1941; Toynbee 1942). Such appraisals forecast the direction of positive response the novel subsequently generated.

In an introduction to the 1950 New Directions edition of *Reflections,* Tennessee Williams lauds the "lapidary precision" of the novel's design, emphasizes its superiority to *Hunter* in demonstrating "mastery over a youthful lyricism," calls for a "fresh evaluation" of its merits, and praises McCullers for "such intensity and nobility of spirit as we have not had in our prose-writing since Herman Melville." Williams framed much of the future critical discussion of the book by setting it in a modernist rather than a strictly southern tradition, discounting the influence of Faulkner and attributing McCullers's so-called Gothic effects to a keen artistic apprehension of "an underlying dreadfulness in modern experience," a "Sense of The Awful" that motivates "nearly all significant modern art, from the *Guernica* of Picasso to the cartoons of Charles Addams" (xviii). International audiences, he implies, are better able than Americans to appreciate her genius: "in Europe the name of Carson McCullers is where it belongs, among the four or five preeminent figures in contemporary American writing" (xx).

Williams's defense of this novel, along with reassessments occasioned by the 1951 collected edition of McCullers's fiction, generated the first serious academic criticism of *Reflections.* Nicholas Joost (1951) misreads Williams's attempt to separate McCullers from a strictly regional Gothicism and sets out to rescue her from the category of "Poe-esque fiction which flourishes in the South, literature that titillates without meaning very deeply anything." *Reflections* "contains depths of meaning of which its violence and grotesquerie are the outward symbols" (285). The first substantial discussion of McCullers, Dayton Kohler's analysis (1951) of her themes, devotes little attention to the novel except to acknowledge its highly developed symbolism, in which all structural elements "exist as one great metaphor" for human cruelty and self-deception (7). Oliver Evans (1952) discusses the consistency with which McCullers explores the theme of spiritual isolation unredeemed by love, finding *Reflections* an exemplar – if not a cornerstone – of this pattern. A curious neglect of *Reflections* occurs in Jane Hart's discussion of McCullers as a "Pilgrim of Loneliness" (1957), an otherwise synoptic article, especially since Hart quotes from Williams's introduction to make a point about *Hunter*.

Frank Baldanza (1958) offers one of the first analyses of the novel's tightly symmetrical structure, suggesting that the demonstration of animal passion between Leonora Penderton and Morris Langdon and of spiritual love between Alison Langdon and Anacleto recalls the Platonic balance in "the myth of the two pairs of horses pulling the chariot of the soul in *Phaedrus.*" He also observes that McCullers "invariably focuses on the spiritual – and, in a sense, the asexual – relation, without, however, ignoring or denying the patently sexual basis from which the experience stems," and calls this conjunction of the spiritual and the sensual "the curiously disturbing synthesis of ideas which gives her writing the haunting flavor that one finds so hard to isolate in analysis" (158).

The decade's series of thematic studies culminated with important syntheses in 1959 and 1960 by Ihab H. Hassan and John B. Vickery. Hassan's article on "The Victim" in American fiction (1959b) quotes Williams's introduction to buttress a view that "terror and violence are the means by which the contemporary writer exorcises evil. They are a form of prayer" (145). That enticing observation is not applied to *Reflections,* one supposes, because the novel contains no lover capable of "redeem[ing] evil, by offering himself as a willing victim" (145). In a more extended essay on McCullers, Hassan (1959a) judges the work less successful than her other novels in embodying the complicity of love and pain. In *Reflections* "all relations fail," including, he implies, the relation between writer and reader. Though he admires the "skillful structure" that keeps "suspense and revelation . . . in check" and McCullers's sure sense for finding "the right if lurid gesture for each character" (319), Hassan complains that "the novel remains somehow inert, brutish," without the defiant energy of truer primitivists such as D. H. Lawrence or Faulkner, and without a "lucid consciousness" to interpret the events described. Liken-

ing the novel to the image of its title — "the disquieting symbol" of a peacock's eye — Hassan implies that the work mirrors without insight and,
"haunted by the need to suffer, lacks the energy that redeems suffering"
(318). In subsequent reprintings Hassan slightly modified this section of
the essay to make more pronounced the novel's failure to embody his thesis.

Vickery (1960) explores the conjunction of love and violence in the
novel, especially "the horror invested in thwarted sexual love"(18). "Each
of the characters is caught in a trap from which it is impossible to escape
save through violence or death itself" (19). Weldon Penderton and Alison
Langdon, driven to extremes by their spouses' infidelity, can communicate their desperation only through violence. Extending the interpretation
of love in McCullers's fiction to include concepts of questing and dreaming, Vickery sees Penderton and Langdon as victims of a society unsympathetic to their dreams. Langdon cuts off her nipples in "a wordless
attempt to wake the other dreamers" to her desperation; Penderton's violent assault on Firebird and his slaying of Ellgee Williams result from the
"accidental intrusion [of others] into the captain's dream of himself" (20).

The narcissism implied in Vickery's observation about Penderton became the focus of Irving Malin's analysis of the novel's Gothic features
(1962). Malin sees the psychological distortions of the contemporary
Gothic mode figured in McCullers's images of "the 'living' . . . squeezed
into the 'mechanical'" (24): Alison Langdon's unusual means of self-
mutilation, or Penderton's shoving a shivering kitten through the slot of a
mailbox. The characters are driven by narcissistic compulsions echoed in
the rigid, repeated patterns of life on the army base. Given his focus on
the Gothic, it is not surprising that Malin ranks *Reflections,* as well as *Ballad,* as McCullers's best work (157). Mark Schorer (1963), on the other
hand, finds the novel "a horrid dream" that inverts McCullers's typical
themes by portraying "people whose self-engrossment, malice, contempt,
or sheer stupidity have for all their desperation, put them outside the possibility of feeling either loneliness or love" (89).

Barbara Nauer Folk (1962) finds redeeming qualities in the portrayal
of the houseboy Anacleto, "one of the most delightful characters in modern fiction" (206). McCullers's association of music with the relationship
between Anacleto and Alison Langdon is consistent with her use of musical imagery to symbolize the ideal. Other critics have averred that *Reflections* is the least musical of McCullers's novels.

John M. Bradbury (1963), calling *Reflections* "an impressive achievement in the New Tradition" of southern literature, emphasizes the work's
symbolic dimensions, concentrated in "a complex of natural images, par-

ticularly the autumn sun and animal or bird eyes which reflect back the self who seeks meaning in them" (111). Wayne D. Dodd (1963) places Anacleto's "painting" (it is actually only a vision, not a painting) of the golden-eyed peacock within the larger pattern of children's grotesque art-work that is emblematic of private, isolated visions which "must of necessity seem grotesque to others" (209), the symbolism thereby advancing McCullers's theme of human aloneness.

German critic Klaus Lubbers (1963), one of the first to reassess McCullers's achievement after the publication of *Clock Without Hands* (1961), judges her fiction harshly for failing to duplicate Faulkner's interest (and that of other southern writers with whom she is assigned kinship) in themes of the past and the land. Lubbers calls *Reflections* an "abortive attempt to deal anew with a concatenation of bizarre feelings" (196), failing principally because it lacks "the necessary observer," a narrator willing to make sense of its tragedies. Alison Langdon, among the characters, affords too little in the way of a norm to explain the novel's moral chaos.

Chester E. Eisinger (1963) argues that McCullers, in practicing an "aesthetics of the primitive" (243), does not care to make moral or ideological judgments about the "half-people" whose deficiencies preoccupy her. He describes the novel's six characters as evenly divided into conflicting camps of nature (Leonora Penderton, Morris Langdon, Ellgee Williams) and culture (Weldon Penderton, Alison Langdon, Anacleto), which "destroy each other" (252). Captain Penderton's shooting of Private Williams is a fatal "denial of nature," by which Eisinger means "masculinity." Similarly, Alison Langdon cuts off her nipples in "a physical act which is symbolic of her psychic mutilation" – the failure of her femininity (254). Given her relentless belief in human inadequacy, Eisinger says, McCullers could hardly have imagined a wholesome or integrated outcome.

The novel's extremes of grotesquerie, and critics' preoccupation with them, are parodied in *Saturday Review*'s "The Man in the Gray Flannery McCuller-Alls," a four-paragraph spoof set near "Gomorrahburg, Georgia," where "the evening sunset burned fiery red over the swamp like a rabid peacock's eye" and the heroine is "almost completely saved from burning by the window-peeping Chinese dwarf from across the street" (Schaefer 1963, 6).

Three important studies in 1965 deepened the analysis of McCullers's Gothicism. Louis Auchincloss criticizes Tennessee Williams's introduction for the self-serving suggestion that "artists and lunatics [exist] apart from the generality of readers in a kind of twilight zone where they experience horrors not felt by the rest of humanity" (163). Williams, he says, makes a point of horror, whereas for McCullers "the horror is a regretted necessity" reported in a "muted, hasty fashion" (164). Auchincloss, however, concedes that the "remarkable shock effect of this novel is hard to explain" (164). Discussed principally in terms of the conflict between the man of civilization, Weldon Penderton, and the man of nature, Ellgee Williams, *Reflections* symbolizes the triumph of nature and death in the various eyes suggested by the title (that of Williams, the voyeur, and those of the great dark bird Penderton imagines and the ghastly peacock Anacleto sees). Penderton shoots Williams "to extinguish the eye that has tormented him to lunacy" but is tragically mocked by the animal warmth Williams displays even in death (165).

On the other hand, Louise Y. Gossett (1965), in a deft comparison, describes the silent Private Williams as an "entirely unreflective counterpart" of Captain Penderton (163). Both characters' violent impulses arise from "the fear of loneliness." Two particular acts, Penderton's "psychotic" beating of his wife's stallion and Alison Langdon's mutilation of her breasts, compel attention to "the psychological depravity of man when the impulse to love has been fatally thwarted" (169). Gossett further observes that, unlike Faulkner, for whom history and geography were as causative as psychology, McCullers created characters purely as psychological case studies.

In the first book-length study of McCullers, one of three within the decade, Oliver Evans (1965a) analyzes *Reflections* in a chapter titled, after the reported complaint of one reader, "Not Even the Horse Is Normal." Evans calls it a French novel, Flaubertian in technique, deriving its contemporary Gothicism from the "school" begun with Faulkner's *Sanctuary,* and somewhat dated by "the impact of Freudianism" (79). Evans rates McCullers's treatment of the themes of voyeurism and tragic homosexual attraction superior to that of her probable models, Faulkner, Lawrence ("The Prussian Officer"), and Melville *(Billy Budd).* He acknowledges that *Reflections,* for better or worse, earned McCullers a reputation for Gothic effects, but he argues that she is no "pornographer . . . of terror" (80), using horror merely for horror's sake (a characteristic he is willing to assign to *Sanctuary* and some of Poe). Rather, he says, readers are apt to misunderstand the "fusion . . . between realism and allegory" in the novel, which, because of its compression, is not entirely successful.

In noting the similarities between Captain Penderton's love-hate response to Private Williams ("the man of animal grace and freedom" to Penderton's "man of will" [63]) and that of John Claggart to Billy Budd or the Prussian officer to his orderly, Evans suggests that McCullers rises above mere allegory by making Williams as warped a character as Penderton and through such "complication and irony" provides "a dimension that is lacking in Melville's and Lawrence's [works], where the men of nature are truer to type" (67).

Evans's analysis emphasizes Penderton's sadomasochism (observing that in brutally whipping Firebird, Penderton may symbolically punish himself for his animal passions) and connects his ascetic, unfulfilled homosexuality with the fastidious sexual ambiguity of Biff Brannon in *Hunter*. Moreover, Evans fits *Reflections* neatly into patterns of failed love established in the earlier novel. By making the affair of Leonora Penderton and Morris Langdon successful on a physical level ("a mere mating of animals" [70]) and Alison Langdon's spiritual relationships with Anacleto and Lieutenant Weincheck reciprocal, "McCullers seems . . . to be saying that physical love has the greatest chance of success where the spiritual potential is slightest, and here, as elsewhere in her work, spiritual love (where the potential for it exists) compensates for the failure of love on a physical level" (70). Such strictly physical or spiritual attachments frame the doomed longings of Penderton for Williams and Williams for Penderton's wife. Evans's desire to establish parallels between this novel and *Hunter* results in a forced analogy between Penderton and Singer as "typical romantic lover[s]" who idealize their beloveds. Evans does, however, acknowledge that Penderton's ambivalence toward Williams undermines the comparison: Penderton "both loves and hates the soldier, and it is a subject for speculation whether his hatred is a mere device for masking his love, or whether it exists independently, as the complement to it" (70).

Evans makes two other notable observations about the similarity between *Reflections* and *Hunter:* the prevalence of dreams and fantasies as compensations for failed or unachievable love and, most strikingly, the persistence in the later novel of a naturalistic view of life. Evans is one of the remarkably few critics who link McCullers's eerie blending of realism and symbolism with a pessimism traceable to the tradition of Stephen Crane and who do so during an era when "naturalism" was an outmoded critical label. The peacock's golden eye is "the mirror of art" held up to "a world that is lacking in moral dimension [and, one might add, freedom of choice] but which is strange to the point of freakishness" (71), he says.

Though Evans generally admires McCullers's achievement in *Reflections,* particularly its mature and "formidable command of technique," he joins others in convicting her of youthful excess in her choice and control of subject matter. "To make her allegorical point it was scarcely necessary for her to construct so complete a chamber of horrors: is it not sufficient that Captain Penderton be a homosexual, an algolagnist, and a drug addict without also being a kleptomaniac?" Evans asks, concluding, "It is as

if Flaubert . . . had made the discovery of Freud and placed all his technical resources at the command of that ingenious intelligence" (80).

Later critics would perceive trenchant irony and satiric hyperbole
where Evans and others saw excess, but not immediately. In a damning
assessment written just after McCullers's death and the debut of the film
of *Reflections* (though published two years later), A. S. Knowles, Jr. (1969)
accuses the wunderkind of an unsympathetic, adolescently superior attitude toward her material and a perverse championing of sexual abnormality. McCullers, he says, implies "that normal heterosexuality is associated
with the coarse and vulgar, and that, once again, any marked degree of
sensitivity is likely to have as its corollary a departure, in some direction,
from normal sexuality. For Leonora and Major Langdon, the stud and his
mate, there is no sympathy. For the Captain, with his fixation on the faun-
like Private Williams, there is some. It is a sterile and morbid book, and
one wonders why Carson McCullers wrote a novel in which she so obviously felt superiority to and distaste for her characters" (94). Robert
Drake (1968) adds little new to the view of McCullers's detractors in saying that "the kinked up" *Reflections* exemplifies the "tragic disjunction" in
her life and career when her head overbalanced her heart and "she forgot
or ignored her real story and started to examine pathological specimens"
.(51). Drake believes McCullers might have maintained the harmonious
balance of her best works had she stayed in the South.

Robert M. Rechnitz (1968) admires McCullers's narrative voice, finding in it the principal source of the novel's grotesque effects and an ac-
companiment to the theme of failed love. Identifying the tone as that of "a
precocious child" horrifying her elders, Rechnitz says, "It is her attitude of
decorous, almost prim impassivity in the face of almost unspeakable violence that fascinates and appalls the reader" (455). The impassivity bor-
ders on coldness and suggests the incapacity to love that plagues all
characters but one. Rechnitz is surely mistaken in singling out "the
amoral, near-animal Ellgee Williams" as the only character capable of
love. Seeing Williams as "the embodiment of life itself, an innocent, almost mindless god of life" requires the reader to make the same mistake
as Penderton. As Evans (1965a) makes clear, Williams is as much a moral
cripple as the others, and it is this fact that deepens and complicates
McCullers's version of the *Billy Budd* plot. More usefully, however, Rechnitz, by an analysis of the first confrontation between Williams and
Penderton – the scene in which Williams cuts the branches Penderton intends to shield his lawn from the adjacent woods – derives what he calls
"the fundamental movement of the novel": "Each character in his own

way attempts to shut out the unknowable, some aspect of life which he deems threatening" (455).

Francesco Gozzi (1968) focuses on the symmetry of the novel's relationships organized around "l'antitesi di vita e spirito" (350), reflected in the more or less successful pairing of Leonora-Morris and Alison-Anacleto and extended disastrously in Penderton's obsession with Williams. Williams represents the unformed conscience to Penderton's deformed conscience, repeating in parallel Leonora's animal innocence and Alison's tortured interior life. McCullers's handling of this antithesis and her use of catalyzing, epiphanic visions – Williams's response to seeing Leonora nude and Penderton's delirious visions while riding Firebird – remind Gozzi of *Death in Venice* and the coincidence of McCullers's friendship in the 1940s with Erika Mann, Thomas Mann's daughter; however, by all accounts, *Reflections* was finished – except for revisions – before McCullers met Mann's children, Erika and Klaus, in the summer of 1940.

In pamphlets published in 1969, Dale Edmonds and Lawrence Graver take opposite views of *Reflections*. Edmonds praises its technical control and describes it as "a modern morality play with metaphysical overtones [cast] in taut, sardonic prose" (17). Reading the title image as a symbol of narcissism, he proclaims each of the characters a narcissist and his or her condition a reflection of "the state of man." His neatly packaged generalization ends with the observation that Weldon Penderton's "distorted, death-wishing, sexually ambivalent, intelligent, driven, ascetic, sensuous, corrupt being . . . suggests the disorders to which modern man is subject" (19). Graver, on the other hand, damns *Reflections* as "the most pompous and disagreeable of all her books" (21), claiming that it exploits rather than illuminates the psychological maladies of its characters. McCullers "takes three mutually contradictory attitudes toward her subject matter": the objective reporter whose detachment yields "a poised monotonic response to everything miraculous and mundane"; the satirist "whose aim is to demolish everyone in sight for the assorted vices of pride, moral vacancy, and self-deceit"; and the poet or "mythopoeic explorer who sees in this grotesque domestic drama a monumental conflict of will against instinct, the artificial against the natural, and death against life" (22). Graver pronounces McCullers's talent inadequate to her conception and berates her for mocking the characters "with such relentless sarcasm [that] she makes it difficult for us to care for their inhumanities" (23). What ought not to be lost in Graver's condemnation is the recognition, largely for the first time, of the role of satire in this novel, a feature which was more productively analyzed in the ensuing decade.

Ray Mathis (1970) reads *Reflections* as a satire on Christianity, calling the book "a series of jokes upon the characters and the readers, especially the 'Christian' middle class" (54). Mathis identifies three categories of religious behavior and groups the characters accordingly: Alison Langdon and Leonora Penderton represent secularism; Weldon Penderton, Ellgee Williams, and Anacleto are would-be mythmakers; and Williams and Morris Langdon reflect "characteristics of religiosity" (546). Alison Langdon, formerly a Latin teacher, is something of a stoic, unable to accept Christian consolations for the deformity and death of her infant daughter. Her "Platonic shadow," Anacleto, may be "the East whom the West failed to Christianize"; he is, at any rate, a myth seeker attached to a false savior (Alison the neoclassicist) who abandons him by her death. Morris Langdon responds to his wife's death and Anacleto's disappearance with a temporary and hypocritical religiosity consisting of prayer and platitudes. Williams, raised by a Holiness preacher to fear women, is a ritual sun worshiper who responds to Firebird and Leonora Penderton with "a mythic appreciation for the source of fertility" (549). Mathis makes his best case for the satiric symbolism of Weldon Penderton, a perverted monk, and Leonora Penderton, a debased Madonna, "a twentieth-century virgin-harlot, the modern mother goddess, the secular anti-heroine" (558). Ironically, she embodies as much of Christian goodness as can be found in the novel, so McCullers's portrayal of her as mentally deficient and capable of remembering little else from the Bible than that Jesus was crucified on "Cavalry Hill" implicitly criticizes traditional Christianity. Yet the novel "portrays a vast need for grace, or love" and, while suggesting the failure of modern religion, paradoxically reveals the spiritual longings Christianity, in Mathis's view, is best equipped to satisfy. (A similar irony has been recognized in McCullers's association of the deaf-mute Singer with Christ in *Hunter,* though Mathis does not mention this parallel with the earlier novel.)

Alice Hamilton (1970) enlarges our understanding of Weldon Penderton's obsession with power and military rule but is less convincing in applying to *Reflections* a thesis about the tyranny of the "outside" over the "inside" rooms of McCullers's fiction. Quoting Morris Langdon's renewed vow after his wife's death "to be a good animal and to serve my country," Hamilton proposes that patriotism in this military setting involves the expectation of having "one's freedom checked abruptly from without" (224), an expectation that might be shared by "a good animal," a trained horse. Penderton's mad ride on the uncontrollable Firebird and its aftermath – Penderton's cruel beating of the animal and the naked Williams's leading the horse away – cause Penderton to transfer to Williams the mixture of love and hatred his powerlessness over the horse arouses. Like Firebird and Leonora, Williams is a symbol of "freedom from rule" (225). Such an approach leads Hamilton to the arresting observation that Penderton's Seconal-induced dream of a "great dark bird" with "fierce, golden eyes" alighting on his chest and wrapping him in its wings is presumably a dream of the country's symbolic bird and therefore evidence of Penderton's willing surrender to "the brilliance and power of the State" (224).

Tracing sexual aberration in McCullers's fiction to Oedipal desires, Irving H. Buchen (1973) asserts that "almost all the violence in McCullers is castrating in nature": Weldon Penderton is representative of homosexuals in her fiction who "always bewail their lot as having to scrape the square peg into the round hole," and, "when Alison Langdon cuts off her nipples with a pair of garden shears, it is not accidental that her favorite companion is then the dwarfish Filipino eunuch Anacleto, who safely matches her own dwarfed or diminished guilty sexuality" (24). Charlene Kerne Clark (1975a), focusing on McCullers's "heavy reliance on humorous parody," suggests that Alison Langdon and Anacleto are a modern version of the archetypal pairing in American literature of "the mistress and the devoted but foolish dark servant" (165).

Richard M. Cook's monograph on McCullers (1975) for Ungar's Modern Literature series goes farther than any earlier Vietnam-era study to identify the novel's setting on an army base as the key to its meaning, the depiction of "the horrors of a modern, regimented hell – a nightmare world of isolation, repression, boredom, and violence" (57). Only Alison Langdon (along with Anacleto the clearest outsider on the base) can view army life for the brutal life it is. She provides "a counter-consciousness, a sensibility in impotent rebellion against the stupid animality of her husband and the empty repressive ritual of military life." Cook calls Weldon Penderton "one of the most extreme cases of eclectic deviancy to appear in modern American literature" and, as well, "quite possibly the most thoroughly isolated character that McCullers ever created" (51). He has been shaped by the military and has used its regimentation as an escape into "a mask of impersonality" – or, as later critics recognized, a mask of approved masculinity. Cook verges on a recognition of the novel's gender inversions in focusing on the pattern of doll images associated with Penderton, but he interprets the pattern in terms of the mechanical "toy-soldier" mask Penderton has sought but is impelled to discard. His ride on Firebird and his obsession with Private Williams express his desire to "make contact with the sensual passionate world he has cut himself off from" (55). But killing Williams, like beating Firebird, is a futile gesture that leaves Penderton isolated and "more irrelevant than before" (56).

Cook finds this novel more despairing than *Hunter* because its characters "have lost all capacity and will to express themselves" (57). It is less satisfying because of the price McCullers pays for her aloof – and Cook thinks, contemptuous – perspective: "the book's characters may have the hard, brilliant intensity of concentrated reflections, [but] they lack the warmth of feeling, the humor, and the psychological depth that are the result of a more complex, expansive and sympathetic view of human nature" (58).

Of the dissertations on McCullers that began to proliferate in the 1970s following her death and encouraged by the publication of Virginia Spencer Carr's biography (1975), the most valuable is Judith Garrett Carlson's study (1976) demonstrating that visual art is the structuring principle in *Reflections*. She describes relationships among the characters as a series of four overlapping triangles: (1) Weldon Penderton, Ellgee Williams, and Leonora Penderton; (2) Morris Langdon, Anacleto, and Alison Langdon; (3) Leonora, her husband, and Morris Langdon; and (4) Leonora, her husband, and Firebird. Carlson's discussion of this structure uses Taoist and Jungian concepts of complementary opposites to reveal the theme that "love is what happens when another becomes a symbol to us of something within ourselves" (118). Setting aside homosexual attraction, which Carlson views as significant in a symbolic but not in a physical sense, she describes Penderton and Williams as "archetypal twins" – "a disembodied intellect" and "a mindless body" (100). Cut off from his own body, Penderton inflicts pain on himself and others to counter his "inner deadness, the fear of life" (102). Parallel scenes in which he responds with rage to his wife's and then Williams's nakedness emphasize the structure and the meaning of Penderton's divided self. The triangular and dualistic patterns are reinforced in other parallel scenes, notably the irritable intrusion of Morris Langdon into the delicate 4:00 A.M. diversions of Alison Langdon and Anacleto, whose comedy is balanced by the fatal intrusion of Penderton into Williams's silent vigil beside the sleeping Leonora. Carlson's method also yields a useful analysis of the narrative voice, whose ironic distance she sees as intended to remind readers that "the story is not real in itself but a symbol of the real," like the function of narrators in the plays of Bertold Brecht (127). The kindly bachelor Lieutenant Weincheck, having failed to marry or otherwise certify heterosexuality, will leave the army without his captain's bars. Weldon Penderton, whose homosexual tendencies have been so obvious as to discourage other officers from visiting his quarters alone, finds refuge and protection in his awkward marriage to Leonora. Ellgee Williams is another of McCullers's orphaned or single-parented children warped by lack of love.

Ellen Moers (1976) calls *Reflections* McCullers's finest work and finds in it "abundant evidence of [her] participation in a tradition at least as feminine as regional." Moers places McCullers midway in a tradition of the Female Gothic that stretches from Mary Shelley to Sylvia Plath. The portraits of Alison Langdon and Anacleto, Moers believes, were drawn from Isak Dinesen's *Out of Africa:* "a woman who is wife, mother, and queen (yet has neither husband, child, nor subjects) and a grotesque, devoted servant of another race, perhaps a homosexual, certainly a gifted, sensitive, ridiculous, mad, dwarflike creature, as diminutive as a monkey or a child" (109).

When Lawrence Graver's pamphlet (1969) was reprinted in *Seven American Women Writers of the Twentieth Century,* editor Maureen Howard (1977) partially rescued the novel from Graver's Olympian disgust by demonstrating its importance in a unified pattern of "fear of full adult sexuality, heterosexual or homosexual" that explains McCullers's portraits of Morris Langdon as "sexually competent but stupid," Weldon Penderton as "brilliant, precise, dandified but blocked from all insight about his own homosexuality," and Ellgee Williams as a lustful creature "blocked by a perverse religiosity" (21). This pattern explains as well the characterization of Alison Langdon as "all quivering ineffectual soul without body" and the sexually attractive Leonora Penderton as "a moral idiot" (21). The fear of adult female sexuality turns McCullers's "grown women" into grotesques and accounts for the striking presence in her fiction of "boyish, presexual girls" who "sense that grown-up womanhood is tainted and corrupt and that the pain of being powerless and innocent is preferable to maturity" (20). With Moers, whose work she quotes, Howard raises issues of gender and sexuality in new ways that critics of the 1980s explored more fully. Representing a shift in emphasis driven by advances in feminist criticism and increasing scholarship on women generally, the comments by Howard and Moers prefigure the work to come by focusing more minutely than before on McCullers's female characters and attempting to read her fiction in terms of a female tradition that is more comprehensive than standard categories – modernism, southern literature – permit.

Margaret B. McDowell (1980), in the Twayne's United States Authors Series introduction to McCullers, offers a multidimensional reading of the novel to avoid imposing a single critical approach or arbitrary pattern of unity. Starting with the assumption that "McCullers' books vary so much from one another that one must be cautious in using them as a group in expounding a theoretical approach" (149n), McDowell provides the fullest discussions yet of similarities between *Reflections* and "The Prussian Officer" and the influence of Isak Dinesen. She considerably advances as well the appreciation of McCullers's ironic narrative voice. McCullers's attitude toward egocentricity in this novel differs from the compassion shown in *Hunter* and represents a deliberate experiment "with techniques whose intended effects are comic" (49). McDowell takes seriously McCullers's description of the novel as a hilarious "fairy tale" and cites her "incongruously casual tone," "catalogs or lists which . . . become comic by virtue of their exaggerated specificity or their mixing of significant with trivial items," and her "dramatic fusion of the horrible with the ridiculous" as hallmarks of her "dark comedy" (48). Such comedy sharpens "a satire on the military ethos" (50): "Military activity in peacetime simply appears to be a game without point, whose players are complacent, enervated, maladjusted, or decadent" (49). The novel's irrational, grotesque, and "grimly humorous" personalities and events suggest McCullers's "profound distrust of the intelligence as an exclusive means for interpreting human experience and her growing distrust of realism as a literary mode which relies upon rationally stated motives for its characters" (50). She creates a world where "instincts and unreason dominate" (53). McDowell traces McCullers's experiments with the Gothic "combination of the violent and comic" to the influence of Isak Dinesen, whose *Out of Africa* and *Seven Gothic Tales* McCullers reread annually. Dinesen's Gothicism is a stronger influence on *Reflections* than Lawrence's "The Prussian Officer," which, McDowell acknowledges, may exist "somewhere in the background" of the novel (55). McCullers's "flashes of ironic comedy" (54) provide the clearest contrast between the two tales.

McDowell admires the novel's "technical virtuosity" and describes the narrative voice as "marked by emotional detachment, formality, concision, and some artifice suggest[ing] an undeviating attitude of superiority, on the speaker's part, and his awareness of the absurdity of the characters and situations" (61). At some points McCullers approximates "the style of the teller of the tall-tale of frontier days" (61), as in drolly explaining why Leonora Penderton's feeble-mindedness does not represent a liability to the men in her life, who do not require or expect intelligence in a woman, or to her success in the highest social circles of army post life. The mocking of individual characters extends to Anacleto, whose devotion to Alison Langdon might be overestimated were it not for passages designed to portray him as a "foolish and vindictive" troublemaker who prefigures Cousin Lymon in *Ballad* (62). Only Alison Langdon, in her concern for her dying child, escapes egocentricity and the narrator's mockery to any appreciable degree; she is also "the most clear-sighted character," but her vision is distorted by self-hatred and self-pity (59). While she finds the work remarkable, McDowell does not see its satire as unblemished: "It is unclear whether McCullers implies that the cosmos is fundamentally askew or that the limitations of human beings themselves give rise to a society that has little continuity and meaning" (64).

A dissertation by Helen Fiddyment Levy (1982) calls the army post a "metaphoric miniature of the post-industrial society" so regimented and stultifying that "only the dim-witted, the mean-spirited, or the mentally ill survive." In such satire McCullers is a precursor of writers like Ken Kesey, Joseph Heller, and Thomas Pynchon who "use . . . the monolithic institution as the central metaphor of Post-World War II fiction" (321). Such a world transforms masculine energy into sadism and feminine nurturance into masochism. Captain Penderton succeeds in the military hierarchy "precisely because of his neurotic compulsiveness" (322). Both he and Alison Langdon are "maimed in the expression of their sexual identity" (327).

Frederick R. Karl (1985) likewise sees McCullers as a precursor of later postwar writers such as John Hawkes or J. D. Salinger, but he objects to the mannerisms of "excessive drinking, the suggested or actual homosexuality, the helpless artistic sensibility" he finds in McCullers and some of her contemporaries – a reference as much to reputed lifestyles as to the contents of their work – McCullers's private life having become highly visible with the publication of the 1975 biography by Virginia Spencer Carr. Karl, for example, describes Anacleto as "a Tennessee Williams type," presumably alluding to the dramatist himself as much as to his characters (123). Karl calls *Reflections* a "dance of fading forces" and praises its rhythmical innovations which blend "broad elements of movement and silence, intense frenzy combined with withdrawal" (124). Like its title, the novel is almost totally devoid of sound and emphasizes "stealth, voyeurism, watchfulness" (124). Although the setting specifies an army post in peacetime, Karl maintains that "the sense of some kind of war is never beyond us" (124).

Pratibha Nagpal (1987) studies the grotesque elements in the novel and emerges with the insight that all characters, except for Alison Langdon, reside in "a spiritual wasteland and . . . [a] private hell." McCullers contrasts "the rigid pattern of life imposed by military discipline and the uncontrolled vast universe of nature" to show that regimentation interferes with self-expression and the formulation of identity. Nagpal believes as well that the failure of love in the novel is symptomatic of McCullers's rejection of "physical relationship as an anodyne to loneliness" (64).

Arleen Portada (1988) examines Weldon Penderton and Alison Langdon as sex-role misfits in an "oppressively phallic community," the army base where sexual roles are exaggerated and enforced for women as well as men (66). Penderton's richest relationships exist entirely in his imagination, his erotic impulses stifled and distorted by his repressed homosexuality and his unfulfilling marriage. Langdon, potentially the healthiest character because she is aware of and articulate about her emotions, is driven by grief and humiliation to reject the maternal role by cutting off her nipples. Portada concludes that "McCullers created particularly incompatible marriages as a paradigm for . . . [conformity] to particularly alien social conventions" (68).

Donna Bauerly (1988), in developing a thesis about the shift from eros to agape in McCullers's fiction, determines that in every instance the movement away from eros is frustrated in *Reflections* by lack of self-knowledge. Raphael B. Johstoneaux (1989) devotes an entire article to the dehumanizing forces he attributes to narcissistic self-involvement; a "dehumanized position . . . [is] one wherein only the self matters" (101). He describes Ellgee Williams, Weldon Penderton, and Alison Langdon as "emotionally abandoned" beings without clearly demonstrating in every case how this is so. Williams is motherless; Langdon has been abandoned by her faithless husband, and her daughter has died, but Johstoneaux does not address these circumstances directly. Williams, he says, "lacks even the hard companionship of conscience" (98), a trait that might equally apply to the sadistic Penderton.

Virginia Spencer Carr (1990) provides a lucid survey of the novel's origins and movement, emphasizing McCullers's use of seasonal imagery and the play of light and dark. Structurally unrelieved by music or imagery associated with music, the novel does make use of "a subtle kind of mirror counterpoint . . . in the dissonant/harmonic relationship among the five characters and the horse, all inextricably unified, yet developed with linear individuality. Whereas in counterpoint, two dissimilar themes or melodies run counter, yet concurrently, and combine eventually into a harmonious whole, in this dissonant tale the chords are too harsh, the melody too broken to ever result in anything more than scattered musical strains" (49–50). She also remarks on one feature of the narrator's remoteness from the story: McCullers "in no way discloses the gender of her narrator" (40).

The question of tone has been central to the developing body of criticism on *Reflections in a Golden Eye*. With what degree of irony, compassion, comedy, or disdain does McCullers regard her bizarre assortment of characters? Although punctuated by a few superficial or misguided studies in every decade, the pattern of critical response has generally grown in the direction of expanded range and subtlety. Tennessee Williams's insights into this novel's stylistic precision and its existential themes have been profitably elaborated as readers have, through the medium of its narrative world, attended to the fashions and exigencies of their own times, from the cold war politics of fear and isolation to postphallic ideologies of sexual freedom. Perhaps the most striking shift during four decades of criticism has occurred in the increased visibility and meaning of the novel's setting. McCullers's earliest critics, responding in the middle of World War II or close to its end, barely noticed the regimented, peacetime army base where the unsettling events occur. Its significance was not profitably explored until the disenchantments of Vietnam-era war-making encouraged readers to interpret the novel as a satire on repressions of several kinds, chiefly institutional. The principal result from more than forty years of critical understanding has been an enlargement of our estimate of McCullers's craft, particularly our appreciation of the complexity and surprising sophistication of vision she brought to her work.

4: *The Ballad of the Sad Café* (1943, 1951)

> *Mrs. McCullers has elevated her primitive*
> *characters and their grotesque actions to the*
> *wild, extravagant, and beautiful level of myth.*
> (Albert J. Griffith 1967)

*T*HE BALLAD OF *the Sad Café* is customarily regarded as McCullers's fourth significant work of fiction, but its publication in *Harper's Bazaar* in August 1943, two and one-half years before the appearance in that magazine of part 1 of *The Member of the Wedding*, makes the novella McCullers's third important work. Confusion arises from the fact that it did not appear as a book until May 1951, five years after the book publication of *Member* (March 1946) and little more than a month after publication of the dramatic adaptation of that novel (April 1951). *Ballad* is treated here in the order of its composition and serial publication, although a case could be made that its role in shaping McCullers's reputation depends on the widespread, antecedent estimate of *Member,* as both novel and play. In fact, there is only one notable response to its appearance in *Harper's,* a tribute from Kay Boyle, "I Wish I Had Written *The Ballad of the Sad Café"* (1946).

Another complicating factor in gauging the impact of *Ballad* is that it appeared as the title work in an omnibus volume that also reprinted the stories "Wunderkind," "The Jockey," "Madame Zilensky and the King of Finland," "The Sojourner," "A Domestic Dilemma," and "A Tree. A Rock. A Cloud." as well as *Reflections in a Golden Eye* and *Member.* Both U.S. and English editions were effectively marketed, and the collection was simultaneously issued by Houghton Mifflin as a Book Find Club edition. As intended, the collection was viewed as a testament of the strength of McCullers's reputation. Most reviews focused on the total achievement, or the newly gathered stories, taken as a whole, rather than on *Ballad* individually. The significance of the collection for McCullers's reputation as a writer of short stories is treated in chapter 8, below; the focus here is on the academic response to this arresting novella.

That response has been considerable. The importance of *Ballad* for an understanding of McCullers's stylistics and thematics, poetics and erotics, was recognized immediately. The physical abnormalities of its characters marked it as a further stage in McCullers's handling of the grotesque, and its overt ballad form confirmed critics in connecting McCullers's narrative techniques to musical models. The role of the narrator, the significance of the coda, and the function of a long and justly famous digression on the nature of love have been recurrent concerns.

Viewed as a credo by many critics, and often quoted to illuminate her handling of other novels or stories, the digression lays out with syllogistic precision a statement that any person or thing can be the object of love; that the value of love derives solely from the lover; and that the state of being beloved is well nigh intolerable, producing, inevitably, fear and hatred of the lover. These tenets are demonstrated in the novella by Miss Amelia Evans's love for the hunchback dwarf Cousin Lymon Willis, Lymon's love for the reprobate Marvin Macy, and Macy's erstwhile love for Miss Amelia. The present time of the story begins with the appearance of Cousin Lymon. The love Miss Amelia forms for him transfigures her and the entire town. Outsized, manly, and notoriously stingy, Amelia becomes, as a lover, jovial and generous, opening her house as a café where townspeople find a welcome and festive fellowship. Marvin Macy, the husband Miss Amelia disdained and rejected, returns to town after his release from jail. Lymon, conceiving a love for Macy, joins him in humiliating Miss Amelia. The triangle ruptures in a final battle in which the two men conspire to defeat her utterly. The novella ends with a reminder that, outside of the town, "twelve mortal men" sing together the song of the chain gang.

Dayton Kohler (1951) finds in *Ballad* the paradigm that accounts for the structural and thematic unity of McCullers's fiction to date. He identifies "the chief elements of her narrative pattern: a plot of double conflict, external and internal, between the individual and a hostile environment; a dramatic structure unfolding the tension of crisis, when the individual realizes that he is separate and lost; a theme of moral isolation presented in terms of social disunity and the wasted human effort to escape the loneliness which life itself imposes; style as technique, to disclose thematic meanings which parallel the dramatic line of action" (4). Such a catalog could with only slight modification serve as a sketch of fictional devices to which Cleanth Brooks and Robert Penn Warren directed student readers in their classic introduction to New Criticism's value for *Understanding Fiction* (1943). As a critic adept at this approach, Kohler establishes patterns of interest in *Ballad* that hold for more than a decade. *Ballad,* he says, "has the casual tone of an old wives' tale, retold with touches of horror and wry humor . . . . It is also a story of compassion and insight, for deeper meanings lie under the simple narrative pattern, meanings which are prefigured at the beginning in the brief glimpse we have of Miss Amelia peering from a window of her boarded-up house." McCullers triumphs in making Miss Amelia "grotesque without letting her become ridiculous, just as Cousin Lymon is sinister without being melodramatic. In this fable the writer ponders the mystery of love and the hatred which lies close to it, and the ways by which character is shaped for betrayal and ruin. *The Ballad of the Sad Café* is an impressive story because it takes a long, steady look at the moral evil which is also the devouring obsessive evil of modern society, the isolation of the loving and the lonely" (5).

Responding to the English edition of the omnibus collection which features *Ballad,* the *New Statesman and Nation* offered a surprising assessment, in this case surprising for its enthusiasm. V. S. Pritchett (1952) calls McCullers a genius and

> the most remarkable novelist . . . to come out of America for a genera-
> tion . . . . What she has, before anything else, is a courageous imagina-
> tion; that is to say one that is bold enough to consider the terrible in
> human nature without loss of nerve, calm, dignity or love . . . . Like all
> writers of original genius, she convinces us that we have missed some-
> thing which was plainly to be seen in the real world. So that if it is a mat-
> ter of freaks like a gangling, mannish, hard-spitting, hard-hitting old
> virgin, or the hunchback dwarf she falls in love with, we are made to see
> that ordinary human love can transform them as it can any other crea-
> ture . . . . It may be objected that the very strangeness of the characters
> in a story like *The Ballad of the Sad Café* is that of regional gossip . . . . But
> the compassion of the author gives them their Homeric moment in a
> universal tragedy. There is a point at which they become "great." (137)

Frank Baldanza (1958) calls *Ballad* "a short and powerful exemplum on the impossibility of being loved"; it echoes the Socratic dialogue in *Phaedrus* on the relative value of loving or being loved. But, unlike Socrates, McCullers denies a positive outcome: "not only are the attentions of the non-lover and the sensual lover unworthy, she says, but the attentions of the spiritual lover are invariably unwelcome, and he is bound to come to grief too" (162). *Ballad* shows McCullers's "insistent push toward allegorizing fantasy" and Baldanza's approval of the work's elevation above "all the distracting profusion of naturalistic observation and social inclusiveness of *The Heart Is a Lonely Hunter.*" In *Ballad* "every detail of the matrix of scene blends into the overall design of the meaning" (161). The tone of this passage offers clear evidence of the "insistent push" among critics of this period toward discovering just the sort of ultimately unified or unifiable matrix of self-contained meaning Baldanza applauds as McCullers's highest achievement.

The desire to classify McCullers's treatment of love is evident in John B. Vickery's reading of *Ballad* as a parody of romantic love in which "each of the three main characters is successively lover and beloved" (1960, 14). "Each, then, is in turn a slave and a tyrant, depending on whether he is loving or being loved. The refusal or inability of the characters to synchronize their changes of heart produces the interlocking romantic triangles which constitute the plot, while the grotesque comedy arises out of their each in turn conforming to a role they contemptuously rejected in another" (15). For Amelia, Cousin Lymon "is simultaneously the lover-husband she has rejected and the child she will never have." Like Marvin Macy, "by loving she herself creates the beloved tyrant who eventually repudiates and destroys her" (15). Cousin Lymon, in loving Marvin Macy, "becomes imbued with the masculinity which Marvin has regained in the world outside the town" and is thereby capable of asserting himself. "Indeed he himself becomes a psychic projection of Marvin, and by stealing Amelia's love, he amply redresses the latter's failure" (15). As "the child of Amelia's heart," Lymon is "a homuncular incubus, the product of a nightmare marriage and the dark, secret perversion of her own soul. And it is only with the flight of the hunchback and the victorious Marvin . . . that she grasps the solitary nature of love and accepts its suffering. It is this awareness which constitutes the first stage in that agon of experience which is human love" (16). In an essay of highly variable quality, Vickery's discussion of *Ballad* is particularly insightful.

Willard Thorp (1960) propounds four characteristics shared by southern humorists, from late-nineteenth-century tale tellers like George Washington Harris and A. B. Longstreet to mid-twentieth-century novelists like Faulkner, Capote, and O'Connor: characters who operate outside conventional society; a "war" between the insiders and outsiders; "incidental satire" on the agents of respectability; and a tendency to "resort to a grim and outlandish fantasy which carries their writing way beyond realism" (172–73). *Ballad* provides an example of the fourth characteristic. The bizarre relationship among Miss Amelia, Cousin Lymon, and Marvin Macy builds toward a cataclysmic conclusion, what Thorp calls "another of those house-destroying, community-shattering battles which Southern humorists, old and new, write about" (174).

The significance of the coda is addressed by Barbara Nauer Folk (1962), who sees the novella's last lines, an "invitation to 'go listen to the chain gang,'" as a "reminder that the piece is at one and the same time a literary ballad and a folk dirge enclosing a cosmic statement" (203). "It is this sad and tender vision of humanity which is central to Carson McCullers' writings: the race of men a grandiose chorus, a body in chains but nevertheless able to transcend itself in expression which is as variously toned as painfully beautiful, as its own mysterious nature." McCullers's "use of music and musical references is always intelligent, functional, and openly reverent" (202).

Mark Schorer (1963) says, approvingly, that "with the novelette, *The Ballad of the Sad Café*, the theme remains the same [as in her previous novels] but the method pushes farther away from social realism than anything she had yet written. It is probably her most successful work and attains most completely the objectification of myth" (92).

> The whole melodramatic action, the somehow depersonalized characters, the objective narration, the indifference to psychological as to social realism, the refusal to comment on even the most mysterious elements in the action, the frame in which the action is set (it begins and ends with a doomed, closed building inhabited by a haunted, crazed, and solitary figure), and by the now well-known legendary style, here much heightened – all this and more detailed matters of stylistic device and texture as well as more general matters such as the brooding, fated atmosphere of the work are characteristics familiar to us in the ballad form. In the prose version of this form, Mrs. McCullers' talent finds its most complete consolidation. (92)

Schorer points out that the men on the chain gang are "Together, of course, in their captivity" (93).

John M. Bradbury (1963) finds *Ballad* "a return to her symbolic, or perhaps better parabolic, manner . . . . The characters again [as in *Reflections*] are extremes, the action somewhat fantastic, particularly in the climactic stomp-and-gouge match between the female protagonist and her ex-criminal husband, but, like Faulkner, Miss McCullers here manages to heighten the language and atmosphere of her story to the point where it acquires a sort of legendary credence." Bradbury believes the story represents the climax of McCullers's pessimism. *Ballad*'s "obsessions are exclusively those of love and its counterpart, hate, and all the characters exhibit the fatal tendency to learn hatred for those who would envelop them in love, and love for those without love or merit. The central action is neatly framed by the haunting lonely songs of a chain gang and emphasized by repeated descriptions of the 'dreary' mill town, offering lifetimes of boredom" (112).

Wayne D. Dodd (1963) calls attention to Cousin Lymon's unfinished painting on the right side of the front porch, which allies him with the child-as-creator figures of John Henry in *Member* and Anacleto in *Reflections* as artists of the grotesque. The self-preserving isolation which McCullers's characters both fight to keep and long to discard is portrayed in Miss

Amelia's confinement in the dilapidated house at both the beginning and the end of the novel. However, Dodd sees some relief from the bleakness depicted in the coda, where the twelve mortal men "represent the plight of all mankind in her world, caught, bound together by the chains of circumstance and necessity, yet unable to achieve a harmony that transcends their individuality . . . . They are forever bound; yet there is something beautiful and noble about their struggle" (212).

Walter Allen (1964) in his history of the modern novel calls *Ballad* "the strangest, the most haunting of Carson McCullers's work. It has the timelessness and remoteness of a ballad." The novella "describes a sort of ritual dance in which the loved one always turns from the lover to love another who also turns away. It is told with a beautiful economy and precision in a prose of singular purity that transmits both the ambience of the town and its inhabitants and the timeless quality which broods over the action" (136).

In a source study, Robert S. Phillips (1964b) traces the inspiration for *Ballad* to "The Monkey," one of Isak Dinesen's *Seven Gothic Tales* that McCullers read in 1938, several years before writing her novella. McCullers's story parallels Dinesen's in several particulars: corresponding characters, a dilapidated house, the hint of incestuous love, an unwanted marriage proposal, and a brutal "battle royal" (188). Most striking are the resemblances between characters. Dinesen's corrupt Boris, a "priest of black magic," may beget Marvin Macy. Miss Amelia has her parallel in the six-feet-tall Athena; both "will not tolerate being loved by any other than their fathers" (187). Dinesen's monkey, the pet of a Prioress, is the counterpart of Cousin Lymon. Both "are small love objects for strong, sexless women" (185). Even McCullers's chain gang has its parallel in "Dinesen's wandering crew of hangmen, who have seen so much horror that they can weep on command." Phillips acknowledges that "both stories are constructed upon the foundation of ancient fairy tale and myth" (189), but his case for influence, or "literary affinity," as he prefers, is persuasive — at least until the comparison is revaluated by Louise Westling below (1982).

In a subsequent essay, Phillips (1966) argues that *Ballad* is not vintage McCullers Gothic but "something unique in the context of her work" (80), a parable more than a novel. He sees the Amazon Amelia and the little "lie-man" as "characters who are the physical embodiments of Freudian symbols," but inverted as to sex: Amelia, "ugly, oversized . . . elongated and masculine, suggests of course the phallus. The small, round-backed Lymon is the female organ" (82). Amelia's masculine identification with her father is none too subtly figured in the acorn she saves from the day he died and her own two kidney stones (Phillips calls them gallstones), removed and preserved and frequently fondled. The gesture "suggests Amelia's subconscious desire to possess male genitals," an odd formulation if, in fact, she is, as phallus, the very symbol of them. By draping Lymon in a lime-green shawl, she "makes him a suitably feminine love object" (81). She disguises Lymon because, like Mick Kelly and Frankie Addams, Amelia "fears heterosexual relations." In the Oedipal dynamics of all three works Phillips recognizes that "unconscious hostility against the phallus is the constant and impelling motive." Phillips cites as an example of gender inversion the scene in which Amelia wrestles Macy "over the love of a beloved, also a male, who stands cowering in the corner like a Victorian heroine, pale and wan." The pattern of inversion counters Irving Malin's "theory that Amelia and Lymon are intended as mutual doubles" (83). It also sets *Ballad* apart from the other novels, being altogether outrageous and hyperbolic in the manner of a burlesque or the tall tale. It is "the greatest departure from realism in all her writings" and her "most didactic work" (85). *Ballad* is "a breakthrough" in McCullers's use of "Southern Gothicism." The genre "with its traumas and tortures – can create the hallucination and exaltation of fright, but it also can be used for both burlesque and didacticism, the exaggerated actions and physical mutations calling attention to the moral and sexual conflicts involved. The material is much the same; the effects are quite different" (85–86).

In an overview of a "new comic realism in American fiction," Ihab H. Hassan (1964b) puts McCullers in company with Welty, O'Connor, and Purdy as writers who aim "to describe spiritual distortion in our time" and do so by portraying "physical distortion": "The one incarnates the other. They create freaks of love or loneliness, or monsters of holiness . . . . But freaks and monsters are the subject of veiled mockery; their abnormality shocks and shames us into ironic laughter. This is why the comedy of the grotesque often seems acerbic. Only children can laugh at hunchbacks or fanatics with glee. Adults learn to transform their discomfort into irony, which serves to domesticate the monsters roaming the inner landscapes of the soul" (638). Hassan believes McCullers's grotesques and comparable characters in Bellow, Purdy, Salinger, Ellison, Capote, and O'Connor signal "the birth of a new sense of reality, a new knowledge of error and of incongruity, an affirmation of life under the aspect of comedy. For comedy, broadly conceived, may be understood as *a way of making life possible in this world, despite evil or death.* Comedy recognizes human limitations, neither in broken pride nor yet in saintly humility but in the spirit of ironic acceptance. It is, therefore, the antic child of realism." The younger novelists he cites are "relearning the old art of improvisation

in fiction; they cultivate the picaresque or fantastic modes; they are re-
pelled by the neat formulations of style or structure that formalist critics
once pressed too hard. Their sense of order admits of potential disorder.
In short, they have acquired a tolerance for the mixed, causeless quality of
experience: its loose ends, its broken links, its surprises and reversals.
Knowing how outrageous facts can be, they do not pretend to subdue
them with a flourish and a symbol" (636). "Modern European literature,
which is largely existential, is really a raucous record of absurd laughter."
Hassan credits Fiedler with noticing the "gothic or supernatural strain in
classic American fiction, black with laughter" (637).

Oliver Evans (1965a) says, "Cousin Lymon is outlandish enough for
anyone's taste: he is a dwarf, he is hunchbacked, he is tubercular, and he
is homosexual. His relationship with the man-like Amelia constitutes one
of the saddest and most grotesque situations in modern fiction" (130).
Ballad itself "must be among the saddest stories in any language." Indeed,
Evans sees it as a declaration that McCullers has moved a step beyond
the earlier novels, in which reciprocal love was still held as a possibility, to
unredeemed pessimism: love is always an unequal and opposite experience; the beloved actually hates the lover. "This, according to Mrs
McCullers . . . is the terrible law of nature that has sentenced man to a life
of perpetual solitary confinement. There is no longer even a possibility of
escape." However, "the impulse to love is a good impulse, even though it
is doomed to end in frustration" (131). For a time Miss Amelia and the
town are happy. Amelia's love for the dwarf is credible. "A freak herself,
she feels for him the same kind of affinity that Singer feels for Antonapoulos . . . . The same mixture of love and pity [and, no doubt, recognition] is
also found in the relationship between Anacleto and Mrs Langdon" (132).

The meaning of the epilogue is "richly symbolic": "The twelve mortal
men represent all mankind, and they are prisoners because they cannot
escape the fate of spiritual isolation. There is paradox and irony in the fact
that *what joins them together is exactly what keeps them apart:* that is, the predicament of their loneliness. They escape temporarily through their singing (love), which it is significant that they do *together* in an attempt to
resolve, or rather dissolve, their individual identities; but their music is
'both somber and joyful' (love, that is, mixed with despair). The effect of
this music of chained humanity upon the casual listener is also paradoxical, a mixture of 'ecstasy and fright'" (133–34). The café is as well an important symbol, "serving the microcosmic function . . . noted in . . . earlier
work"; it is "the stage for an elemental allegorical drama of love and
hate"; "a refuge and a solace for the townspeople" – "a kind of bulwark
against the impersonal and the inimical" as is Biff Brannon's New York

Café. It serves "exactly the same function" as the bodega in Hemingway's "A Clean, Well-Lighted Place," "as a fortress against loneliness and disorder, symbolized in both stories by the darkness outside" (134).

Like Phillips, Evans reads the acorn as generative, but not necessarily masculine. Like the egg in Sherwood Anderson's story, the acorn stands for "life itself, by which the protagonist in both stories is baffled. When we read that Miss Amelia's face was 'saddened and perplexed' when she contemplates the acorn, we remember that the one disorder which, in her role of amateur country doctor, she refuses to treat is a 'female complaint' . . . and we remember also the fury with which she repels Marvin Macy on her wedding night. Her sadness and perplexity are caused by the realization of her failure to accept the vital principle" (135). Evans points to the "extensive use of the magical numbers three and seven" but does not connect it with ballad form. He remarks as well the resemblance of McCullers's novella to Faulkner's "A Rose for Emily" in the image of the recluse shut away in her decaying house. Both women, Evans notes, are "victims of a father complex," and both stories turn on love and revenge, but he says, "I think there can be no doubt that Mrs McCullers's is the better story" in that Faulkner's is merely Gothic – horror for its own sake – whereas McCullers's novella "can lay claim to universality" (137). Faulkner "sacrificed the universal to the sensational. On the other hand, Mrs McCullers, whose purpose is didactic and whose treatment is allegorical, has made her characters unique for a purpose: their eccentricities are the badges of their isolation" (137–38). Evans concludes that the novella shows that "an eternal flaw exists in the machinery of love, which alone has the power to liberate man from his fate of spiritual isolation" (143).

Soviet critic Inna M. Levidova (1966, trans. 1972) comments in passing on the grotesque elements of the novel. "In her best work, *The Ballad of the Sad Café*, the three heroes are locked together – like the prisoners who work on the roads near the unnamed town, the setting of the story – by one chain of incomprehension, love and hate . . . . The author unfolds this rather depressing Gothic story like an ancient fairytale – epically, smoothly, harmoniously and somehow in an amazing musical fashion." Unlike most U.S. critics of the decade, Levidova notices the realism of the setting. McCullers, she says, "is not talking about some never-never land in her strange fairytale about the fantastic whims of the human heart. This all occurs in a very realistic, briefly but well described town in the American South of our time, where the heroine sells whiskey, engages in petty but persistent lawsuits against the neighboring farmers, where . . . . 'The soul rots with boredom'" (92–93).

Louis D. Rubin, Jr. (1966) compares the handling of the grotesque by Faulkner, O'Connor, Caldwell, and McCullers. Like Caldwell, McCullers "goes in for the physically deformed and maimed in her work; for her, however, grotesqueness is designed not to provoke amusement but to convey the sense of loneliness and isolation that comes with abnormality. Pain is the motif of her fiction; her characters move about in a haze of *Angst* and misery. In her best work, the strange novella . . . a tall, sexless, masculine woman and a hunchback dwarf convey through their very oddness and deformity the loneliness, the pain of thwarted and unfulfilled love that is Miss McCullers' picture of our experience" (242–43).

Albert J. Griffith (1967) says that the novella is "as grotesque in characterization and incident as anything in American literature"; but it somehow "sublimates its unpromising ingredients." Griffith points out that "even the violence of the denouement – a primitive bare-fisted agon between the woman and her one-time bridegroom over the hunchback – fails to mar the poetic serenity of the tale for most readers" (46). The "quasi-poetic stylistic devices, the fairy-tale atmosphere, the non-literal meanings – are the marks of the mythic imagination, and their combination in this story suggests the making of a modern myth" (46). Noting the quality of inevitability in the action, Griffith says, "The events as narrated seem, furthermore, to be fore-ordained, the result of destiny, not free will . . . . The famous disquisition on love . . . is no psychological explanation at all; at best it is a philosophic hypothesis which only begs the question" (54). Miss Amelia has superhuman drive and energy; Marvin Macy has a "demonic degeneracy" (50), and Cousin Lymon has "certain affinities with the deformed gods" of Greek myth (51). "The style is presentational, however, rather than representational: we are always aware of the mediating influence of the narrator" (53). "Most of the major events . . . are carried out in a solemn and ceremonious manner, suggestive of rituals, both sacred and satanic." The final battle "is no private skirmish entered into in the heat of passion but a public encounter with all the ceremony of a gladiatorial contest or a knightly joust" (55). McCullers's "central insight . . . – that the operations of love are not amenable to nor explainable by reason – is not one to be demonstrated scientifically, but by an appeal to those very sources of irrational knowledge from which love itself springs. To treat of love 'wild, extravagant, and beautiful as the poison lilies of the swamp,' Mrs. McCullers has elevated her primitive characters and their grotesque actions to the wild, extravagant, and beautiful level of myth" (56).

Robert N. Rechnitz (1968) takes the unorthodox view that failed love stems not from the selfishness of the lover but from the recalcitrance of the beloved: "one's acceptance of the world is ultimately determined, not so much by loving, but by allowing oneself to be beloved, to be known by another and ultimately, through this process, by oneself." The three grotesques symbolize the refusal to be loved. Miss Amelia "denies her inner nature, her femininity"; Cousin Lymon does not know his own age, and that fact, to Rechnitz, is, like his deformity, a sign of "willful ignorance"; Macy "never sweats" and seems therefore "part machine" (459). What is it, one wonders, that Macy thus denies? Each of the characters is childlike. Even the narrator uses a childlike pose "to increase the reader's apprehension that [she] is treating matters so frightful that she must hide behind a façade of childlike innocence. The style then becomes a kind of buffer to fend off what would otherwise be unbearable." Miss Amelia's "desire to be a lover conflicts with her fear, perhaps her hatred, of being loved" (460). But this observation does not hold. She has no desire to love Marvin Macy and no demonstrable qualms about being loved by Cousin Lymon. The desires do not arise in tandem and therefore do not conflict. Rechnitz is somewhat more astute about the coda, whose vision of twelve mortal men making music together he dismisses as "mere wishful thinking" (462).

Lawrence Graver (1969) praises McCullers's handling of "the urgent, atmospheric, and primitive" elements of legend and romance in *Ballad.* "The boldness and precision with which she creates the sense of a town estranged from the rest of the world is the first of Mrs. McCullers' successes" in this work. "Unlike those narrators in the earlier novels who move uneasily from realism to myth and back again, the invented voice in this story has an obvious authority and grace" (25). Amelia is larger than life: "Since her liquors relieve melancholy, her foods hunger, and her folk remedies pain, this perverse cross between Ceres, Bacchus, and the neighborhood medicine man is the one indispensable person in town" (26). "Much of what is permanently haunting in this grotesque little story is the product of Mrs. McCullers' easy relationship with the properties of the ballad world. Experience heightened far beyond the realm of plausibility is given a valid, poetic truth by the propriety of those conventions that make the miraculous seem oddly real. Dreams, superstitions, omens, numbers, musical motifs, all operate here to provide an authentic atmosphere for this perverse triangle of passions, and to make the inexplicable longings of the characters seem like dark elemental forces in the natural world" (29). "The richly patterned, sinister dance in which Macy, Amelia, and Lymon play at different times the roles of lover and beloved dramatizes the wayward nature of human passion and the irreconcilable antagonism inherent in every love relationship." Graver explains, "Everyone wants to be a lover because the lover is the archetypal creative spirit: dreamer, quester, romantic idealist" (30). "Having created the beloved in the image of his own desperate desire, the lover is open to rebuff and betrayal" (31). Because of her love, Amelia has become "a force for good in the community, and the destruction of her dream is a cause for genuine mourning." *Ballad* is "an elegy for Amelia Evans, and it has all the brooding eloquence and eccentricity to stand as a fitting tribute to that very peculiar lady" (32).

Dale Edmonds (1969) examines the extent to which the novella emulates the ballad form in theme, setting, and tone. He cites the "impersonal, oracular tone to the authorial voice": that of a balladeer. "Like a ballad, [it] unfolds as a series of vivid, effectively juxtaposed pictures." "Miss Amelia is crosseyed, a physical characteristic with occult overtones – at least in folk understanding." Noting also the association of hunchbacks with mystical powers, Edmonds says, "Together Miss Amelia and Cousin Lymon suggest a witch and her familiar, and they are regarded as such by the townfolk" (20). The novella's "three major plot 'movements' may be considered analogous to the three stanzas of the old French ballade form, and the concluding 'Twelve Mortal Men' passage may be likened to the envoy of this form" (21). Because the prisoners sing together, the envoy indicates McCullers's belief that "mutual love is possible" (23).

Alice Hamilton (1970), exploring the inner and outer worlds of McCullers's fiction, reads *Ballad*'s digression on love with particular astuteness: "The lover sees his beloved as the object of his stored desires; and that makes him aware of his loneliness, because the inner world of this love is inhabited by him alone. The beloved reveals the soul of the lover, making the nature of the lover more clear. The beloved has merely objectivized the 'ego.'" The lover desires to invade the inner room of the beloved. The ideal of the outer world is embodied in the café. Its function is "to give worth to life – to make men proud. In the café gaiety, satisfaction, and fellowship can be bought cheaply. The bitter feeling that one is worth very little can be 'laid low'" (226). Hamilton notes that only the preacher failed to partake of the communion offered by Miss Amelia's café. Miss Amelia is defeated in the climactic battle because "she could no longer function in the 'outer' world, since her 'inner' world was dead. The result for the town was spiritual stagnation" (227).

Dawson F. Gaillard (1972) locates the success of *Ballad* in McCullers's construction of a narrator who is also a member of the community. His perspective, "characterized by wisdom and reflections that give to the ballad a sense of timelessness, [moves] the story out of history (the record of irreversible events) into tradition, or myth" (420). "The narrator's seriousness, empathy, and sympathy for man's soul-pains and his assurance that he speaks from common experience bring to the telling the presence of a human being trying to make sense of the events he recalls. Because of this presence, the reader cannot . . . distance himself from the emotional impact of the action. Such is the magic of the oral quality in literature" (422). The significance of the coda is explicable to Gaillard in these terms: "With the loss of the café, the narrator almost instinctively seeks to fill the dark void of his soul by listening to the singing of the twelve mortal men of the chain gang. Their music is the music of life itself, being 'both somber and joyful.' This moment cannot last, but like the café, it can provide, for a short time, a sanctuary from total darkness of the soul. And like the music of the twelve mortal men, the balladeer's tale can cause the heart of the reader-listener 'to broaden and the listener to grow cold with ecstasy and fright'" (426). "He also tells his story, as a balladeer sings his song, and in these actions of vocalizing the spirit of man, the speaker or singer dramatizes one moment of victory over time and mortality . . . . It is the sound of the human voice, the action of a human mind coming to grips with what has occurred in time that provide the power of *The Ballad of the Sad Café*" (427).

John McNally (1973) likewise offers a reading in which the third-person narrator is taken to be a townsman, a character intimately familiar with the people, the weather, the liquor he describes. McCullers's enigmatic epilogue, "The Twelve Mortal Men," serves to balance the bleak story of Miss Amelia. By rousing himself to listen to the chain gang, the narrator signals his growth away from the stagnant dreariness of the town: "What we have in *The Ballad of the Sad Café*, then, is a beautifully sculptured piece of writing in which we overhear the internal monologue of a character whose haunting recollections enable him to overcome his own *ennui* and to resist the atrophying pressures of the familiar world" (43). Such a reading seems an attempt to recuperate this dark ballad into the dominant patterns of canonical American fiction: the frame tale in which an Ishmael, Coverdale, or Carraway profits from the tragedy he witnesses.

Joseph R. Millichap (1973) asserts that the novella's "unqualified success" stems especially from the "integrity . . . of narrative voice" (330). He, too, describes the narrator as the ballad maker and focuses on McCullers's use of ballad conventions to refute claims by other critics for the universal significance of the novella's pronouncements about love and hate. "Strangely enough, the same critics, intent on demonstrating their Procrustean theories in all of her work, often misunderstand *Ballad* by insisting on the universality of elements which are obviously peculiar to the point of aberration. The use of the bizarre theory of love offered by the narrator of *Ballad* as a formula for interpreting all of McCullers' fiction has hampered analysis not only of the *novella* itself but of her other works as well" (329). In the process of displacing earlier readings, Millichap departs from the approach to McCullers's fiction for which he is best known: his insistence on its social realism. "Unlike the larger mill city which serves as the setting of most of her fiction, the mill village is not used to probe economic conditions or regional problems in a realistic manner. Even the chronological setting is unimportant; it might be 1920 or 1940; for the village in *Ballad* exists in the temporally imprecise world of human passion." Certainly "this is the traditional world of the ballad, a world of passion and violence, of omens and portents, of the full wild impulsiveness of archetypal human behavior" (330). Citing traditional ballads which concern "analogous love-hate relationship[s] . . . between the courtly lover and the disdainful beloved" (332), Millichap argues that the novella exaggerates one dimension of love; it does not propound a universalized theory about inequality in love. The famous digression on love is merely a convention of the ballad expressed as the localized observations of the ballad maker.

The three characters, likewise, are rooted in ballad tradition: Miss Amelia, an Amazonian enchantress with supernatural healing powers; Marvin Macy, a demon lover; and Cousin Lymon, the mysterious stranger physically "akin to the fairy children of folk tale and ballad – pixies, elves, leprechauns." Noting the good luck thought to come from rubbing a hunchback's hump, Millichap observes that Cousin Lymon "becomes a strange combination of man, child, and pet that Amelia can love as she could not love her husband." In an often quoted description, Millichap says, "He is a man loved without sex, a child acquired without pain, and a companion which her limited personality finds more acceptable than a husband or a child. Their relationship, like Amelia's marriage, is symbolically incestuous and immaturely formed" (335). The triangle is shattered in an epic battle that leaves Miss Amelia defeated and alone. The presence of the chain gang "illustrates the prison house aspect of the human condition. The coda, entitled 'Twelve Mortal Men,' emphasizes how man can achieve creativity, in this case the beautiful work songs and ballads of the gang, even in the most difficult situations if there is harmony and cooperation" (338). Their harmony contrasts the last view of Miss Amelia. "McCullers' other novels demonstrate this condition [isolation] in the modern social world; the strange ballad of the café that becomes sad traces the roots of these difficulties in the timeless province of the lonely human heart" (339).

By focusing on the human pride and conviviality fostered by the short-lived café, Panthea Reid Broughton (1974) squarely observes the novel's long unnoticed social criticism.

> McCullers makes a comparison between useful commodities which have a clearly established value [products of the mill] and human lives which do not. The comparison is seminal here because it is a lack of confidence in their own human worth which renders the townspeople incapable of sustaining the transcendent affirmation which was the café. For the dreary desperation of the town with its one-industry economy has conditioned the people to hoard themselves as well as their money. As Tocqueville long ago surmised, spiritual isolation is closely aligned with competitive capitalism. Here the normative pattern for dealing with the world and its people is the transaction. Now the transaction may be efficient, abstract, uninvolved, and profitable, but it is also dehumanized [and joyless]. To expend the soul in an open give-and-take relationship with another is too much of a risk; it seems safer, and more expedient, to approach another only to take rather than to risk being taken. (37)

Broughton goes on to trace the extent to which the three central characters are marked, and undone, by their exploitation of human relationships. "As the lover, each is a slave; as the beloved, each is a tyrant." Their cruelties are tragic, not comic; they are the inevitable consequence of the mill town's contempt for "the human virtues of tenderness and sensitivity [which] are considered to be exclusively feminine and decidedly superfluous" (38). "Sexual characteristics, then, are so rigidly dichotomized that they cannot be held in balance. One is either servile and feminine, or, preferably, dominant and masculine" (38). Written during the brief vogue of androgyny as a solution to gender inequalities, Broughton's article focuses on the pernicious "sexual stereotypes of extremity" and the need to reject them: "The problem, then, is to reclaim the virtues of tenderness and receptivity from their exclusive association with whatever is female and weak, and to reinstate them as virtues which are essential to all humanity; for, without accepting these virtues as a dignified aspect of mankind, the human community cannot survive." Broughton cites the taunt of Marvin Macy near the end of the story as he laughs at Amelia and says, "'Everything you holler at me bounces back on yourself.' His denunciation provides an apt image for the entire novella. For *The Ballad of the Sad Café* may be interpreted as a fable which shows us that rejecting those characteristics labeled as exclusively feminine bounces back on the rejector and renders men and women alike incapable of loving and thereby escaping the prisons of their own spiritual isolation" (42).

Charlene Kerne Clark (1975a), investigating McCullers's participation in the tradition of southern literary humor, says *Ballad,* "despite its forlorn theme of unrequited love, is strongly infused with backwoods folk humor superimposed on violence. The murderous wrath of Miss Amelia against her prodigal husband, Marvin Macy, is undercut by humorous blunderings as she bungles several attempts to murder him, the most humiliating of which occurs when she accidentally receives the poisoned plate of food intended for him. Humorous brutality sets the tone for much of the ensuing action" (163). In the final battle, "despite the tragic implications of Miss Amelia's defeat, the fight is in many respects a ridiculously comic affair described in as much deadly earnest and trivial detail as a Howard Cosell sports report (at one point, we are told, one of the spectators, his mouth open in amazement, swallows a fly)." Clark credits Leslie Fiedler with identifying "the classic example of this combination of violence and humor . . . in that sordid spectacle in *Huckleberry Finn* where Pap lies dead on an abandoned [boat] in a cabin scrawled with obscenities, and Fiedler notes that such a fusion of horror with humor is the hallmark of American fiction." Clark also treats the "ludicrous parody of courtly love" in the role reversal of Miss Amelia and Cousin Lymon (164): "In her desperate but comic effort to woo Lymon, Miss Amelia feeds and clothes him in grand style, plies him with gifts, and caters to his every whim. But all is not laughter in this romantic affair, for in the end Lymon deserts his benefactor-lover, and Miss Amelia, in despairing resignation over her rejection in love, becomes a recluse. This tragicomic depiction of the human pair is a distinctive mark of McCullers' fiction" (165).

Richard M. Cook (1975) notes that the novella's theme is "the miraculous power of love" and that the café is its "true subject" (85). The measure of Amelia's magical love and "her most elaborate gesture of affection" (88), the café inspires in the townspeople "a 'freedom and illicit gladness' that makes them forget their dull work in the factory and their grinding poverty . . . . Miss Amelia's feed store turned café symbolizes a profound shift in values that has occurred within the community" (89). Like Amelia herself, the townspeople become more generous and sociable, less inclined to regard themselves or others in monetary terms. The townspeople "have begun to take pride in the fact that there is more to their lives than mere survival" (89). "It is a pride that makes them act with dignity and finds expression in social ceremony." However, "in the final reckoning the love felt by Miss Amelia for Cousin Lymon is an unbalanced, disorderly love, containing in its single-minded intensity the seeds of its own destruction" (90). "The beloved's fear and hatred of the lover injects a new destructive element into Mrs. McCullers's love relationships" (92).

"The events leading up to and following the fight in the café run a dramatic course encountered before in McCullers's novels. It may be described as one of rising hope leading to a sharp, violent confrontation with reality, followed by disillusionment and despair – the pattern of the interrupted fantasy or daydream, of emotional intoxication plummeting into emotional withdrawal" (97). "Without love the town is thus left in a state of living death" (98).

Cook sees in the song of the chain gang a characteristic use of music to express meaning. "Trapped in the cruelest and most hopeless of physical conditions, the prisoners display an elemental capacity for joy that transcends and changes, if only for a moment, the miserable conditions of their lives . . . . The beauty of their song . . . is the more intense and upsetting for the extraordinary pain and despair out of which it grows. We are moved by the contradictions in this scene just as we are moved by the contradiction of a giantess falling in love with a hunchback dwarf " (100). The novella is McCullers's "most daring excursion into the contradictory and the grotesque. It is composed of material so disparate, comic, ugly, drab, and bizarre, as seemingly to defy harmonious organization into art. Yet the strangeness of the mixture is undoubtedly what makes *The Ballad* so startlingly, hauntingly beautiful. Like the watch chain Miss Amelia gives to Cousin Lymon, that she has had decorated with her own kidney stones, like the table in the café decorated with 'a bouquet of swamp lilies in a Coca-Cola bottle,' *The Ballad* and its envoy reveal through all the surface contradictions and incongruities a deeper beauty of shared human feeling, of people who are together" (101).

Richard Gray (1977) turns to *Ballad* to illustrate his contention that McCullers's South is a "ghostly, private world" instead of a real territory (266). He does, however, stand in awe of its complete evocation. McCullers's description of the town leads Gray to remark that

> the effect of McCullers's prose is accumulative. She does not work in a series of detached, glittering phrases as, say, Truman Capote does. Nor does she, imitating Faulkner, write sentences that coil up snakelike and then strike, suddenly, before the period. Her language is cool and lucid, almost classical in its precision, her descriptions clipped and occasionally cryptic. A nuance in one place, a repetition or a shading somewhere else: this is all she needs really because, like the painter Edward Hopper, she tends to rely on the resonance given to a detail by its total context – and to use concealment almost as a medium of communication. The inertia, the desolation, and the brooding violence of the small-town South are caught in images that are hermetic, despite their apparent candor, and in incidents brimming with undisclosed biography . . . . McCullers has cre-

ated here . . . a world where emotion and vision can coalesce – in which through the agency of her prose, her own particular sense of life can be externalized. The town is no dream kingdom . . . . It is anchored in this world, in a firm if understated way, by such details as the references to the bus and train services and by an implicit understanding of its economic function. (267–68)

Gray reads the digression as a succinct and explicit summary of McCullers's theories about "the delusions attendant upon the human need to love" (268). The plot of *Ballad* is "like something borrowed from the comic legends of the old Southwest. There is a kind of crazy, comic logic of frustration behind everything that happens: the beloved is always turning away from the lover to create a false idol of his or her own" (269). The portrait of Amelia is particularly revealing of McCullers's control over her material: "By reducing her appearance to a series of conflicting angles, by emphasizing her physical defects and her masculinity (or, rather, her sexual ambivalence), McCullers effectively transforms Miss Amelia into a freak here – as much of a caricature in her own way as Sut Lovingood is, say, or any of the subhumans populating *Tobacco Road*." The "epic fight" resembles "those almost operatic trials of strength which enliven so many of the tales of the Southwestern school." Miss Amelia, as a grotesque, is intended to be representative. "Like an image seen in a carnival mirror, she is meant to offer us an exaggerated, comically distorted, and yet somehow sadly accurate reflection of ourselves" (270). McCullers's style "manages to be lyrical and colloquial, lucid and enigmatic, at one and the same time" (271). The result is distancing as well as intimate. "This is an extraordinarily subtle relationship to set up between character and reader – far subtler than anything we are likely to come across elsewhere, in the work of other writers who have experimented with the Southern comic mode. It has its origins, of course, in McCullers's belief that a paradox lurks at the heart of experience, naturally attaching itself to the idea of a *shared* isolation. As for its issue, that we find in the mood or *ambiance* to which our minds first return when recalling a McCullers novel – our memories of a quiet, but peculiarly inclusive, pathos" (271). Noting that the term has "acquired an odor of sentimentality," Gray says that McCullers's fiction at its best shows "how tough and really critical an emotion pathos can be. Her characters are pathetic, but they are pathetic in the finest sense" (271–72). Given his admiration for *Ballad*, it is not difficult to see why Gray believes the quintessential McCullers to lie outside the South's major literary themes – history and the social world.

Margaret Bolsterli (1978) includes *Ballad* among the "prerevolutionary" works by McCullers, Welty, and Porter that show women struggling against a patriarchal status quo. "If *The Ballad of the Sad Café* is not about the frustrations of Miss Amelia's desires to run her own life, then, frankly, I do not know what it is about" (96). In a spirited analysis, Bolsterli admires Amelia as "that rare creature in literature, a 'tomboy' grown up who has never bowed to either biology or societal expectations" (103). Amelia is "beyond public opinion"; she "runs the only store, carpenters, practices medicine, lays bricks, lends money, slaughters hogs, and personally makes and sells the best whiskey in the county." She is vulnerable only "within herself" (104); and it is on this level that McCullers allows her defeat "by the one thing she cannot control – love" (103). Calling Amelia and her counterparts "bound" characters because they were created prior to women's liberation, Bolsterli concludes with sweeping hyperbole: "So Miss Amelia, surely one of the most independent women in modern literature, loses just as surely as any stereotyped 'feminine' character who surrenders herself in return for a subtle dominance over males, or as any character who wants to be independent but cannot because she must work without equal opportunities. She loses because she cannot win in fiction at a time when she could not win in real life; the author is bound by a degree of verisimilitude, even in this fairy tale, and at this time in history the princess, no matter what her own desires are in the matter, cannot love a toad and get away with it, especially at the expense of the prince. Fictional women must 'lose' until real women can 'win'" (105). Bolsterli, who mistakes the date of composition, misses the rather important irony that the novella was written in the era of Rosie the Riveter and her sisters. In fact, McCullers's prescience about the postwar fate of women might be claimed in this work as much as in the portents of racial conflict in *Hunter*. Marvin Macy's return from prison – his time spent in uniform – fatally disrupts Amelia's autonomous empire, leaving her boarded inside the dreary prison-house that counts for home.

Charlene Kerne Clark (1979) remarks on the structural similarity of *Ballad* and *Member* in the triangular relationship of characters, among whom are, in each work, "an aggressive female-passive male pair" who are cousins. While comparable in these terms, the patterns yield opposite effects: "In the more realistic work, *The Member of the Wedding*, the children behave like adults, whereas in the fabulistic novella, *The Ballad of the Sad Café*, the pair of adults behave like children" (12).

Margaret B. McDowell (1980) locates the genesis of the novella's strange triangle in McCullers's personal love relationships: "the love and hate she felt for Reeves, whom she was divorcing; the strong, but frustrated, love she felt for her new friend Annemarie Clarac-Schwarzenbach; and the bewildering, but warm, affection she was discovering for David

Diamond, who was attracted both to her and to Reeves" (65–66). *Ballad* was "conceived and almost completed" at Yaddo in 1941 during a period in which Reeves McCullers and David Diamond lived together in New York. The work "explores such themes as sexual ambivalence, destructive infatuation, the pain of being rejected by the beloved, the problematical configurations implied in any love triangle, and the paradoxical closeness of love and hate" (66).

Miss Amelia is "a sorceress" on whom the townspeople depend for healing, foodstuffs, and prognostications about weather and crops. She is not beneficent, and the townspeople are not beholden. They constitute "a sinister chorus to comment on the action" (67). "Though she denies her own femininity, she expresses maternal concern for children and is infinitely gentle in her treatment of them, making sure they are thoroughly anesthetized by drinking enough of her best liquor before she performs any painful operation" (68). Faced with the loss of Cousin Lymon, she is capable of humbling herself by admitting Marvin Macy to "the best room" in her house. "She concludes: 'It is better to take in your mortal enemy than face the terror of living alone.'" The confrontation between Macy and Miss Amelia on Ground Hog Day has "overtones of the Grendel-Beowulf encounter." Each possesses "mythical strength." "Only the intercession of the demonic Lymon, a still more powerfully mythical figure, finally defeats Amelia in the agonizingly protracted wrestling contest" (69). The coda repeats the paradoxical quality of love asserted by the story proper. The twelve prisoners "have escaped the solitary existence – but . . . are together only because they are in chains" (69). "Spontaneous and lasting fellowship is an impossibility in this novel. The forced and uneasy fellowship in the café, like the harmony and solidarity of the chain gang, lacks genuineness" (70). "McCullers claimed that in *The Ballad of the Sad Café* she tried to illustrate the superiority of Agapé (communal affection) over Eros (passionate love)"; but her concern with Agapé is "at best minimal" (70). McDowell views McCullers's treatment of love from novel to novel as evolving: *Hunter* focuses on loneliness as "an affliction" of the lover who can be cured only by love. The "mere narcissism" of Singer's satellites, however, strongly suggests a pessimistic view (70). In *Reflections,* "lust rather than love dominates the vortex of sadism, masochism, self-pity, and violence so dramatically presented" (71). Returning to the ambiguous nature of love explored in *Hunter,* McCullers extends her pessimism in *Ballad:* "love becomes in this novel a force which drives the lover into deeper isolation by driving him in on himself. Love is the dreadful result of an individual's isolation and its intensifier, rather than its cure" (71).

McDowell believes that *Reflections* and *Ballad* show McCullers developing in her own work the Gothic qualities she defined in her essay on "The Russian Realists and Southern Literature " (1941). In *Ballad* she "dramatically blends realistic detail with romantic and supernatural elements" (72). Both *Reflections* and *Ballad* focus on closed societies; explore the effects of psychic stress in terms of irrational, macabre, or supernatural evil; and suggest a correlation "between evil and human solitude" (73). In these ways McCullers returns to eighteenth-century principles of the Gothic. Amelia "has been set apart at the beginning by the townspeople as a woman with special understandings and powers, and at the end she is isolated as one who, through a series of peculiar incidents and relationships, has been overcome by incomprehensible forces of evil" (74). Her fate is poignant and affecting. "Even more a prisoner" than the men on the chain gang, Amelia becomes at the end "a mythic figure representing the deep, chronic isolation which McCullers saw at the center of human life" (78).

Mary Roberts (1980) focuses on Miss Amelia as androgyne. She

> is an Amazonian, hermaphroditic figure: tall and dark, "with bones and muscles like a man" . . . and contemptuous of any "female complaint" . . . . She begins and ends solitary and, like Singer, Biff Brannon, and Penderton, desexualized. At nineteen, she is married to the handsome and virile mischief-maker, Marvin Macy, whose love for her has reformed him. But his attempt at love-making threatens the "masculine" element of Amelia's psyche, her self-sufficiency; she rejects him violently and he vanishes from town to lead a life of crime . . . . Whatever its sexual roots, her love for Lymon requires no fleshly union. Instead, it effects in her a spiritual transformation, and she becomes the generous owner of a café which unites the townspeople in a short-lived and precarious fellowship. (94–95)

Miss Amelia ends "sexless and white, with two grey crossed eyes which are turned inward so sharply that they seem to be exchanging with one another one long and secret gaze of grief " – "the grief which sees the human condition as that of spiritual isolation and unfulfillment . . . . In such a universe, the complete androgyne (he who makes himself whole by marrying the sexes within his own psyche) cannot come into existence." Like Eliot's Tiresias, McCullers's incomplete androgynes "remain mysteries to themselves, ravaged by conflicting needs: the urge to remain inviolable and longing for conjunction with that god-like 'other' who will cure the breach in their natures. It is Carson McCullers' supreme achievement to have illuminated, in patterns of extremity, those images of wholeness which haunt the fragmented consciousness" (95–96).

Louise Westling (1980) reminds us that McCullers was exploring "the consequences of androgynous identity" in *Ballad* as she worked on *Member*. "The folktale atmosphere . . . gave her liberty to create her greatest freaks – the hulking man-woman Miss Amelia and her twisted dwarfish lover Cousin Lymon. The story is a nightmare vision of the tomboy grown up, without any concessions to social demands for sexual conformity. This understanding of the grotesque extreme of masculinity in a female must have contributed profoundly to the undercurrent of fear McCullers creates in *Member*" (345). Westling expands this view about ambivalence toward female identity in a subsequent essay (1982) and features it in her book on McCullers, Welty, and O'Connor (1985). In exploring such ambivalence as the site of the grotesque, the novella represents "dangerous psychological territory" for its author. The "flat, childlike narrative tone" constitutes a "strategy for placing the action at a safe enough remove from ordinary life to allow forbidden impulses free scope" and thereby allows McCullers "to indulge the impulse to appropriate male power and thus escape the culturally inferior role of woman" (1982, 110). "Behind the dream of independence represented by Miss Amelia's 'masculinity,' however, lies the fear of male vengeance which triumphs in the story's conclusion" (110).

Westling acknowledges McCullers's debt to Dinesen's "The Monkey" but believes that Robert S. Phillips (1964b) "overstates" the extent of similarity between the two stories. "The only clear parallels are the motifs of the amazon and her bitter hand-to-hand combat with a hated male suitor. These motifs are developed in very different ways by the two writers, and the stories move through entirely different atmospheres to almost opposite conclusions about the sources of female autonomy . . . . McCullers's novella is a kind of challenge to the arguments implied by Dinesen's story" (110). Westling focuses on the Prioress, who brings about the marriage of the Amazonian Athena and the decadent Boris by shape-shifting: "the prioress emerges as the very incarnation of the Wendish goddess of love, half-monkey and half-human. Because Boris and Athena witness the prioress's grotesque exchange of shapes with her monkey on the morning after the seduction attempt, they are united as initiates to the mystery of her power. They submit to her insistence that the sexes cannot remain separate; Boris must pay homage to female power, and the proud young Athena must renounce her heroic virginity in an alliance with him" (112). *Ballad* concerns the refusal of such union.

Amelia's helplessness before complaints of female trouble is the only dent in her power. "Her embarrassed confusion is a natural consequence of her total identification with masculinity and her childlike sexual innocence. Even in adulthood, Miss Amelia preserves the tomboy attitudes we encounter in Mick Kelly and Frankie Addams" (112). The grotesque triangle raises a central question: "why Miss Amelia should have rejected a vigorous normal man, only to fall in love with a twisted midget" (113). McCullers endows "qualities of 'normal' masculinity" with evil: "Macy may be tall, brawny, and good-looking, but he is also violent and viciously lustful. He is the devil male who mutilates animals for fun and has ruined the tenderest young girls in the region" (114). "The sexual dynamics of *The Ballad of the Sad Café* are an inversion of traditional heterosexual patterns. Contrasts with Dinesen's 'The Monkey' help reveal the masculine sources of Miss Amelia's autonomous strength and point up McCullers's complete rejection of heterosexual union. Rather than accepting her femininity by consummating her marriage to the aggressively masculine Marvin Macy, Miss Amelia focuses her affections on the little hunchback who seems to function simultaneously as child, pet, and rather feminine companion" (115).

McCullers's theorizing about the inevitable hatred of the beloved for the lover and her comment that the novella is "intended to show the inferiority of passionate individual love to *agape* fail to account for the individual peculiarities of her characters and for the sexual dimensions of their problems in love. The real force of [the novella] lies in its depiction of a masculine amazon whose transgression of conventional sexual boundaries brings catastrophic male retribution. Unlike Dinesen, who portrayed an uneasy compromise between proud female autonomy and reluctant masculine homage, McCullers sought to deny the feminine entirely and to allow a woman to function successfully as a man. She could not sustain her vision because she knew it was impossible." Westling believes that "the consequences of her experiment in this novella play a part in determining the final form of *The Member of the Wedding*, ... [in which] Frankie would have to submit as Miss Amelia had not" (116).

In her 1985 study of McCullers, Welty, and O'Connor, Westling adds to her analysis of *Ballad* an observation about the code of feminine dress in the novella. The yellow satin wedding gown worn by her mother and by Miss Amelia on the occasion of her marriage to Marvin Macy symbolizes a promise of which Amelia is ignorant.

> When her new husband tries to make love to her that night, she is just as indignant as Frankie is when the soldier attempts the same thing with her . . . . Upon Macy's vengeful return to town at the end of the novel, Miss Amelia once more wears a dress, but this time a red one and in full cognizance of the danger in which it places her. She will defy Marvin Macy even as she wears the clothing of a sex object he can never enjoy.

> After her near victory in the wrestling match has been upset by Cousin
> Lymon and she is left beaten almost to death, it is the unmistakable
> body of a woman we see lying on the floor of the café, for the red dress
> makes her a symbol of her sex, with all its attendant connotations of
> menstrual blood and the suffering of childbirth. The preferred clothing
> of Mick, Frankie, and Amelia shows their fundamental identification to
> be masculine. Wearing dresses seems to destroy the freedom achieved
> by that identification and to make them vulnerable. (177–78)

Westling dismisses earlier interpretations of the red dress: Broughton's
statement that it is "a symbol of Amelia's accessibility" and Rechnitz's notion that she is "trying to lure Macy away from Cousin Lymon"; Amelia's
behavior is "the opposite of seductive" (193n).

Mary Ann Dazey (1985) concludes, through a syntactical analysis of
the novella, that the narrator has two voices. In this she follows a line of
critics who have commented on the duality as both a strength (Graver
1969) and a weakness (Kohler 1951), as well as more thorough but less
systematic studies by Gaillard (1972) and Millichap (1977). Dazey finds "a
single narrator with two distinctly different voices": one, "the ballad
maker, who actually tells the tale"; and the other, "the voice of the
lamenter," who generalizes on and directs the reader's attention to specific
events or behaviors (118). "The ballad voice tells the story, and the second voice provides the sad background music." The voices differ in syn-
tax; the ballad voice relatively uncomplex, the lamenting voice
characterized by multiple clauses. "The transitions from one voice to the
other are smooth, almost unnoticeable" (122). Dazey says that the duality
identified by Barbara Nauer Folk (1962) – that the novella is both a
"literary ballad and a folk dirge" – is accounted for by this theory of dual
voices from a single narrator. "The harmony of the voices of the 'twelve
mortal men, seven of them black and five of them white boys from this
county' is precisely the kind of harmony McCullers achieves in the blending of the two voices of her single narrator" (123).

Pratibha Nagpal (1987) writes that the three grotesques "have lost contact with human values and lead an estranged and forlorn life" mirrored
in their surroundings (66). Nagpal's article focuses on the setting and its
symbolic or allegorical function, noting, for example, that "the drastic cli-
matic changes presage the unusual and often gruesome incidents of the
novella. The sticky and sultry weather after Marvin Macy's arrival from
the prison and the unprecedented snowfall before the climactic fight between Marvin Macy and Miss Amelia indicate the presence of some sinister design in the whole bizarre pattern of things" (65).

Mary A. Gervin (1988) writes that McCullers uses three "frames of reference" in the novella: ancient myth, folk epic, and philosophy. Miss Amelia and Marvin Macy are versions of "the elusive mythological goddess Artemis and her consort Orion" (37). From the folk epic McCullers derives her plot and its embellishments; the events of the novella are "highly reminiscent" of "The Flight" by Augustus Baldwin Longstreet (39). She also seems to profit from Friedrich Nietzche and René Descartes: "Taking her cue from Nietzsche, McCullers sunders Amelia Evans' womanhood by endowing her heroine with masculine attributes . . . . Miss Amelia's repression of her feminine psyche evokes an element of masculine protest similar to that of Nietzsche because the nature of woman represents a threat to the masculine Will to Power" (40). Descartes's "Passion of the Soul" is said to prefigure McCullers's treatise on love: "Both she and Descartes acknowledge love as a relationship between two beings who do not have reciprocal feelings for each other . . . . Cartesian in spirit, McCullers' love is an opposition between benevolence and concupiscence" (41). Gervin practices a criticism of coincidence here, providing little evidence that McCullers knew or had reason to be influenced by these works.

Margaret Walsh (1988) offers a convincing reading of the novella as an anti-fairy tale. "A fanciful text filled with country humor, outlandish characters, and bizarre happenings carries McCullers' disturbing message, and it is the author's choice of ballad context that permits fantastic exaggeration, a feature common to ballad and fairy tales. Other shared properties . . . are the stock characters of dwarfs and giants; enchantments and marvelous transformations; magic numbers, spells, and elixirs; and the telling of a story dramatically, with emphasis on action and climax and without deep characterization or analysis" (43). Lymon "is an amalgam of [fairy tale] dwarfs, helpful in his influence, mischievous in his ways, and finally nasty and ungrateful, leaving destruction in his wake" (44). Macy "has the makings of a handsome prince waiting to be released from imprisonment in a terrible form; when overcome by his unlikely love for Amelia, he is transformed into a thrifty, mannerly, pious suitor" (45). "The simultaneous metamorphoses of Amelia, Lymon, and the town are accomplished within the traditional mythological period for symbolic deaths and regenerations: 'And so ended three days and nights in which had come an arrival of a stranger, an unholy holiday, and the start of the café'" (45). "Lymon is an unsettling chimera, the unstable element at love's center. We might consider him as other than an actual or concrete character; if, in the land of enchantment a lowly toad can represent inchoate sexuality, then surely this dwarf can manifest psychological reality, specifically the psyches of Evans and Macy; read in this way, *Ballad* becomes for each of them a terrible story of self-revelation" (47). Furthermore, McCullers tips the scales of justice to punish "those traditionally female components of the binary male/female equation (e.g., emotion, intuition, gentleness, sensitivity, candor)." Walsh offers these examples: "when a beastly male like Macy is tamed by love, it is unrequited, and he is defeated, leaving his unreformed, violent mate richer and more powerful; when the previously unfeeling Amelia shares everything in her life with Lymon, he forsakes her; when Lymon receives love, he abandons the person who gives him a new life of affection and self-respect." *Ballad* is an anti-fairy tale because it reverses the "redeeming love of fairy tales." "Though the tale is recounted with good humor, ultimately these characters seem the victims of a grim cosmic joke." In the novella "the moral seems to be that a visitor to the Sad Café should not plan to live happily ever after" (48).

Ann Carlton (1988) says that the key to Miss Amelia is her tragic dependence on masculine models. "The only power she knows is male power; the only language she possesses is the language of the dominant culture. Yet she is a part of the muted culture and expected by the onlookers to act like a woman. The result is one of the most poignant figures in all of American literature, and a parable of the distortions created when one culture so completely dominates another" (60). She cannot win in either cultural guise. "It is reverting to her female self, as defined by the culture, that defeats Miss Amelia" (61).

Peter Messent (1989) writes of the southern novella as "a genre marked by a 'combination of intensity and expansion' resulting in a type of fiction which both focuses on a specific incident, or on an individual consciousness at a moment (or moments) of crisis, and from there circles outwards to reveal and examine the cultural conditions which give such an incident or crisis its larger meaning" (114–15). Its thematic development parallels that of other southern fiction, and, as a consequence, it epitomizes a post-Southern Renaissance shift in thematic concerns, especially the portrayal of the decline of the southern family.

McCullers's treatment of insular communities and her focus on "the subject of gender relations" in *Ballad* and in *Reflections in a Golden Eye* characterize her work in the genre. "Her explorations of gender roles and community mores in these contexts lead though in the direction of dead ends: to violence, alienation and isolation. Her concern with gender roles in traditional communities extends in the direction of that concern with debilitating alienation . . . central to Southern fiction in recent years." McCullers's concern with community, however, plays a *secondary* role to the "grotesque" characters and behaviour which are of central interest to her. She does question in her fiction the traditional rigidities of Southern social and sexual hierarchies; the new life and energy which are allowed to surface and replace such rigidities are, however, brief lived, and in *[Ballad]* what is left behind is a rural culture in terminal decline. But it is the concern with loss and loneliness which is her most central subject, with individuals who *finally* are in no way defined by their cultural context. And gender relations in McCullers reinforce her message of *personal* dislocation and loss of centre as the very conditions of twentieth-century life, a dislocation realized in "parable" form by her use of protagonists who are disfigured either physically, psychologically, or both. (132)

In *Ballad* the renewal of community on a different basis than the family, within the café, is "a location where normal gender and social hierarchies become irrelevant" but where the happiness of the group "is dependent . . . on the relationship between Amelia and Lymon" (133). Amelia's "failure to fill an ornamental function but willingness to submit herself to [Lymon's] varying demands (carrying him on her back in the swamp, for example), leads to a relationship in which gender roles are peculiarly distributed, but which forms the basis both for Amelia's greater happiness and sociability and for the burgeoning of the café and its importance to the local community" (133–34). "Her use of the 'grotesque' cuts strongly against any realistic reading of the texts, and means that no norm is offered the reader against which he or she can measure the excesses of the characters." Her true subject "is the difficulty of contact and communication . . . together with the power of love as potential medium for transcending alienation . . . . Finally, though, her fictions close with death, derangement, isolation; alienation is seen as the end condition of individual existence in a Southern world where social and individual bondings are presented as merely superficial or temporary" (134).

Kenneth D. Chamlee (1990) analyzes Miss Amelia and the sad café in the context of McCullers's portrayal of cafés and their proprietors in other novels. "Despite the 'communal warmth' which Amelia's café projects, it is not a center of genuine communication any more than the New York or Blue Moon cafés. Though Amelia dotes on Cousin Lymon and spoils him, they have no meaningful dialogue" (237). "Most significant, of course, is the distance apparent in their love relationship: Amelia as the lover is generous and spoiling while Lymon is a selfish and indifferent beloved. As the narrator says, the fact that love 'is a joint experience does not mean that it is a similar experience to the two people involved'" (237). Marvin Macy dominates Amelia "physically in a brawl since he was unable to do so sexually in their marriage bed" (238). "Over the next three years, Amelia allows the café to wither, and when it dies, the town dies as well" (238). "Cafés are an important aspect in McCullers' depiction of the ambivalent struggle of living. This common social setting does not always foster sociability, but the potential is there, and sometimes, as in Biff Brannon's case, a transient understanding occurs. Amelia Evans's store is transformed by love into a thriving communal gathering place, but when the love is lost (or torn away), the café fails and is closed. Perhaps it is only by chance, McCullers is saying, that characters and café owners 'find truth, a moment of pure love, a sudden illumination'" (239).

Virginia Spencer Carr (1990) adds to the autobiographical background of the novella recounted first in her biography and later by McDowell – that relationships with Reeves, Annemarie Clarac-Schwarzenbach, and David Diamond figure in the background of the work – the anecdote about McCullers's calflike infatuation with Katherine Anne Porter at Yaddo in 1941 as displaying "the very manner in which the characters she was creating moon over one another" in *Ballad* (54). She reminds us as well that the hunchback dwarf is modeled on a denizen of a local bar described in McCullers's "Brooklyn Is My Neighborhood" (1941). Unlike other critics, Carr leaves the question of the narrator's gender open, referring to "he (or she)"; and says that the function and character of the narrator (though not gender) has received "more critical discussion" than any other element in the novella (57). In contrast to other works with tripartite structure, the novella is "tightly compressed into one continuous narrative" and "told as one long flashback" (58). Carr cites McCullers's statement about agape/eros in "The Flowering Dream" (1959) but divulges that shortly after the novella appeared in *Harper's Bazaar* McCullers inscribed beside the famous pessimistic digression on love, in a copy presented to a friend, the observation, "This is true . . . only when you are *not* in love" (63). "McCullers's coda . . . stands as a paean to survival and a moving illustration of the power of brotherhood, even when the union is brought on by chains of bondage" (66–67). Carr points out that in recording the "Twelve Mortal Men" passage in 1958, McCullers wept on reaching the final line.

The novella's critical history bears out the suspicion that this may be McCullers's strangest and most magical work. Critics have been in nearly total agreement on its enchantment – that is its distance from the world of actual human events and its links with the archetypal world of legend and tale. It may in fact be not so much *about* that world but an evocation of the powers that create it. Like the sparrow whose flight through the mead hall gives us one of our most poignant images of the transience of human happiness – the fragility of warmth and light in a world of storms and darkness – its first readers in 1943 may have found the sad evocation of this ancient fear particularly relevant in a world at war. But there are only fragments of response from this period to allow us to know whether those readers sensed in the story a deeper social relevance than did its larger audience in 1951 and after. It is, however, clear that from one decade to the next this work has epitomized more strikingly than any other McCullers's skill at holding in unsettling tension the grotesquely amusing and the grotesquely horrifying.

Two features of its reputation deserve emphasis by way of conclusion: first, the digression which pronounces love an odd, unequal, and ultimately doomed condition ought to be examined with some skepticism in its local setting (in the mind of a narrator who may have the bias of one whose powers of observation are truly finite and limited to the events before him or her). To what extent has McCullers's "philosophy of love" been unfairly defined by generalizing the pronouncements made so authoritatively here – but with an authority whose limits McCullers meant to imply by the very tropes of imprisonment and enslavement in which the novella abounds. And second, though recent critics have remarkably expanded our understanding of gender ambiguity and the fluidity of boundaries once taken for granted, we still await a sophisticated analysis of the uses of enchantment to suggest the conjunction of psychological and political and spiritual truths. What, for example, is the significance of a story built on the conflict among Outsiders played for the benefit of a town full of menial Insiders? And does it matter that Amelia and Marvin and Lymon are positioned narratologically as objects of fascination and dissection, as Beloved, to the reader's and town witnesses' Lover?

5: *The Member of the Wedding* (1946)

At times, the reader of the new school of
adolescence may feel that the only hope of the
boy-hero is that he may some day achieve the
relatively positive vantage-point of existentialism.

(James William Johnson 1959)

F EW OF CARSON McCullers's works were initially more misunderstood
than her novel of Frankie Addams's adolescent crisis, *The Member of the
Wedding*. More than a decade after book reviewers had pronounced it either a case study in "child delinquency" (Dunkel 1946) or a sensitive portrait of "the confusions of life" (Young 1947, 152), James William Johnson
continued the pattern of gender-blind reading. The experiences of Frankie
Addams, as well as those of Katherine Anne Porter's Miranda Rhea and
the male adolescents of Wolfe, Faulkner, Joyce, and Hemingway, are said
to epitomize the loss, isolation, estrangement, and uncertainty of the twentieth-century myth of adolescence, "the contemporary novelist's fable of
the half-man" (8). Like Mick Kelly in *The Heart Is a Lonely Hunter*, Frankie
Addams would wait thirty years for a reading of her dreams and behavior
as specifically female experience.

There is good reason for the blindness to gender difference in "the
postwar celebration of consensus," whose effect in literary culture was to
resolve internal tensions in claims for unity and universality. As in the
civic arena, where the celebrated consensus of "the American way of life"
was being constructed as "a defense of masculinity and whiteness" just at
the moment that major social, economic, and cultural changes threatened
dissensus (Breines 1992, 1, 10–11), the world of literary criticism persisted
in wrapping the problems of difference in a normative cloak of male,
white, middle-class experience.

The result in the case of *Member* is revealing, and occasionally astonishing. In addition to ignoring the insistently feminine expectations which
Frankie both resists and desires to fulfill, reading her summer's dis-ease as
symbolic of "mankind's" spiritual longing, critics read the youthful passions and middle-aged compromises of Berenice Sadie Brown, black cook
and caretaker, as Platonic wisdom. She is "the Socrates of the novel"
(Evans 1965a, 111); she conducts "a long twilit kitchen seminar," convey-
ing, like Aristophanes in *Symposium*, "the frenzied search of humans for

love simply as a pursuit of one's own other half-soul" (Baldanza 1958, 159). Six-year-old John Henry West, Frankie's cousin and playmate, and the most nearly central male character, is credited with "philosophic calm and detachment." Like Biff Brannon's amused distance in *Hunter,* John Henry is said to be "fascinated by the human spectacle in which the real is ever the miraculous and the delight is in comprehending the unbelievable" (Vickery 1960, 23).

Citing such instances of overreading does not deny that Frankie and her attendants serve a symbolic purpose and reward multilayered understanding. It does, however, demonstrate the determination with which her earliest readers attempted to see palatable truths of universal scope, preferring with few exceptions the rarefied safety of philosophical unities to localized meanings mired in routine social conflicts or mundane, often selfish desire. What critics of the 1940s, 1950s, and early 1960s by and large avoided noticing are those very tremors that foretell and accompany seismic social upheaval. Growing racial unrest, a teenage counterculture, rebellion against confining gender roles, sexual norms, and other brands of social conformity were already subterraneously in motion beneath postwar consensus culture. Novelists like McCullers registered the tremors minutely.

Frankie's turbulent summer consists of a short but perilous journey out of the stifling womb of Berenice's kitchen and into the riskier world of her small Georgia town, a community partitioned by class, race, and war, the masculine adventure which has taken her older brother to far-off Alaska and returned him a grown man ready to marry. Frankie lives with her widowed father in a neighborhood of grape arbors, lawns, piano lessons, and "colored" help who come and go, returning to Sugarville at day's end. Berenice's foster brother is a talented young black man stifled and ruined by the desire to escape a racial ghetto. Soldiers on leave frequent another section of town where bars and beer offer the illusion of a good time. When Frankie escapes the kitchen and interminable card games and conversation with Berenice and little John Henry, she wanders the town, eager to impart to anyone who will listen her plan of accompanying her brother and his bride into the larger world. Her odyssey takes her to every sector: the commercial district where her father runs a jewelry store; Sugarville, where Big Mama tells her fortune; and the dockside district of the Blue Moon Café, where a drunken soldier tries to rape her. Oblivious to the physical dangers she faces, Frankie fears only the prospect of failing to belong, to be accepted as a member of some group. Her dream of becoming a member of the wedding reflects a desire to enter a gendered adulthood on her own terms, without sacrificing her tomboy fantasies of power and entitlement. The three of them, she tells Berenice, will become world travelers and celebrated adventurers asked to speak over worldwide radio.

McCullers worked five years to shape Frankie's story, in the belief that "it's one of those works that the least slip can ruin . . . . It must be beautifully done. For, like a poem, there's not much excuse for it otherwise" (qtd. Evans 1965a, 100). It is told in close third-person narrative, no word or observation beyond the vocabulary or capacity of twelve-year-old Frankie, as well as in dialogue, through the voices of the permanently or temporarily disenfranchised: a middle-aged black servant, a boy child, and a girl almost teenaged. From the earliest reviews to the most recent critical essays, readers, with one or two notable exceptions, have praised McCullers's dexterity with style and point of view. Trends in interpretation for this work are easily mapped by the focus or lack of focus on several key features that shape or reflect changes in Frankie's sense of self: the contrast between the world of the kitchen and the world outside it; the role of the drunken soldier; and the meaning of the coda, in which Frankie becomes Frances, Berenice agrees to marry a man who fails to make her "shiver," and John Henry dies twisted and screaming from meningitis.

The earliest reviews were striking in their agreement on McCullers's management of the novella form, proclaiming the work "exquisitely wrought" (Bond 1946, 17), told with "the utmost delicacy and balance" (Dangerfield 1946, 15), "a tender and gracious and oddly impressive little study" (Straus 1947, 3), a "little tragicomedy" (Match 1946, 5), "planned on a small scale . . . [and told] with an exquisite nervous tension" (Gannett 1946, 23). "Rarely has emotional turbulence been so delicately conveyed," says the reviewer for the *New York Times Book Review* (Kapp 1946, 5). In this gender-sensitive age, such diminutive attributes are recognizable as decidedly feminine, and prejudicially dismissive. Other reviewers were more explicit. *Kirkus* calls it "an *odd, unhappy little* story" (1946, 20, emphasis added); the English *New Statesman and Nation* is perplexed by Frankie Addams: "the strangest little monster who ever opened her eyes to a bottle of coca-cola" (King 1947, 241).

Only the rare reviewer noticed that its subject was female adolescence. Marion Sturges-Jones remarks that "F. Jasmine is such a convincing portrait that no one reading 'The Member of the Wedding' will ever again be able to think of a junior miss in terms of Sally Benson's Judy" (1946, M11). The more typical reaction was to interpret Frankie's experience as genderless, representative of the "No Man's Land of Childhood" (Match 1946, 5) or even "a parable on the life of a writer in the South, the alienation and withdrawal the sensitive Southerner must feel" (Rosenfeld 1946, 634). Academic reviewers, particularly, found it distastefully specific, its grotesqueness lacking sufficient "symbolic value" (Frank 1946, 537). Of such reviewers, Diana Trilling is the most explicit in revealing the standard to which McCullers was being held. The novel brings us "too close to the adolescent state of mind," and Frankie is "too specific" to serve as "a universal child case" (1946, 406–7).

The most famous review and the one that rankled longest in McCullers's memory is Edmund Wilson's pronouncement that "the whole story seems utterly pointless." Calling it "a formless chronicle of Frankie's musings," he says, "I hope that I am not being stupid about this book." The event which causes him the greatest perplexity is the "one violent incident" in which Frankie, or F. Jasmine as she calls herself at this point, knocks the soldier unconscious with a water pitcher "at his first attempt to make a pass at her." By failing to notice the soldier's drunkenness and Frankie's total misperception of the man's intent, Wilson reads Frankie as the transgressor: "one finds it rather difficult to believe that even the vagaries of a frustrated adolescence would either lead to so drastic an act or allow such complete indifference" (1946, 87).

F. Jasmine's "drastic" act begins in fear. As she starts to leave the soldier's room, he grabs her skirt and pulls her to the bed. Finding "she could not push away, . . . she bit down with all her might upon what must have been the crazy soldier's tongue – so that he screamed out and she was free." When he staggers toward her, she breaks the glass pitcher over his head and flees down the fire-escape, leaving him unconscious: "whether he was dead or not she did not know" (McCullers 1951, 760–61). A faithful reading of this incident, much less an interpretation of its meaning in context, eluded the novel's first critics. The problem arises, as in the example of Edmund Wilson, from a tendency to hold the soldier relatively blameless, attributing the violence to F. Jasmine. The soldier "attempts familiarities" (Evans 1965a, 104), attempts "seduction" (Baldanza 1958, 159; Eisinger 1963, 255; Cook 1975, 74), "attempts to make love to her" (Edmonds 1969, 26); he represents "the alluring mysteries of the adult world" (Vickery 1960, 22); the experience constitutes a "frustrating evening adventure" (Lubbers 1963, 197). These are not strictly euphemisms for sexual aggression but a genuine failure to recognize it. In forty years of commentary, the word 'rape' has rarely been applied to the soldier's motives or to F. Jasmine's perception of them.

Likewise, interpretations of the function of the incident suffered from misreading. Oliver Evans explains its presence in the novel as a sign that McCullers's definition of love does not include "the possibility of love as a physical experience" (1965a, 105). Frank Baldanza concurs. Love for McCullers is asexual and spiritual. The soldier represents "the aura of physical passion" which Frankie rejects (1958, 159). A. S. Knowles, Jr., too, says the "encounter" shows Frankie to be "above all, utterly ignorant of adult sexuality." As if to make explicit the implied normality of the assault, Knowles concludes, "she is moving toward maturity, but she is not there yet" (1969, 95). In a similar vein, Dale Edmonds suggests that the "soldier's interest in her" may reassure us about her eventual ability to "appeal to *male* friends" (1969, 28). For John B. Vickery, the soldier stands at the nexus of the child and adult worlds Frankie seeks "to fuse," and the incident is an extension of child's play: "she crushes his quite inexplicable advances in the same way as she has been accustomed to dealing with neighborhood bullies" (1960, 22). Vickery identifies an important comic dimension to Frankie's naïveté which – as is often true in the affective operation of the grotesque or of black comedy or absurd humor – attenuates or (for these critics) obscures the equally strong terror that competes for a reader's attention. Does McCullers give us farce or melodrama or tragedy in this scene? Her aim, she says, was "lyric tragicomedy in which the funniness and grief coexist in the same line" ("The Vision Shared" qtd. by Cook 1975, 64). For readers accustomed to laugh at thwarted seduction, at drunkenness, and at female naïveté, Frankie's genuine danger, her fear, and its effects are readily, perhaps unconsciously, suppressed. Many academic critics from the 1950s and 1960s fail to treat the incident at all (Joost, Kohler, Dodd, Felheim, Hassan, Allen, for example).

Among these, Ihab Hassan offers an interestingly cautious comment on the novel as a story of initiation:

> It is characteristic of initiation in the modern world that its course must be oblique and its rewards ambivalent. Mrs. McCullers' treatment of the traditional theme of sexual initiation is to the point. The sexual impulse, as we might have been led to expect, is diffused through the novel; it acts as a faint, persistent scratching on Frankie's consciousness; and it is never really understood . . . . The point is simply that initiation no longer requires the commitment of action, the definition of choice, or the confirmation of self-knowledge. (1961, 225)

To recognize that Frankie's is a different sort of initiation story is one thing; to attribute the difference to a shift in the character of recent fiction, in general, is another. It does not occur to Hassan to consider whether the difference might inhere in the gendered nature of the experience into which Frankie is initiated.

That recognition waited more than two decades for its fullest statement in a work by Barbara A. White which examines *Growing Up Female:*

Adolescent Girlhood in American Fiction (1985). Embracing a central tenet of the feminist critique of literary studies – that what is asserted as "universal" or "human" or "normal" experience is often masculine experience writ large – White takes exception to readings of this novel that assume adolescent sexuality is either "normal" (i.e., the same for girls as for boys; or at least more same than different) or "abnormal" (i.e., homosexual). Assailing Leslie Fiedler's "sexist interpretation of McCullers's 'boy-girls,'" White reads Frankie Addams not as a grotesque or as a protolesbian freak but, more simply, as a girl unwilling "to relinquish the privileges of boys" (91), which growing up female would require her to do. Like the protagonists of other novels of female adolescence White examines, Frankie resists adult sexuality, resists sexual initiation, and resists it actively (not passively, as Hassan implies) both physically and mentally.

The incident with the drunken soldier occurs in the middle section of the novel where, as F. Jasmine, Frankie wanders the town in relative boldness and freedom, making the stifling security of the summer kitchen all the more vivid by contrast. In the juxtaposition of these two worlds, the kitchen and the town or world at large, critics have found tensions between microcosm and macrocosm that elucidate the novel's meaning. The most conventional awareness of the two worlds of the novel takes the dichotomous forms of childhood (inside) vs. adulthood (outside) or "spiritual isolation" vs. membership made possible by love.

Nicholas Joost (1951), like many early critics, mixes the two. He views Frankie as "an adolescent who must grapple with the spiritual problem of loneliness and love even as she must somehow come to terms with the fact of her maturing. Frankie's development to F. Jasmine and then to Frances means not only the gain of a new peace of mind but also the loss of the old certainties of childhood: a loss of innocence, an agonizing loneliness before the emergence into young womanhood with its acceptance of adult convention . . . . Carson McCullers has not compromised with her vision of individual solitude, but she does seem to suggest that it can be mitigated through the force of human love" (285–86).

In *Member* McCullers "makes us feel that adolescence is the thing she says it is, a haze of loneliness and groping shot through with private fantasy and furious outbreak against a complacent adult society," according to Dayton Kohler (1951, 7). Tracing the thematic unity of her fiction, Kohler emphasizes that the dream of becoming a member of her brother's wedding is to merge the world of private fantasy with the world of adult commitment.

Jane Hart (1957), examining the functional use of the grotesque in advancing McCullers's "constant theme of human loneliness," sets Frankie's adolescent solitude against the desire for meaningful participation in the world at large. "Frankie is youth in its hurt, fierce searching, in a time cut off from the world and desiring it more violently than ever." Her experience of the "oppression of solitude, of adolescent longing, . . . causes Frankie to burst out passionately and positively, ecstatically banishing all the deep haunting of her mind: 'We will have thousands of friends. We will belong to so many clubs that we can't even keep track of all of them. We will be members of the whole world'" (56–57).

Frank Baldanza (1958) views the microcosm in Platonic terms. Berenice articulates, in reverse, "the essentials of Aristophanes' speech in *Symposium*" (159) in her pathetic pursuit, husband after husband, of the wholeness she knew in her marriage to Ludie Freeman. "Aristophanes maintains that at one time each human being was a double creature with two heads, four arms and legs, and the like; and that Zeus, in a moment of fury, punished mankind by splitting each creature in two; Aristophanes interprets the frenzied search of humans for love simply as a pursuit of one's own other half-soul; as a consequence, obviously, success and failure in love are dependent on whether or not one actually finds the other half of his own soul in the beloved. Thus love is synonymous, almost mathematically, with wholeness" (159–60). "However, Berenice's commitment to sensual love puts her in a category of lesser beings, and the real concern of the tale is with F. Jasmine's spiritual discoveries about love and being. She realizes that she is no longer the child who was hustled out of a movie for hooting at a showing of *Camille,* and now actually participates as an equal in the kitchen discussion of love" (160). The movement of the novel is predicated on a successful emergence into the macrocosm.

Published in *Phylon* in 1958 and responding to two of the decade's sociocultural motifs, racial disharmony and the loneliness of individuals in mass society, an essay by Charles B. Tinkham focuses on those incidents in the novel which support the idea that loneliness manifests itself in violence – incidents such as Frankie's contemplated suicide and her abuse of John Henry and Berenice, especially with the angry epithet "nigger." Tinkham advocates the view that microcosmic disturbances yield macrocosmic upheaval. Frankie is "a girl whose family has all but disintegrated and whose neighbors ignore her [and who] seeks to include herself, unrealistically and dangerously, in the very idea of inclusion, and at the same time she shows unrealistic 'destructive' suspicion of groups seemingly opposed to her best interests." In an interesting disavowal of the spiritual value of Frankie's love for the wedding, Tinkham criticizes loving "from the abstract to the particular" because it can lead to judging people "not individually, but altogether," thereby fostering divisiveness and group hatred (389). He points out that "Frankie has fallen in love with the very idea of love, has fallen in love not with another human being, but with a particular instance of attraction between two people which she almost instantaneously generalizes into a kind of universal love. To join the wedding party means that she will be fully accepted wherever she goes" (388). The three of them will be "members of the whole world." If his observation is just and capable of being extended, it may be possible that McCullers criticizes in this work, as in *Hunter* and in "A Tree. A Rock. A Cloud." the tendency of some lovers to devote themselves to the abstract – a strong true purpose, justice, freaks, inanimate objects, nature in general, a wedding – that is, to the idea of loving, rather than to any act of love generously, concretely, microcosmically realized. Devotion to the abstract, Tinkham suggests, confirms the devotee in his or her superiority and serves thereby as a divisive force, a force for misunderstanding rather than comprehension, false knowledge instead of truth.

Subsequent commentary begins to make clear the relationship of theme and structure in propositions about the inside/outside and micro-/macro-worlds. John B. Vickery (1960) reads Frankie's experience conventionally, as "the quest of the lover for a center other than the self but this time within the context of the family" (21). The wedding promises that "miraculously she will possess a family of her own selection, dedicated to the fulfillment of those adventures in the marvelous of which she has dreamed for so long," and the chosen family will connect her with the world. "This desire to be enveloped in an organically complete pattern such as is symbolized by the wedding is motivated by the contradictory emotions of the adolescent who wishes both to explore the alluring mysteries of the adult world and to retain the comprehensible familiarities of childhood." Frankie's simultaneous need for and rejection of the comradeship of the kitchen is evidence of this vacillation. But neither Berenice nor John Henry can provide the understanding Frankie requires. "For sympathetic as she is, Berenice is nevertheless committed to an adult's view of Frankie's trials with the result that most of her advice cannot be absorbed into the imaginative world of the child; adult and child, like lover and beloved earlier, are from different countries" (22).

Wayne D. Dodd (1963), tracing the symbolic development of themes associated with love, especially the godlike image of the beloved, the child-as-creator trope, and the pattern of inner worlds jealously guarded, focuses briefly on John Henry's creations, the doughman and drawings, as species of the grotesque. They are "careful, deliberate productions; they are not defective because of any haste in design, but rather because of lack of understanding and foresight." Coupled with the worlds that

John Henry, Berenice, and Frankie say they would create if they were God, the trope of creativity shows the isolation of each in a limited point of view, a perspective that would appear grotesque to others. This motif blends with the broken off tune from the blues horn and the piano tuner's unfinished octaves to suggest that "the world is somehow unfinished, incomplete. Thus once again we can see a reason for the inability of men finally to communicate" (210). It is interesting from the point of view of our late-twentieth-century expectation of gender-neutral language to note that Dodd can write a sentence about the inability of men to communicate when the examples adduced come from a black woman, a boy child, and a prepubescent girl.

In a journal published by the Catholic Renasence Society, Robert S. Phillips (1964c) discourses on twentieth-century literary Gothicism and makes a strong, though occasionally overstated case for the Gothic design of *Member*. Several of his observations appear linked to his particular audience – those, for instance, about sexual deviancy and anti-Catholicism as traditional Gothic features resurrected in McCullers's fiction. Phillips, too, in this essay is influenced by the definitions and theories of Leslie Fiedler, though he sidesteps allegiance when it suits him. He concludes, "Universally proclaimed a novel of tender adolescence by the critics, *The Member of the Wedding* provokes frightening responses in the reader which for too long have been overlooked. With its moribund setting, fear of sexuality, terrifying death scenes, dark dreams and nightmares ... the novel is yet another manifestation of the author's Gothic vision" (72). Spiritual isolation, McCullers's professed theme, is often a Gothic theme, as Phillips says, "a theme which obsessed an earlier writer of Gothic stories in America, Edgar Allan Poe .... All the tales of Poe are, according to [Mario] Praz, a 'symbolical, mythological translation of the same thirst for unrealizable love and of the desire for that complete fusion with the beloved being which ends in Vampirism.' The same futile quest for unity in love is a recurring theme in Mrs. McCullers' fiction" (61). "Frankie's fears are the fears of all human beings, and the last name of Addams indicates her archetypal function in her initiation into worldly knowledge. The self-chosen nickname of Frankie (like the name Mick Kelly) is a feeble effort on the part of the adolescent to assert her individuality in a patriarchal culture, as is the crew cut which makes her a neuter being" (66).

Some 1960s and 1970s critics in retreat from the New Criticism looked for but perceived little social seriousness in the work. Chester E. Eisinger (1963) chastises McCullers for restricting herself to "the child's self-centered world in which the macrocosm plays no part" (255–56).

Lawrence Graver (1969) agrees with the observation but sees the lack of connection to a larger world as "precisely the source of its strength" (42). Graver rates the novel as McCullers's best principally because it is circumscribed and "complete in itself" (41). Such views appear short-sighted, given the world disorder reflected in the reminders of war and racism on the streets of Frankie's town and reflected as well in the drawings on the kitchen walls.

Irving H. Buchen (1973) also takes a contrary view, but one heavily invested in the psychological acuity of McCullers's perceptions. He calls McCullers a visionary writer on the model of Kafka and Dostoevsky. Like theirs, her works are "aberrational"; they tantalize and repay the critic skilled in blending psychological and literary analysis. Ironically, this is so because McCullers provides minimal psychological and historical information about her characters. "McCullers' world is so dispersed rather than concentrated and so dominated by symptoms rather than causality [that] it is a world poised for violence, especially gratuitous violence; because violence seems to be the only way of terminating symptoms or to be the supreme symptom itself" (20). Focusing on adolescence as the site of incestuous pressures, Buchen arrives at the idea that love in McCullers's fiction, especially in *Member,* is incest-driven. Here are the steps in his reasoning: "Adolescence is the time of maximum sexual contradiction and pressure"; the adolescent is sexually indeterminate, "a normal freak" (22). The "permanent opposition between lover and beloved" is rooted in "the law of [adolescent] bisexuality." Adolescence is "a microcosm of all later life. The adolescent thus tyranically acts out in miniature a span of failure that will not so much change directions as change partners. It is this pervasive theme of permanent infidelity that comprehends both all the unfulfilled relationships and all the odd couples and peculiar marriages that regularly sustain her work" (23). Like Frankie Addams, McCullers's adolescents are typically motherless, attached to their fathers, and "are regularly voyeuristic." Buchen believes that "the absolute taboo of all taboos" lies behind "the voyeurism, fear of castration, and homosexuality." Guilt over incestuous desire explains "why almost all the violence in McCullers is castrating in nature" (24).

> In McCullers' world, adolescence may be coupled together with incest because at that stage the quest for sexuality moves through the maximum contradiction of bisexuality and inevitably partakes of the original family cluster. When Frankie Addams unreasonably demands to be a member of the wedding, what she is really asking for is to be a voyeuristic observer of parental sex or an active participant in the bed of her brother – surrogate for that of her father. In either case, as long as incest

is a taboo, she will remain, as Honey Brown is in the novel, eternally unfinished or unsatisfied. Moreover, as the tyranny of adolescence reveals,
that secret desire for a forbidden incestuous wholeness will haunt her
adult life as well, and although she may find love, she will resent being
an object of love and seek to become a lover in her own right. That such
a desire in childhood or adolescence could have such a tyrannical grip
on later life would not surprise Freud, who maintained: "The reason
money does not bring happiness is that it is not an infantile wish." (24–
25)

The Freudian paradigm, used in this way, makes Frankie and her peers
sexual agents. (No wonder critics of the 1950s and 1960s hold her responsible for the behavior of the drunken soldier.)

Buchen's article is important in its self-consciousness of violating certain fraternal taboos: "When to use and when not to use the resources of
psychology? That is the question for the literary critic. If one were to follow one of the classic texts on literary criticism, *Theory of Literature,* the answer would be never. Speaking of psychological insight, René Wellek and
Austin Warren maintain . . . . 'psychology is unnecessary to art and not of
itself of artistic value'" (26–27). Buchen does not entirely disagree with
this tenet of New Criticism, saying only that some writers repay the insights of psychology. He himself opts for half measures, to remain open to
the requirements of the work: "Unless the critic is at least part chameleon,
the artist cannot be protean" (27). In so saying, Buchen acknowledges the
extent to which the relationship of the critic to the artist is constitutive.

Delma Eugene Presley (1974) links the themes of entrapment and betrayal in *Member* to McCullers's feelings about the South. The conversation in which Berenice, John Henry, and Frankie enumerate the ways in
which all people are somehow "caught," trapped in prisons of self or social or generational ghettos, does not constitute "an existential confession.
Despair is not so much a sobering truth as it is a whining lament that,
somehow, things have a way of going sour" (27). Presley sees such plaints
as projections of McCullers's adolescent disdain for her region. In keeping
with his contention that McCullers's talent diminished after she removed
herself from the South, Presley sees *Member* as inferior to *The Heart Is a
Lonely Hunter,* lacking the earlier novel's "broad ethical landscape" (29).

For Richard M. Cook (1975) the relationship between the outside and
the inside is explicable in terms of McCullers's "new theme" in this work:
"the role of time in human affairs" (80). The kitchen is the world of adolescence, of being trapped in the middle space; the outside world is the
world of adults. The middle section of the novel and the events of the
second day represent "a preliminary test of Frankie's membership in the

wedding and the adult world it represents" (66). Even so, the outside world is experienced almost exclusively in personal terms. It is the world of "private problems" not the world of "social, racial, and political problems that were important to [McCullers] in her first novel" (80). Although McCullers's narrative strategy keeps us focused on the interior meanings of Frankie's experience, as Cook says, to see the novel as wholly invested in the world of "private problems" he must ignore the omnipresence of war and segregation and the impact of these exterior forces on Frankie's imagination.

An interesting approach to the novel emerges from a 1975 dissertation from the University of Gothenberg (Sweden). Eleanor Wikborg uses the tools of computational linguistics to embellish insights into the novel's style and structure. Wikborg anchors a definition of the novel's "poetic prose" in a statistical demonstration of its "high degree of organization at several levels and [its] symbolic technique" (163). By tracing recurring language patterns, Wikborg documents the encoded desperation of Frankie's personal crisis in the repetition of such words as *sick, tight, afraid, wrong, crazy, strange,* and in the sinister undertone of sounds from the world outside that play against the interminable kitchen conversations: unfinished music, the radio, a clock, the rat behind the wall.

In one of the fullest and most insightful analyses of the novel's structure, Margaret B. McDowell (1980) demonstrates the close counterpoint between the world of the kitchen and the world outside it. In the hot summer afternoons behind kitchen walls "decorated with plane wrecks and other catastrophes," Frankie and Berenice and John Henry listen and wait. "Their anxious waiting mirrors the nation's anxieties during that summer as it waits for the shift in the balance of power in the war, while few suspect that mankind is about to split the atom, with all the possibilities for destruction that that event will bring about" (83).

The most important correspondence between micro- and macrocosm McDowell identifies is the mirroring of Frankie's experience by Berenice. "The problems and responses of Frankie, echoed in those of the older Berenice, achieve a universal significance, because they are seen to be the preoccupations and the aspirations of another generation and another race" (85). McDowell cites the tender exchange in part 2 in which Frankie tells of a vision nearly seen on her odyssey downtown. Turning a corner she thought she glimpsed her brother and the bride beside her only to realize it was two black boys. Berenice recognizes the experience as identical to her own occasional experience of the felt presence of Ludie Freeman, her first husband and only love.

> If one central theme of the book is Frankie's need to achieve a sense of identity with others, the sharing of a supernatural experience marks the closest approach to the imaginative conjoining of Frankie and Berenice. It is followed, in fact, by a kind of communion ceremony. Frankie reaches over and takes one of Berenice's cigarettes. Berenice allows her to do so; for the first time, Frankie sits smoking with an adult. Frankie and Berenice are at several other times remarkably congruent in their preoccupations and insights, considering their antagonism and the fact that one lives in anticipation while the other lives in memory. (87–88)

It is through the balancing of Frankie and Berenice that McCullers effectively counterpoints Frankie's fear of a world turning too sudden, fast and loose, with Berenice's frustration at being caught, trapped within relationships dictated by racism, poverty, gender, and age. Frankie would put the world to rights by becoming a member, with the rules, uniformity, and stability membership might imply. Berenice would keep whatever freedom and individuality her circumstances permit. McCullers "balance[s] the turmoil and self-centered egotism of Frankie with the agony, courage, and cynical humor of Berenice. Frankie wins neither of her conflicting goals – to become perfectly joined and to become independent. Similarly, Berenice cannot find Ludie alive and become a member again of that perfect wedding, nor can she 'bust free.' She settles for a life with T. T. Williams, which promises a measure of congeniality and of independence" (94).

In a methodically developed Jungian reading, Clifton Snider (1984) views the novel as a drive toward wholeness in the first stage of a child's progress toward individuation. He cites McCullers's essay "The Flowering Dream: Notes on Writing" (1959) to indicate how congenial her own view of writing as born in the unconscious is to Jungian theory and observes that the novel was written at a time "when the world was collectively split" by war and in need of wholeness (33). Following are some of the archetypal elements Snider finds in the novel. 1. The name Addams "suggests her case is primal; she is an 'everyperson'" (34). 2. The wedding is "the *hieros gamos,* or 'sacred wedding,' an archetype of wholeness, symbolizing the union of opposites" (35). 3. Her obsession with the wedding corresponds to the Jungian observation that an archetype, once activated, can compel a compulsiveness in the personality. Frankie's compulsiveness takes the form of a desire to escape her immediate environment, but the Jungian pattern dictates that in the individuation process appropriate to Frankie's stage of life, her most urgent need is to adapt to the conditions of her immediate environment. "Her fervent wish is to go, as it were, to an Eden of her imagination" (35), which constitutes an evasion of the developmental task she must face. 4. One dimension of the prescribed pattern of growth is the development of "'an appropriate persona' . . . . the 'mask' or conscious public identity an individual takes on" (37). That she does not successfully complete this phase of growth is foreshadowed by the unfinished scale of the piano tuner and the tears which displace the customary singing in the kitchen after the last meal together of Frankie, Berenice, and John Henry. 5. The progress she is able to make toward individuation requires her to break with her father and her symbolic mother and to undergo "a symbolic rebirth from the womblike kitchen" (37). 6. As characters, John Henry and Berenice are archetypal and "numinous"; they are symbolic guides to the inevitable and the possible on Frankie's journey from one stage (or world) to the next.

Mary Jane Kinnebrew's linguistic analysis (1985) finds that language shifts in *Member* are used effectively in characterizing the different stages of Frankie's identity. "Frances' language lacks the non-standard structures and expressions she uses in the earlier sections. Her linguistic precision becomes another sign of her superficiality and her quickness to forget the previous summer" (89). Such variations in dialect "reflect the changes in [Frankie's] character and her movement away from a child's world of communication and commitment toward an adult world that seems to promise only superficial concerns and artificial community" (90).

Barbara A. White (1985) reverses the earliest standard reading of place in the novel (that the microcosm of the kitchen and the confusion of the town alike emphasize Frankie's symbolic isolation). To White, Frankie's problem "is not isolation but exclusion" (96). "Frankie cannot find relief beyond the kitchen, for the outside atmosphere is just as stifling." The heat suggests "boredom and restriction"; cold suggests "liberation" (97). Moreover, the world that she seeks to enter is stratified by limits placed on gender as well as age, race, and class. Berenice, acutely aware of the effects of racism, serves ironically as the agent of Frankie's intended acceptance of her limited female role. "Berenice correctly interprets Frankie's concern with the wedding as concern with her own future as a woman" (94). Even the names that structure the three parts of the novel function ironically. White points out that "the new 'feminine' name 'F. Jasmine' is ambiguous because it is generally a male practice to use an initial and a middle name. One might conclude that Frankie is unconsciously subverting her outward attempt to become more womanly" (93).

Louise Westling (1985) also identifies a crisis of conformity to gender roles. "The images which define this crisis for Frankie Addams are the images of sexual freaks in an ambience of androgynous longings, homosexuality, and transvetitism" (111). The particular development of freakishness in this novel may have been forged by McCullers's experience with *Ballad*. She "knew that Frankie would have to submit as Miss Amelia had not. The conclusions she reached in her nightmarish folktale must have contributed profoundly to the undercurrent of fear McCullers creates in *The Member of the Wedding* through the image of the freak show which haunts Frankie's mind and indeed the whole novel" (126). Westling describes the world of the kitchen as "a living freak show peopled by a transvestite boy, a black cook with a left eye of bright blue glass, and a gangling tomboy. It is a horrifying prison for Frankie" (181).

Karen Sosnoski (1988) follows Westling and White on the problem of gender conformity in McCullers's works. Using the theories of feminist psychologist Nancy Chodorow, she discovers an alternate microcosm, a privileged female world. "Frankie's conflicting feelings for Berenice are typical of those Chodorow attributes to her particular stage of feminine adolescence: A girl alternates between total rejection of a mother who represents infantile development and attachment to her, between identification with anyone older than her mother, and feeling herself to be her mother's double and extension" (85). In the scene of shared cigarettes, "in this moment of bonding with Berenice, Frankie is an insider, a 'woman' with all of the mythically connoted attributes: insight, sensitivity, intuition. She is incomprehensible to the male outsider, a mystery. Frankie's sense of superiority is intensified by the presence of her younger cousin, who as a child and a boy is doomed, in her opinion, to be excluded from this feminine world" (85).

Kenneth D. Chamlee (1990) examines the function of the Blue Moon Café as "an adult world from which Frankie has previously felt excluded . . . but in which she [temporarily] feels welcome; thus, it is the first place F. Jasmine chooses to reveal her plans" (235). "Though Frankie Addams initially feels the Blue Moon Café is a place where she can assert her new adult identity and make the human contacts she desires, it turns out to be a sterile place characterized by its ghostly, apathetic proprietor, a place where Frankie is more isolated in her adolescence than ever before" (236). It is, as well, the site of her escape from the drunken soldier and, on the night of the wedding, the place where her father and the police find the runaway Frankie.

Views of the novel's micro- and macrocosmic structure, then, may be seen to have evolved from the common assertion in the 1950s and 1960s that the outside world is the world of adulthood, characterized as either positive, because it is the normal goal of human development, or problematical, in being complex and just as isolated as the childhood Frankie wants to leave, to the distinctive readings of the 1980s that see adulthood as a gendered condition and Frankie's passage into a culturally defined female role as fraught with danger. Interpretation of the novel's brief and jarring part 3 follows a similar trajectory. How readers come to terms with the Frankie of this final section reflects changes both in the practice of literary criticism and in cultural attitudes toward the proper role of women in society. Frankie, now Frances, turns from the world of the kitchen, from John Henry's death from meningitis, from Berenice's multiple losses (including the loss of a job as Frances and her father prepare to move to the suburbs), from the memory of her humiliation at the wedding, to the happy anticipation of her new friendship with Mary Littlejohn. Is her isolation now appropriately and beneficially ended, or is she caught in an even more pernicious trap than the world of the kitchen once seemed?

For Ihab Hassan (1961), the ending offers "a final affirmation of youth's resilience. Frances, entitled at last to her full name, outgrows the humiliation of her first defeat. Unlike Mick Kelly, she moves beyond the acrid feeling that the world has cheated her. And with the heedlessness of youth she takes up new friends and other illusions, remotely conscious of the death of John Henry and the separation from Berenice. There is change; there is no knowledge or confirmation" (226).

For Irving Malin (1962), the ending completes the pattern of images associated with liminality, of hanging around in doorways she cannot truly enter. As Frances, she will emerge once and for all from the kitchen, "the world in which everyone is trapped," and enter a new home in a new suburb (85). This pattern, like the pattern of cracked and distorted reflection, is typical of postwar American Gothic fiction. One sign of her "leap into 'maturity'" is the relative absence of images of "narcissistically distorted" reflection (137).

Mark Schorer (1963) believes that the novel rightly ends on a note of equipoise with Frankie on the verge of "discover[ing] the nature of her identity. The materials necessary to that discovery she already possesses: the painful inevitability of separateness, the moderate mitigations to be found in love" (91).

Walter Allen (1964) reads *Member* as a novel of initiation "into the acceptance of human limits" (134). Taking a middle view, he points out that the freaks at the fair remain but no longer constitute a threat. Frances is able not to dwell on them because Mrs. Littlejohn believes they are "morbid."

In the service of his thesis about the novel's "Gothic architecture," Robert S. Phillips (1964c) rather overstates Frankie's reaction to the death of John Henry, seeing the intensity most readers expect but do not find.

"With the loss of this rapport [with John Henry], Frankie finally feels any meaning to her life has vanished. All that remains is the spirit of John Henry which seems to visit her . . . . Time and again she is to recall his torturous death" (67). "Frankie clings to Mary because she does not think she will ever be loved by, or be able to love, a man. Mary is a little John, then, a surrogate male lover" (70). Frankie is "the frail heroine alone in the night – again we find the typical Gothic situation. Frankie is isolated and always will be. The trip around the world with Mary Littlejohn is merely another pipe dream like that of the wedding . . . . Both Frankie's mother and John Henry are dead, and Berenice deserts her to marry for a fifth time in her never-ending search for fulfillment. Berenice's departure signals the total collapse of Frankie's 'family'" (71). This is a singular and quite wrongheaded reading of Berenice's motives.

Louis Auchincloss (1965) says that Frankie is catapulted into adolescence by "the violent crisis of a single weekend. Frankie Addams, poised between childhood and maturity, crosses the line on the eve of her brother's wedding" (165). "Then it is all over, suddenly over, and in the last pages, some time later, we see a new Frankie whom we hardly like, talking airily about Italian art and her new girl friend and desperately hurting the feelings of Berenice who has loved her with such devoted sympathy. Worst of all, she has almost forgotten John Henry who, we learn, has died of meningitis. The sense that the novel conveys of the recuperative powers of childhood at Frankie's age is shocking to the extreme, but as Carson McCullers always manages, with the eerie intimacy of her style, to imply: would one have it otherwise?" (166).

Oliver Evans (1965a) defends John Henry's death and Frances's presumed callousness as consistent with McCullers's logic in the novel. The child's death "emphasizes the sense of universal meaninglessness and chaos" that characterizes a brand of naturalism McCullers shares with Stephen Crane. The flat indifference of nature to helpless human pleas for justice is enacted in the novel's swift destruction of "one of the most sympathetic of all her characters." John Henry's death also "parallels and dramatizes" the death of Frankie's childhood (124). Furthermore, as Frances, Frankie has "merely replac[ed] one impossible ambition with another: how likely are her dreams of becoming a great poet or the world's 'foremost authority on radar' – or even of travelling around the world with Mary Littlejohn – to be realized?" Like Mick Kelly's dream of being a concert pianist, Frankie's dreams will collapse or be outgrown. "The materials of the dream will change, but not the necessity for it" (123).

Dale Edmonds (1969) outlines two ways of regarding the ending:

John Henry is dead. Honey is doomed to toil on the chain gang. Berenice has compromised herself in accepting T. T. Williams. Frances has found in Mary Littlejohn only another "wedding" – an illusory object with which to attempt a connection. On the other hand, these eventualities may be interpreted in an entirely different way. John Henry has died, but his death is neither good nor bad: it is simply a fact of the human condition. In the outside world Honey Brown was a restless, unhappy, incomplete individual; it seemed only a matter of time until he met a violent end. While on the road [chain gang], Honey may, at least, find solidarity . . . . Berenice may be marrying a man for whom she has no strong passion, but perhaps she has finally realized that her attempts to "marry off pieces" of Ludie could lead only to disaster. Perhaps Frankie's friendship with Mary Littlejohn will end – but this is the case with many, if not most, adolescent friendships. Mary Littlejohn *is* the first friend Frankie has made in some time, which may indicate that Frankie will be able to attract others in the future. (28)

For Edmonds the novel is intended "to end on a note of uncertainty." Frankie "has *not* matured in the course of the novel, but she has passed through a series of experiences that will contribute toward her eventual maturity" (29).

For Richard M. Cook (1975), the coda enables McCullers "to show the essentially ephemeral nature of Frankie's summer experience by placing it in the context of passing time . . . . maturity being a continuing process rather than any finally achieved state" (76–77). But the change is not an altogether satisfactory or happy one. Rather than representing strictly the death of childhood, John Henry's death and Frankie's almost callous reaction to it serve to confirm her isolation. "McCullers is offering a detached, even ironic view of a world in which a person 'belongs' only at single moments in time and only from the limited perspective of that single individual's needs and desires" (79).

For Margaret B. McDowell (1980) the novel "closes precipitously" with the almost parenthetical death of John Henry and the death of Berenice's (and Frankie's) dreams. "A mundane, and somewhat complacent and insensitive, maturity begins to dominate Frankie" (85). Her "willingness, finally, to ignore all unanswered questions at the close of the book suggests that she has, in fact, failed to develop in any genuine sense. A superficial self-assurance, along with heightened insensitivity and complacency, pass for maturity" (82). The balance and precision of the novel are disrupted by the uneasy ending. McDowell speculates that "perhaps Carson McCullers is saying that in this imperfect world the adult not only has to settle for the second-best but that he is, in a sense, morally obliged to do so" (95).

Clifton Snider (1984), following a Jungian plot, regards the coda as natural and inevitable, evidence that "Frankie has yet to come to terms with the masculine in her psyche, symbolized by her father, but she has begun to accommodate the shadow, that other unrecognized part of the psyche personified by a member of the same sex" (41). Earlier the shadow had been symbolized by the outlaw or criminal side of Frankie. Now it is "symbolized by her new friend, the Catholic Mary Littlejohn, who, unlike Frankie, has 'lived abroad.'" Mary is "a supraordinate personality [and therefore] symbolic of the Self and therefore foreshadows a new awareness for Frankie" (42).

For Barbara A. White (1985), the novel might more truly have ended with Frankie's capitulation at the end of part 2: she "might as well" propose marriage to the drunken soldier. *Member* is "less a novel of initiation into 'acceptance of *human* limits' than a novel of initiation into acceptance of *female* limits" (109).

> Frankie has not merely replaced her old aspirations with new ones just as impossible; she has changed the very nature of her dreams. Frankie's old dreams, of flying planes, of being able to switch genders whenever she wished, of joining the wedding, were protests against the secondary status of women. They were projections of her desire to be an autonomous adult. Now Frankie, or Frances, as she is finally called, wants to write poetry and travel with Mary Littlejohn. Her new dreams are socially acceptable and easily within her reach. Although she will not climb glaciers and ride camels with Mary Littlejohn, she may tour Europe under the aegis of Mary and her mother. It is permissible for Frankie to go "around the world" but not into it. (106–7)

White recognizes the importance of Honey Brown in this novel by suggesting that, like Frankie, he too finds the place society holds for him, a jail cell. Frankie's cheerful contentment with the female role represents "a jail of her own" (99).

Louise Westling (1985) develops the parallel in a slightly different direction. Honey Brown, like Frankie, is unfinished. He "does not fit the categories imposed on him by his Southern town" (129). The identification of Frankie Addams and Honey Brown allows McCullers to assert "a traditional association between the oppression of women and that of blacks" (130). At the end of the novel, Honey Brown is just one of the "deviants" Carson McCullers "has rather ruthlessly removed . . . from Frances's life so that safe conformity can triumph" (131). Now "a giddy adolescent" (130), "secure in her new feminine identity," Frances no longer notices the freaks at the October fair. The repainted kitchen no longer resembles "the freakish prison of . . . summer"; and the spectre of freakishness has been displaced onto John Henry, who has died blind and "hideously twisted." Westling suggests that the price of relief from feelings of her own freakishness has been too dear. Frances "has become a silly girl who no longer produces her own juvenile works of art – the shows and plays she used to write – but instead gushes sentimental nonsense about the Great Masters. The hard edge of her mind is gone, and all that is left is froth" (131).

Virginia Spencer Carr (1990) suggests that the theme of social and cultural determinism may be stronger in McCullers's fiction generally than the movement toward self-determination. In the case of *Member*, "there is no reason to believe that Frankie's new-found contentment will be anything but short-lived" (86).

Readers of each of the previous works, in fact, would be required to suspend their knowledge of McCullers's pessimism about success in love to see Frankie as bound for a "normal" growth toward maturity in any positive sense. There is, however, one solitary suggestion in this work that a fully congruent and successful love is realizable in McCullers's universe. In contrast to the pessimistic digression in *Ballad*, we might set Berenice's story of her life with Ludie Freeman as an overlooked affirmation of equality in love and the possibility of achieving, if not of keeping, such reciprocity. The most affecting moment in Berenice's story, her desperate stretching herself out along the length of his body to share equally in his death as in his life, provides an exact image of the elusive union of souls. In this relationship, for a time, the beloved and lover are one and the same, and love is not wasted.

6: Two Plays – *The Member of the Wedding* (1950, 1951) & *The Square Root of Wonderful* (1957, 1958)

MCCULLERS'S CAREER AS a playwright was brief, distinguished, and personally devastating. Her distinction was secured by the enormous success of the dramatic adaptation of *The Member of the Wedding*, which ran for over five hundred performances on Broadway between January 1950 and mid-March 1951. The play won for McCullers the New York Drama Critics' Circle Award as the best play of the 1949–1950 season and the Gold Medal of the Theatre Club, Inc., as the best playwright of 1950. Moreover, it won substantial awards for its director, Harold Clurman; revitalized the career of Ethel Waters; and won acclaim for Julie Harris and Brandon de Wilde. Her second play, *The Square Root of Wonderful*, closed prematurely after forty-five performances in 1957.

That the dramatic version of *Member* was written and produced at all is something of a miracle in literary history. Reconstructed from sources (Carr 1975, 1987a; Dedmond 1975) and from independent research, the story, briefly, is this: On impulse, after reading the novel, Tennessee Williams invited McCullers to visit him on Nantucket in summer 1946. The first draft of the play was completed there while McCullers sat at a table across from Williams as he worked on *Summer and Smoke*. After the idyllic summer, the trials came. A mistaken attempt at collaboration with a professional "play doctor" mired the script in lengthy arbitration before McCullers could reclaim the play and reassert her own vision of Frankie's story. Before the play reached Broadway, McCullers had suffered two crippling strokes, a therapeutic abortion, and periods of hospitalization for emotional as well as physical illnesses. The four years between novel and play were marked by courageous struggle and despair, including a suicide attempt. Her siege of ill health cannot be blamed entirely on the disastrous collaboration and her consequent battle to free her own script for production. A rheumatic heart, heedless neglect of her health, alcoholic dissipation, and a stressful marriage were, doubtless, more causal factors. She, however, viewed the botched collaboration and her efforts to overcome it as anguishing. Her willfulness in fighting for her conception of the play figured largely in its success; and its success, on both a personal and financial level, was considerable. Gross receipts exceeded $1,112,000, and with the publication of the play script and the omnibus collection of her

fiction in 1951, McCullers's reputation was at its height. When she attempted to repeat her success on Broadway six years later, she failed. *The
Square Root of Wonderful* opened in New York at the end of October 1957
and closed within five weeks. McCullers regretted that the control she
had insisted on in the production of *Member* she had largely relinquished
in the production of *Square Root*.

The Member of the Wedding

Critical opinion about the novel has eclipsed criticism of the play, at least
among academic critics. McCullers's dramatic adaptation has been treated
in only two substantial articles and one dissertation, and these are more
concerned with describing the events which culminated in McCullers's
Broadway success than in evaluating the play as a play. The most incisive
commentary on the play remains available only in contemporary reviews
of the drama in performance. In these, McCullers receives high marks for
vivid characterization and incident but lower scores on dramatic unity. In
fact, the focus of much criticism is precisely the question of genre. Is it a
play or not a play? And, if a play, what manner of play is it?

Following its debut in Philadelphia at the Walnut Theater on 22 December 1949, critics praised its richness and vitality but, as is not uncom-
mon for tryout reviews, complained of technical flaws and unnecessary
length (Martin 1950, 13; Murdock 1949, 20). Most of the complaints were
solved by the elimination of two scenes at the Blue Moon Café, one of
them the attempted rape of F. Jasmine by the redheaded soldier. These
were the only scenes that departed from the single set of the Addams
kitchen and yard. With them the work ran four hours and suffered from
cumbersome set changes. The elimination of the scenes dispelled most of
the serious reservations on the part of tryout audiences.

Following its Broadway debut at the Empire Theater on 5 January
1950, *Member* received mixed reviews, often reflecting the condescension
those allied with one craft display toward an interloper from another. It is
worth remarking that critical commentary warmed to the play over time,
as audiences voted their approval in attendance records and theater associations issued formal accolades for both the novice playwright and her
talented cast and director.

Brooks Atkinson in the *New York Times* struck the note of compromise
in his first-night review, saying, "it may not be a play, . . . [but] it is art"
(1950a, 26). Months later, as its popular success continued, Atkinson reflected that the poetic dramas of Tennessee Williams had helped prepare
Broadway audiences to admire this unorthodox play (1950b, 1).

Robert Garland's opening-night review in the *New York Journal-American* appeared under a headline that was itself barometric, calling the adaptation "Something Special But Not Quite a Play." Garland says, "As a playwright, she remains a novelist . . . so what should be the climax of the play . . . is no more than off-stage action talked about unseen" (1950, 18).

In perhaps the most enthusiastic opening-night review, Richard Watts, Jr., calls it a "sensitive unusual play of genuine individuality"; its faults as theater are "more than atoned for by its sensitivity of feeling, its delicacy of treatment, and its understanding warmth of human sympathy" (1950a, 45–46). A week later Watts took another look, finding, "There is very little suspense or conflict . . . . Its concern is basically with . . . suggestion and implication, with the capturing of intangible qualities of character and emotion" (1950b, M4).

Wolcott Gibbs in the *New Yorker* sums up one line of complaint in saying that McCullers attempted "to transfer her book too literally to the stage . . . . The result is a curiously uneven work – sometimes funny, sometimes moving, but also unfortunately sometimes just a trifle incoherent and shapeless" (150, 44). Gibbs sees McCullers's stage as wider than most other critics of either the novel or play, believing that she takes the whole of adolescence and race relations for her subject. He does not care for the working out of the subplot involving Honey Brown, calling it "contrived melodrama," and objects as well to the whirlwind third act.

John Mason Brown in the *Saturday Review* explains that the delicacy of character and mood work against the drama's characteristic need for change and action. This is "no ordinary play," but it is an appealing one nonetheless (1950, 27). Other critics felt the same: "It is a play written pretty much against the rules, and therefore all the rarer. It seldom amounts to more than half a play, but this half has a sympathy in it . . . . It is infinitely lovely" (Gabriel 1950, 20).

Theatre Arts praises Clurman's staging and calls the play "a rain from heaven to a dry theatre season" (1950, 13). Margaret Marshall for the *Nation* says, "It is not so much a play as it is whatever in the theatre corresponds to the tone poem in music . . . . An authentic experience, deeply felt, has been articulated in authentic character and speech" (1950, 44).

Member received its share of highly negative reviews as well. The *New York Herald Tribune* critic complained of length, pacing, and lack of skill. Howard Barnes says, it "moves at a snail's pace through two acts in which the literary origin is all too apparent to a final burst of hysterics and melodrama" (1950, 12). Although absorbing in many respects, "as a piece of playmaking it is not ideal, for it reiterates one theme for two acts with scarcely any story or character development," according to John Chapman in the *New York Daily News* (1950b, 55). *Time* snidely quips that "McCullers' novel suffers from having been made into a play – or, rather from not having been" ("New Play . . . " 1950, 45).

When it was performed in London, at the Royal Court Theatre on 5 February 1957, *Member* received generally favorable reviews, with the, by now, standard reservations about its generic suitability. The *Daily Telegraph and Morning Post* calls it a "tragi-comedy of mood and atmosphere" (Gibbs 1957, 8). The *Evening Standard* says, "It is charged with . . . brooding frustration, and futility. Its language . . . has the fragile grace of swaying cobwebs." It is "a very tender bloom that has failed to stand up to the rigours of transplanting" (Shulman 1957, 10). The reviewer for the *Illustrated London News* considers the play a weak substitute for the novel and states that, apart from the page, the work might be more successful as a play for radio than for the stage in that the narrator's perspective might be better represented. (Trewin 1957, 10).

Kenneth Tynan for the *Observer* remarks that it is "not so much a play as a tone poem for three voices in two colours, black and white" (1957, 11); its southernness is part of its appeal. The *New Statesman and Nation,* which had reviewed the novel negatively, did not like the play: "Two acts of stagnation and then a flurry of foreshortened activity is nothing more than a mess," the reviewer says. It could "be used as a prime example of How Not to Write a Play" (Worsley 1957, 201–2).

The play's reputation was advanced by Harold Clurman outside the offices of his role as director. An accomplished essayist and effective historian of the theater of his time, Clurman published several accounts of McCullers and her play. The first appeared in January 1950 in the *New York Herald Tribune* at the height of *Member's* Broadway success, which, he says, calls into question standard definitions of what constitutes a play (1950a, V:3).

So vocal were the early reviews in questioning the play's integrity as a play, that Clurman came to its defense again in an article in the *New Republic* within the first month of the Broadway run. There he asserts that the play is not static, that its action comes from Frankie's "struggle for connection" with the world: "It is impossible to direct a play that has no action. When a play is well acted, it means that a line of action has been found in it. It means that action was in it, however obscure it may have seemed at first sight. Without action, it would not play. The reason why Chekhov's 'Seagull' did not seem to have action when it was first produced was that the original company had not found it . . . . 'The Member of the Wedding' . . . was a play to begin with – albeit of a different kind than any other we had previously done" (1950b, 28–29). Clurman speaks of the play as a spiritual experience. Its success with audiences is particularly heartening. "A renewal of faith in the sensitivity and awareness of our New York theatregoing public was perhaps the greatest lesson I learned from *The Member of the Wedding*" (1950b, 29).

Thereafter, Clurman's essays and memoirs continued to laud the production. His director's notes from November and December 1949 constitute one of the most useful historical documents in the play's history. Published in a 1953 sourcebook on directing, the notes include Clurman's interpretation of the play and the means for staging that interpretation in the production's style, pace, and characterization. His commitment to this atypical Broadway offering and the difficulties encountered in arranging for its production are mentioned in his 1954 essay on "The Kind of Theatre We Have" (77–78). And his 1972 account of his career also contains production notes, along with behind-the-scenes anecdotes and impressions.

Throughout the 1950s and 1960s, collections and commentary by John Gassner kept in circulation his characterization of *Member* as an aberration in American theater, a nonstandard play which succeeded despite its violation of norms for playwriting (1954, 1956, 1964, 1965). A contrary view was almost as prevalent in the recurring comments of George Jean Nathan, who thought McCullers "spoiled a commendable novel" by adapting it for the stage. The "primarily psychological and passively ruminative" characterization would challenge even the most skilled playwright, he maintains. "There is no dramatization and little play . . . . What the author has done is rather to diminish what degree of drama there was in the novel and to place its two . . . principal characters on a stage, and, for the greater part of the evening have them engage in a series of inactive dialogues" (1950, 164–66). Oliver Evans, doubtlessly reflecting McCullers's own opinion, charges Nathan with ungentlemanly motives: "Mr Nathan made no secret of his personal dislike of [Tennessee] Williams, and it is not unlikely that he allowed this subjective attitude to colour his opinion of Mrs McCullers, whose friend Williams was known to be" (1965a, 154).

Asserting that "American theater is today in the doldrums" and that loneliness is the quintessential American theme of midcentury in both the drama and the novel, Alfred Kazin (1950) examines the impact of the latter on the former from the standpoint of audiences. He says, "the pressure on the stage of our familiar American loneliness has made impossible the old, ideally dramatic relations between actor and audience," for now actors are not heard but overheard. *Member* epitomizes the condition: "The child speaks to the Negro, the adolescent heroine to the child, the Negro to the poor, the father to his daughter, as if each were always alone, and had no confidence that he can understand the other or be understood. So that something blurred, always touching, yet inherently elusive – human solitude as a fact in itself alone – is shown on the stage before which the audience feels like an amazed onlooker" (527). From that position, the audience "responds by pity, not by recognition. There is no *situation* to enter into. The life of the theater is action, reciprocality. Here there is no action – there is only character, and in the characters themselves nothing but their passive suffering." Given such conditions, the play becomes merely "the occasion for an actor's personal triumph" (528). Ethel Waters, in other words, receives the more adulation the less audiences are engaged by the play.

Fellow playwright John van Druten explains McCullers's success as the result of luck and ingenuousness: it comes from her "total absorption in her subject, with no regard for the theatrical conventions beyond a wish to use the stage as best she could." Although it drew dissenters who "declined to accept it, deciding that it was no play" – a charge leveled often against the successes of George Bernard Shaw – it was a play and, moreover, "a new-born creature in the theater . . . the play of mood" (1953, 36).

In a reading overdetermined by his investment in Freudian influences on American drama, W. David Sievers calls *Member* "one of the most notable modern American psychological plays" and sees Frankie as "sexually eager" – a view slightly more justifiable in the play than in the novel (1955, 431). He gives no insight into what McCullers may have known of Freud or psychological theory and offers only a superficial insight into the characters' psychological motives. His assertion of Frankie's sexual eagerness seems contradicted by his discussion of her naïveté: "her knowledge of sex is limited to a suspicion that men and women 'look at each other and peepee or something'" (432). Sievers concludes, "It is evident that what little plot there is is sudden, violent and insufficiently motivated. But the richness of the three main characters and their freshness of speech make *The Member of the Wedding* one of the notable modern American psychological plays, a superb portrait of the baffling years between childhood and womanhood. Frankie Addams has a secure place in the annals of adolescence" (433), which Sievers points out have been a staple of comic as well as serious theater in the 1940s and 1950s.

Demonstrating that the theme of loneliness has been prominent in U.S. theater since 1920 and that it is most often used to express a condition of modern American life, Winifred L. Dusenbury (1960) discusses

Member as an example of loneliness within the contemporary family, focusing on the absence of parental attention to Frankie's needs. Dusenbury considers the play's staging of loneliness in such techniques as irrelevant or misunderstood communications and unplanned or disrupted action. She focuses on "three dramatic devices: the action seems unplanned and casual; the conversation is frequently desultory and irrelevant; the characters are not always understood by each other and sometimes cannot express their own feelings. All three devices tend to indicate a kind of isolation between people which could not be portrayed in an integrated drama in which characters react to each other in a steady march to a climax" (60). Far from succeeding solely as a result of the talents of its superb cast, "the play has proved successful on the amateur stage as well," a fact that should force its harshest critics to acknowledge that "unorthodox as the dramatic structure may be, it is eminently suited for the portrayal of the growth of a girl from extreme loneliness to a mature self-reliance" (67). In the final scene, Frankie at last belongs. Dusenbury reveals no doubts about the quality of the resolution Frankie's loneliness has reached.

Critics and historians of U.S. theatre soon came round to the view that *Member* is an important play precisely because it violates the rules of dramatic action. An articulate proponent of this belief, Gerald Weales (1962) argues that McCullers's adaptation represents "the most obvious structural innovation in recent American theatre." Both versions of *Member* strike Weales as "self-conscious constructions, built by a clever and talented draftsman out of materials [she] has used successfully before and which have had some vogue." He is, however, disturbed by the climactic violence in both versions. "It is never clear, in the play or in the novel, why violence and death are necessary for Frankie's passage into adolescence; the fall and the beginning of school would have broken open the ring around the kitchen of that summer and, if a more specific event were needed, the wedding could have served. It may be that the double death in the play (in the novel Honey ends on the chain gang) is a kind of emotional mannerism necessary to the genre of Southern writing to which Mrs. McCullers contributes" (176–77).

Oliver Evans (1965a) details important differences between novel and play, adding,

> One rather wishes that some of the speeches in the play had also been used in the novel. Thus, Frankie's remark to Berenice ("I don't know why you had to get that eye. It has a wrong expression – let alone being blue.") suggests that Berenice's blue eye has another purpose besides the obvious one of imparting to her a certain freakishness: it shows *her* de-

sire (which parallels Frankie's) to escape from the identity which requires that her eyes, like her skin, be of a particular colour: she too is doomed to her identity, and longs for the impossible. So viewed, John Henry's remark, "I like the glass eye better" (also missing in the novel), takes on a special significance as showing his childish preference for the ideal world over the real. On the other hand, some important speeches common to both the novel and the play seem to receive greater emphasis in the latter, because the form is more selective. To this category belongs Frankie's speech in the first act: "I wish I was somebody else except me."

One of the most salient differences from the novel is "the relative importance of Berenice . . . . In the play . . . Berenice has almost as many speeches as Frankie, and in this democracy of dialogue she almost succeeds in replacing Frankie as the centre of interest . . . . [Honey's violent subplot] in which Berenice is involved indirectly, also gives greater importance to her story. Finally, she is more valuable in the symmetry of the play than in the novel: she is the last person to leave the stage, and as she does so she hums the first two lines of the same hymn with which, accompanied by Frankie and John Henry, she ended the second act" (150).

Louis Phillips (1968) observes that both of McCullers's plays take the family, and the problems of one or two of its members, as their focus. His analysis of *Member* develops the parallels between Frankie and Honey Camden Brown, the foster brother of Berenice misidentified by Phillips as her fifth husband. Both are members of no clubs, so "they must take out their humiliation on other people" (154). Phillips does not notice that Honey Camden Brown is given an expanded and different role in the play than he has in the novel.

Dale Edmonds (1969) summarizes changes from the novel, including the single setting, the kitchen, and the changes entailed by it.

> Certain other changes were necessary. T. T. Williams, instead of being a middle-class restaurant owner, becomes a handyman who dons a white coat to help out at the wedding. This reduction in status enhances T. T.'s dramatic usefulness, for he can help report events that take place offstage. Mary Littlejohn's role is handled more adroitly than in the novel. She is mentioned early in the drama in derogatory terms by Frankie; thus Frankie's attachment to Mary at the end emphasizes Frankie's quixotic nature. Frankie's sex experience with Barney MacKean is shifted in the play to Helen Fletcher, a member of the girls' club which has excluded Frankie. By this transfer Mrs. McCullers avoids any "cuteness" that might have resulted from an attempt to deal with this on stage. Frankie's near-seduction by the redhaired soldier, which several critics complained of as being tangential to the main plot

line, has been excised from the dramatic version. The beginning of John Henry's sickness is moved up in time to the night of the wedding, and his death takes place the following week – as does also that of Honey Brown, who hangs himself in jail rather than being sent to the chain gang (as he was in the novel). These changes were necessary for the avoidance of lengthy exposition in the short final scene of Act Three.

Like Evans, Edmonds sees the "elevation of Berenice to virtually equal importance with Frankie" as the most important change from novel to play. Edmonds considers other alterations "less satisfactory." Among these, "Honey Brown becomes, rather than a lost individual, a symbol of the subjugation and consequent hostility of his race. The change in Honey's role involves an unfortunate change in the role of Frankie's father. Instead of an abstracted, rather pitiful figure, he becomes a crude racist . . . . In attempting to give Honey Brown's story more contemporary impact, Mrs. McCullers has, instead, given it only an air of spurious timeliness" (36–37).

In one of the few extended critical treatments of the play, Francis B. Dedmond (1975) adduces its psychological (as opposed to dramatic) structure. The first act "is a subjective, inner-compelled analysis by Frankie Addams of her problem – a many faceted problem to which she returns again and again as she gropes for a solution, a solution which will alleviate her sense of spiritual isolation and cure her deep loneliness." The second act "is largely a grotesque parable of love and death designed by Berenice to bring Frankie to a sense of reality, to carry her beyond her fantasies in an effort to make her see that . . . . to confuse fantasy with reality is to invite confusion and heartache." Calling the third act "inferior to the rest," Dedmond focuses on it as a "maturation experience" in which Frankie is seen "developing a proper feminine sex-role identity" and gaining "freedom from the kitchen." Dedmond says, "It is especially significant, symbolically so, that Frankie and Mary got to know each other in front of the lipstick and cosmetics counter at Woolworth's. Frankie's mental picture of herself – a psychic reality, which is the core of her self-concept – gradually changes with the emergence of her female identification, symbolized by the cosmetics counter" (50–52). Readers of McCullers among the Broadway audience might have had a far different symbolic association for Woolworth's, the place where Mick Kelly's dreams dead-end in *Hunter*. They might also recall that Frankie and Mary meet at a raffle in the novel, a detail that makes this intentional departure from that version all the more salient.

Judith Olavson (1981) treats McCullers with other dramatists in the decade 1940–1950 but adds little to an understanding of the play's success. She says, "There was a quality about the play which eluded the critics. Charmed by McCullers' delicate perception of character, nevertheless the critics were unprepared for the liberties the playwright took with dramatic conventions" (68). The final scene is rendered thus: "For Frankie 'fate' has brought her new friends and a new world in which to live; for Berenice it is a sad moment when she realizes that Frankie's new world is already strange to her. In the closing moments of the play McCullers presents a parallel study of loneliness in the rebellious alienation of the child which finds a cure, and the patient isolation of the woman which does not" (71).

Neva Evonne Burdison (1987), in a dissertation comparing the novel, play, and film versions of *Member,* argues that the work succeeds in each medium but that both dramatic versions lack the psychological intensity and depth of the novel. "As an artistic, psychological portrait of an adolescent girl, the novel stands far above its adaptations" (219). In a detailed analysis, Burdison finds that the play lacks the novel's closeness to Frankie's interior responses and thereby foregrounds the relationship between Frankie and Berenice. In another shift of emphasis, "the play is quietly subversive" in dramatizing racial disharmony, especially in scenes focusing on Honey Camden Brown in conflict with Frankie's father (152). "The play subverts the values of Berenice and Mr. Addams by making Honey and Frankie the sympathetic characters" (155). Burdison maintains that balance is restored, but acknowledges as well the reversal of roles staged in the final scene, in which Berenice is left alone holding John Henry's doll. Saying that the play "clarifies the ambiguous ending of the novel," Burdison suggests that "Frankie's hope is counterbalanced by the last image of Berenice's sorrow. The play ends with certain grief " (156), perhaps for both characters.

Virginia Spencer Carr (1990) largely rehearses her 1987 article in discussing the play, but adds to the summary of the accolades and honors it gained the information that "the fact that [it] was an adaptation kept McCullers out of the running for a Pulitzer, which went that year to the musical, *South Pacific.* However, in a *New York Times* article about the awards (entitled 'Second-Hand Drama'), Brooks Atkinson pointed out that only three notable plays written directly for the stage had been produced during the current theater season, and of the three plays that won a Drama Critics' Circle Award for 1949–1950, *The Member of the Wedding* 'came closest to Pulitzer prize specifications' since both playwright and setting were American" (96–97). In both the biography (1975) and her later essay (1987a), Carr says that McCullers relished Tennessee Williams's suggestion that she adapt *Member* for the stage in part as a chance to avenge Edmund Wilson's remark (1946, 87) that the novel lacked drama.

Mary McBride (1990) points to the irony of the play's closing scene in which Berenice "sits in the kitchen alone and motionless, singing a song about being happy and free" (145). McBride compares McCullers's play to assorted works by Tennessee Williams. "Although McCullers's sensitivity to the adolescent complexity revealed in the character of Frankie is not required in the often more predictable reactions of Williams's adults, both dramatists portray the irresistible force of the basic human need for acceptance and the desperation of characters denied fulfillment of this need" (145). McBride concludes, "The close tension between tragedy and comedy in McCullers's plays is also evident in the works of Williams, but Williams wrote of gentle pathos rather than high tragedy. In most of his plays, characters move through quiet desperation, torn by their effort to live in a state of illusion amid the demands of a world in which cold reality rides roughshod over illusive dream" (149).

The Square Root of Wonderful

What is the Square Root of Failure? New York theater critics asked questions as accusing as this one in hooting Carson McCullers's second play off the stage. It closed on 7 December 1957, a notable national anniversary but also, quite sadly, the fourth anniversary, to the week, of Reeves McCullers's suicide in France. Ironically, the play treats the suicide of a mercurial writer, Phillip Lovejoy, who drives his car into a lake when he realizes that Mollie Lovejoy, his ex-wife, will seek her happiness with another man, the stolid architect John Tucker. It is John who explains that "the square root of wonderful is love" and its opposite, the square root of sin, is humiliation. To the extent that the play exorcised the bitter past of her marriage to Reeves, its commercial failure *was* the more abashing.

Conceived as a play, shortly after the success of *The Member of the Wedding, The Square Root of Wonderful* occupied McCullers from 1952 until 1956, a period during which she experienced the deaths of her husband and her mother and grimly contemplated her continuing poor health. A version of *Square Root,* recast as the story "Who Has Seen the Wind?" was published in *Mademoiselle* in 1956. The history of its production as a play is a story of acquiescence that McCullers came to regret. The pattern repeats in reverse the history of her success with *Member,* which she virtually willed into being in the form she wished it to have. *Square Root* was weakened by collaboration. Virginia Spencer Carr (1987a) says, "The play went through more than a dozen drafts, six or eight by McCullers alone, and a handful of assorted other scripts written in collaboration with her several producers and directors" (47). The directorial history is unusually vexed. The first director, Albert Marre, and the producer, Arnold Saint Subber, "worked with McCullers through six different scripts for over a year, but when Saint Subber announced that the script was ready to be cast and produced, Marre was on the West Coast and unavailable. José Quintero, who was selected to replace Marre, worked with McCullers and Saint Subber for several months until the play's disastrous opening at the McCarter Theatre in Princeton" (47). Quintero resigned and substitute directors worked to salvage the play before its Broadway opening. Anne Baxter, who played Mollie Lovejoy in the production, told Carr details of the directorial disasters, speaking of the play as McCullers's dying child. "It was pathetic. She loved the child, but there was no one who knew what was really wrong with it. Nor did Carson have the emotional, mental, or physical strength to take over herself. Joseph L. Mankiewicz took charge and began rewriting the script until George Keathley could arrive, a director secured through Tennessee Williams. But neither of them knew how to fix it either. They somehow didn't put the things back in that shouldn't have been taken out in the first place . . . . It was a very delicate play, a cobweb" (qtd. Carr 1987a, 48). Carr concludes that

> more than a curtain dropped when the play died . . . . McCullers had tried to work out in it – her fantasy – the ambivalent love/hatred emotions regarding her deceased husband and mother, and she had failed. But unlike *The Member of the Wedding,* which had given McCullers emotional release as well as extraordinary acclaim, *The Square Root of Wonderful* had become its opposite for the dejected playwright . . . . Coping with a collaborator on *The Member of the Wedding* before producing a script that, finally, was wholly hers and that became a prize-winning play with a long run was one thing, but to have *The Square Root of Wonderful* carved up beyond recognition by the play's producers and directors was quite another, and she never quite got over it. (1987a, 49–50)

The script published in 1958 is the last version she considered hers, not the script that was produced in 1957.

The Broadway production drew dismaying notices. "The basic flaw is probably the lifelessness of the characters and the flatness of most of the writing. Mrs. McCullers has not been able to impart to this love story the other-worldliness of her best writing," according to Brooks Atkinson (1957, 40); "Carson McCullers can write like a streak. She can, as demonstrated here, also write like a smudge" (Bolton 1957, 2); the play "boasts flashes of beauty, embedded in a basis of the fumbling and sordid. It starts to soar like a bird . . . but too seldom gets off the ground" (Coleman 1957, 32, 33); "Mrs. McCullers' play presents us with a heroine who is . . . a pinhead, and with a hero and villain who are a rather stifling moralist and a boozily grandiloquent psychopath, respectively" (Gibbs 1957, 103); "Where Miss McCullers is content to write comedy, the current entry is better than all right. But where she turns the script into problem drama, it becomes embarrassing" (Driver 1957, 1425); "The plot is implausible, the people are grotesque . . . . It is difficult to understand how the lady who wrote 'Member of the Wedding' could have drifted into such diffuse doubletalk" (McClain 1957, 22); it is "a curious comedy-drama of cryptic elements, uninteresting characters and surprisingly flat writing" ([Morrison] 1957, 72); it "pursues a persistent indelicacy in its factual details of life with an uxorious husband. The title is the best part of this seemingly illegitimate theater child of the very gifted McCullers" (Wyatt 1958, 306); "The general effect of flatness can be written off as an occupational hazard of any author. What is more difficult to account for in this case is the coarseness of her style, which was matched by the production's heavy-handed direction. The only thing that can be safely repeated about the cast . . . is that it failed to disguise the play's defects" (*Theatre Arts* 1958, 24).

Harold Clurman, director of McCullers's earlier play, gave a strong rebuke to José Quintero, saying that the stage direction caused the failure of the play. "As a result, lyric writing, beautifully awry, and wonderfully intuitive character sense have been flattened into semi-caricature." However, McCullers takes a significant share of the blame: "The characters often fall out of focus, and it is one of the mistakes of the play's composition that the author felt constrained to make her story straightforward so that it might appear logical to the prosaic mind. The script might have been better if it had the faults natural to its author's genius" (1957, 394).

Oliver Evans (1965a) observes that McCullers's preface to the published script leads readers to identify Phillip Lovejoy with Reeves McCullers and Mollie Lovejoy with Marguerite Waters Smith, her mother. However, "the careful reader will note at once that it is Phillip and not his wife who was successful as a writer . . . . (The identity of Phillip is further complicated, for in the play it is John and not Phillip who has been a war hero.) And the circumstance of Mollie's having married the same man twice reminds us not of Mrs Smith but of Mrs McCullers. What the author has done is to identify herself now with Phillip (in the speeches in which he discusses his writing), now with Mollie (in the dialogue which she exchanges with her ex-husband)." To Evans "this lack of aesthetic distance . . . from her characters" suggests the reason the play is her "weakest performance" (163). Evans praises John's last word, "one of the best lines in the play: 'When will you be strong enough to love the strong?'" (164).

The play's life-death theme reminds Evans of *Reflections*, in which Captain Penderton is "'heavily weighted' toward death, and in fact the resemblance between him and Phillip is too obvious to be overlooked: Penderton's need of the soldier parallels Phillip's need of Mollie, for both men, whose orientation is towards death, are seeking to correct this imbalance by establishing a vicarious contact with life" (164). Phillip has returned "to feed on [Mollie's] vitality" (164). Evans also says, "John (like Major Langdon) is dull and 'normal' while Phillip (like Penderton) is brilliant and neurotic" (164). He is on shakier ground in the suggestion that, with numerous differences, Sister resembles Alison Langdon and Mollie resembles Leonora Penderton.

There may be too many "minor motifs" in the play to allow for unity. Evans enumerates those beliefs about love that run through McCullers's novels: its irrationality, its loneliness, its association with fantasies, its ideality that permits "the lover to love all things and all persons" (165). "But the most important of the minor themes has to do with time. The relation of time to love is obvious: it is the Great Enemy of love as it is of life, of which love is the surest sign . . . . In relation to loneliness, however, time takes on yet another significance . . . . Phillip does not dislike clocks because they remind him that time is running out; he dislikes them for the opposite reason, because they remind him of how much time he will have to kill before he finds release from his loneliness: for him, as for all unhappy people, clocks do not run too fast but too slow" (166).

"Except in the case of Phillip (and, to a lesser extent, Mollie) the characterization is thin and lacking in complexity." Mother Lovejoy "bears too obvious a resemblance to Amanda Wingfield"; and the play's humor is sometimes "on a rather low level" (167). The play, technically, "is a well-made play (it makes surprisingly good reading), and the fact that it did not succeed on Broadway may merely mean that a popular audience is less interested in the personal problems of a literary has-been than in those of a fourteen-year-old girl — who might be the one next door — with growing pains. In this play Mrs McCullers is concerned with too specialized an area of human interest and experience — another way, perhaps, of saying that she is too close to her materials" (168).

Louis Phillips (1968) examines McCullers as playwright in tandem with James Baldwin and Saul Bellow, who excel more as novelists than dramatists; "but such an evaluation may be quite useless in the long-run. The important fact is that they have all felt the need to use the dramatic form to express, develop, and amplify the themes that have formed the basis of their many novels" (146). Phillips's study is weak in knowledge of the particulars of McCullers's plays and more valuable overall for what it has to say about the second than the first. "If there is any relation at all between Carson McCullers' first play and her second . . . it is perhaps summed up in Berenice's statement, 'When folks are lonesome and left out, they turn so mean.' It may well be the unifying theme throughout all of Miss McCullers' writing, for her second play takes its title from the reversal of an idea set forth by one of its characters – 'the sin of hurting people's feelings. Of humiliating a person. That is the square root of sin. It's the same as murder'" (155). "Mollie . . . must put up a valiant effort to keep both men from being humiliated – the square root of sin – for both men have experienced failure in their chosen professions" (156). Phillips quotes McCullers about the "risk in alternating comic and tragic scenes" in the theater, where audiences are less flexible emotionally than readers because of the immediacy and lack of opportunity to reflect on the feelings engendered. Phillips concludes, "It may well be that the tragic-comic form is more suitable to the novel than it is to the theatre" (157).

Lawrence Graver (1969, 10) dismisses the play as "a maladroit comedy of manners." Dale Edmonds (1969) complains of its "melodramatic plot" and "painfully unrealistic dialogue," citing the example of Mollie's refusal of John's kiss: "To other people a kiss is light and sweet. To me a kiss is sweet as syrup. But it's not light. In fact it leads straight to the dark. To sin, in fact" (38–39).

Margaret B. McDowell (1980) says that in this work McCullers now suggests that scientific thought may account for the mysteries of love, a concept that she once before tentatively explored in her story 'A Tree, a Rock, a Cloud.' In The Square Root of Wonderful she also approaches love rationalistically." John "instructs her that the truth of love lies not in the world of magic, as she had assumed all her life, but in the realm of logic" (141). John's message is "that love results from the exercise of the free will rather than from a spell cast upon one by fate. In John's mathematical formula to explain human emotions . . . love and humiliation cancel out each other. So Mollie's humiliation in her marriage can yield, if she wills it, to a powerful love that will set her free. Love alone can cancel out the debilitating humiliation she has always previously experienced in a sexual relationship" (142).

The characters "generally reveal little emotion and psychic complexity. Only Mollie reveals much depth and complication. She . . . remains the naive Peach Queen, while she also becomes the bold, vulgar woman who picks up an attractive hitchhiker and jokes about coveting her neighbor's ass . . . . She attains considerable self-awareness, furthermore, when she recognizes her solitariness among her self-centered relatives now that she has become an adult but has no one else who is spiritually adult to talk to" (142).

McDowell acknowledges that "some effective comedy arises from the stereotypical characterizations of Phillip's mother and sister. Sister, a librarian who habitually whispers, once fell in love with a man who checked out a book with a call letter in Z, and now creates in fantasy a variety of lovers from every country in the world with whom she can sin zestfully. Phillip's mother is perhaps more sinister than comic as McCullers envisages her. The mother's eccentricities are destructive because of her wish to humiliate her children. The need to humiliate others becomes the square root of her existence as a human being. She is obsessed with pride in her son's genius and with shame over her daughter's spinsterhood but loves neither of her children. To hide Sister's need for glasses as a child, she attempted to whisper the letters to the little girl as the oculist tested her eyes" (142–43).

According to McDowell (via Carr 1975, 453), the intended director, Albert Marre, once "remarked that McCullers may have been ahead of her time in producing a 'black comedy.' He also suggested that replacing Anne Baxter with Carol Channing might have brought out more sharply the ironic and comic elements present in the character of Mollie Lovejoy" (144). Apparently, however, "McCullers did not sustain in her play the comedy to the point that it provided strong dramatic contrast as the play shifted toward pathos and tragedy. In her attempt to maintain pace, she provided for no continuous, interweaving conversations, such as those found in *The Member of the Wedding*. Except for Mollie, the play lacks vital characterization. It lacks, more damagingly, an adequate synthesis of the comic and the tragic elements that had been so insistent in her original conception of the work" (144).

Mary McBride (1990) observes that "a thread of tension between isolation and desire for acceptance . . . runs through the plays of Williams and McCullers. In both authors' plays, the healing, transcending force is, or would be, love – assured acceptance" (146). "Mollie's need, she tells John, is love beyond the physical She needs more now: somebody who will accept her wholly, not only her body, but also her mind and soul. Phillip, she thinks, had loved her only for her body." McBride refers to the similarity between Phillip's mother and sister and Williams's Amanda and Laura Wingfield but does not find it remarkable. She does suggest that Phillip is like Tom Wingfield, also "a frustrated writer" (147). That she does not discuss the issue of indebtedness further in an essay devoted to a comparison of the two playwrights is curious.

Through the perversity of academic specialization, perhaps, the relationship between McCullers's last two major works, her second play and her fifth novel, which she worked on simultaneously, remains unexplored. The dramatic effects labeled caricature onstage may bear resemblance to those given the identical label in criticism of the novel. Furthermore, both struck their first critical audiences as slightly inept in the mixing of comic and somber effects. The management of character and tone from one genre to the next deserves study.

7: *Clock Without Hands* (1961)

*The strongly emotional tone of the reviewers —
ranging from disappointment and anger to
excitement, enthusiasm, and even joy — cannot
be explained by study of the book alone.*

(Margaret B. McDowell 1980)

THE VOLTAGE OF the reviews which greeted *Clock Without Hands,*
McCullers's last important work and her fifth novel, is attributable in
McDowell's view to the expectations created by her "unforgettable" early
success and by the fact that "no critic could be unaware that she, like her
main character, J. T. Malone, faced death" (1980, 97). The reviews, indeed, are haunted by the image of a wunderkind, now tragically disabled,
working slowly and heroically in a battle against time. However, more
was at stake in 1961 than the novel or the circumstances of its author. Reaction to McCullers's last major work was shaped by a division within
critical ranks that intensified in the 1960s and ensuing decades.

The story of an empty life redeemed by an unpopular choice, *Clock*
traces the last days of J. T. Malone as his private burden, leukemia, is
linked at a crucial point to the greater tragedy of race hatred. The middle-
aged pharmacist is pitted against the elderly bigot Judge Fox Clane, who
leads Malone into a conspiracy to bomb the house of a young black man
who has audaciously moved into a white neighborhood. Malone's refusal
to participate is a moral victory only. Sherman Pew, a black foundling
with blue eyes, named for the church pew on which his mother abandoned him, loses his life at age seventeen, defiantly playing the white
grand piano in the living room of the house rented to shock white citizens.
He is mourned by his foil in the novel, seventeen-year-old Jester Clane,
the Judge's grandson, who plans to avenge Sherman's death from an airplane above the town but ultimately chooses not to take another's life.
The novel ends on the day of the Supreme Court ruling in *Brown* v. *Board
of Education.* Judge Clane dissolves in senile rage attempting to denounce
the decision on radio. The only sentences he manages to babble are from
the Gettysburg Address. Having heard the Judge humiliate himself, Malone dies peacefully. The secret of the boys' parentage, Jester's homosexual crush on Sherman, and Sherman's foppish spitefulness figure vividly
in the plot.

In the fifteen years that separate *The Member of the Wedding* and *Clock Without Hands,* a new generation of critics had come to maturity. The academic criticism that submerged McCullers's sociopolitical concerns under the tidal force of formalist universalizing began to ebb in the early 1960s. It is suggestive to note the number of important works published in the years adjacent to the appearance of *Clock Without Hands* that mark for later generations the character of postwar fiction. A by-no-means-exhaustive catalog includes Leslie A. Fiedler's *Love and Death in the American Novel* (1960), Ihab Hassan's *Radical Innocence: Studies in the Contemporary American Novel* (1961), Alfred Kazin's *Contemporaries* (1962), Irving Malin's *New American Gothic* (1962), and William Van O'Connor's *The Grotesque: An American Genre and Other Essays* (1962). Such an assortment, along with others that might be cited if the range were extended to the decade 1955–1965 – for example, John Aldridge's *In Search of Heresy: American Literature in an Age of Conformity* (1956), John M. Bradbury's *Renaissance in the South* (1963), and Walter Allen's *The Modern Novel in Britain and the United States* (1964); and essay collections such as Joseph J. Waldmeir's *Recent American Fiction: Some Critical Views* (1963), Nona Balakian and Charles Simmons's *The Creative Present: Notes on Contemporary American Fiction* (1963), Harry T. Moore's *Contemporary American Novelists* (1964), and Richard Kostelanetz's *On Contemporary Literature* (1964) – suggests several important shifts in the study of literature: first, that the study of contemporary fiction had gained respectability in academe; second, that literary criticism had been institutionalized within the universities; third, that the WASP-ish enclave of academic literary studies had been invaded by outsiders, the sons of immigrants, newly commissioned as instructors and assistant professors courtesy of the GI Bill; and fourth, by extension, that a challenge to the citadel of formalist criticism was stirring.

The meaning of these trends for the reception of *Clock Without Hands* – and, of course, for McCullers's reputation generally, since she is treated in all of the books marshalled above – has been seen repeatedly in previous chapters but can be illustrated with somewhat greater precision or, at least, more minutely in this instance. This pivotal period in U.S. literary criticism registered a new intensity in the perennial struggle between intrinsic and extrinsic approaches to literature. In the fifteen years between McCullers's fourth novel and her fifth, dissent from New Critical formalism as a critical orthodoxy (and quite apart from the academic battles between old-line historical scholars and new critics) had been largely confined to journals of opinion and weekly book reviews. But even there, many erstwhile socialist and Marxist intellectuals sheepishly entered the fold of the modernist canon. The result was the consensus criticism protested by Malcolm Cowley (1954) and John Aldridge (1956). What had been in the 1950s largely a series of skirmishes between public critics and their counterparts in the universities escalated with the steady passage of outsiders in through the gates of academe.

The challenge to intrinsic criticism – the formalists' insistence on the work of literature as a complex verbal structure to be judged by its success in unifying its internal contradictions – came from the realm of the myth critics and their concern with an ultimate source of myth external to the work, whether in culture, racial memory, or a collective unconscious. Freudians, Jungians, and archetypalists à la Northrop Frye led the way out of the crystal palace of pure form into the countryside of ethical, social, and psychological conflict. To be sure, such a pattern imposes too crisp an outline on the highly variable terrain of 1960s criticism, but it does serve a purpose in tracing McCullers's reputation. As applied to the novel, intrinsic standards of this era measured the development of plot and character by structural coordinates, the accretion of images, the logic of symbolism, the management of point of view, and the architecture of irony, ambiguity, epiphany, and paradox. The successful novel offered a complex and unified vision of universal human experience. By way of psychology, the myth critics added flesh and specificity to the generalizations about universal experience, focusing on character psychology and interrelationships, points of contact between the individual and society, and signs of protest, rebellion, victimization, and escape.

As applied to *Clock Without Hands,* these competing approaches split the field of initial response and continue to be seen in more contemporary criticism of the novel. The influence of formalism appears in the preoccupation with unresolved disjunction or disharmony between the novel's two plot strands. J. T. Malone, as a character, is not strong enough to fend off or be reconciled with the vivid caricature of Judge Fox Clane. McCullers's formal control over style and structure is weaker here than in her previous novels. The work seems disjointed, not polished, confusing in the import of its symbols, and marred by propaganda that overshadows the theme of finding "livingness" in the contemplation of death. Extrinsic criticism, though frequently making many of the same points about structural disunity, claims that McCullers's concern with racial bigotry and violence is a meritorious widening of her narrow focus on the lonely individual. Characterization is explored for relevance to cultural beliefs about race, adolescence, aging, death. The lonely individual is seen as an agent of moral choice and courage, and McCullers's use of caricature is justified as well-placed ridicule of narcissism and bigotry.

A sampling of initial response illustrates the intrinsic/extrinsic range. Benjamin De Mott calls it "depressingly underdone," consisting of "two stories but both have little substance" (1961/1962, 625–26). Doris Grumbach in *America* says it lacks "any distinction except the name of its author"; the novel is "studded with the cliches of current events and is written in a style . . . forced and flat" (1961, 809). Under the headline "The Member of the Funeral," a reviewer for *Time* writes, "Novelist McCullers drops the story thread and comes close to losing the entire narrative spool . . . . Motivations are inept and mystifying" (1961, 118–20). Dorothy Parker, writing for *Esquire,* expresses disappointment in the novel's caricature and implausibility: "It is sharply difficult for me to attempt to explain that Carson McCullers has not, to my mind, again written a perfect book" (1961, 72–73). Charles Rolo in the *Atlantic* says, "Readers who have wished in the past that Miss McCullers were a bit less fascinated by abnormality and grotesquerie may find this the most impressive of her novels . . . . The craftsmanship is impeccable . . . . *Clock Without Hands* is a strong contender for the 1961 National Book Award for fiction" (1961, 126–27). Gerald Walker in *Cosmopolitan* calls it a "departure from these private melancholy studies in the futility of interpersonal relationships . . . . It displays an awareness of a larger social drama" (1961, 26–27).

The split among U.S. reviewers was not to be found elsewhere. It should not be surprising that British critics, who in the past had condemned a certain preciousness with McCullers's precocity and regretted the narrow range of her portrayal of loneliness, found much to admire in the bite of social satire in *Clock*. A sampling of the English reviews shows the general unanimity of approval. The London *Times Weekly Review* calls it "marvellously free from the fetters of dogma and of literary fashion" and praises her portrait of "aggressive and tragic old age" ("Free from the Fetters . . . " 1961, 10). John Gross in the *New Statesman* acknowledges it as her "weakest book" but praises her "unsurpassed feeling for the unfledged, the broken down, the estranged" (1961, 614). Julian Mitchell, for *London Magazine,* finds it the equal of her other works and characterizes it as "a meditation on life and death, and a long look into the eyes of the South" (1962, 91). Isabel Quigly in the Manchester *Guardian* says, "Tensions, atmospheres, glories all mount and multiply, the atmosphere of the small town in Georgia is so strong you can smell the fear and enmity, and see the startling physical beauty" (1961, 7). Simon Raven in the *Spectator* remarks, "It is never easy to see just how seriously she wishes to be taken, so blithely does she sprinkle the sugar-icing of comedy over the grimmest possible events," but he approves the jarring mixture: "You may construe this book with profit, on any level from the anecdotal to the tragic" (1961, 551). Philip Toynbee in the London *Observer* sounds a note of hopefulness not characteristic of reviews as a group: "This is a good novel, funny, sad and beautiful"; its "writing is sound and serious." "Perhaps Miss McCullers's next novel will recover the lost zest and freshness of 'Reflections in a Golden Eye' without surrendering this new-found balance and concern" (1961, 29). The *Times Literary Supplement* says, "She has been able by dint of honesty as much as by technical skill to write a good and moving book which comes up to all the demands raised by her reputation" ("From Life . . . " 1961, 749).

The most reviewed of McCullers's works, *Clock* occasioned on both sides of the Atlantic retrospective estimates of the career and tributes to the writer. Although some reviewers showed an especially captious distress over its failure to measure up to the standard of earlier work, the novel was more often treated deferentially. Granville Hicks's *Saturday Review* column (1961) exemplifies the respectful tone of such reviews, a tone that combines praise, nostalgia, and regret: "Again one has to say that Mrs. McCullers has not equaled 'The Heart Is a Lonely Hunter,' but this is nonetheless a fine novel. The familiar themes are here – identity, the meaning of life, the nature of love – and, as always, they are dealt with perceptively" (14–15). Showing the distance between cold war humanism and his 1930s commitment to the literature of advocacy, Hicks here views the race problem, which he acknowledges the book in some "important sense" concerns, as ancillary to McCullers's purposes: "Mrs. McCullers is not trying to underline the obvious fact that there is a problem, nor has she a solution she wants to thrust upon us; her purpose is to show the problem at the deepest possible level, as it penetrates the secret recesses of human souls" (15). Following a catalog of memorable scenes, Hicks wonders, "What more can anybody ask? In all reason, nothing. But one can remember 'The Heart Is a Lonely Hunter,' in which by the grace of some inexplicable power, more was given" (49). In a reminiscence accompanying this review, Tennessee Williams calls McCullers "a gallant invalid" and "the greatest living writer of our country, if not of the world" (15).

Strong and influential praise came from Rumer Godden in the *New York Herald-Tribune* (1961), who calls it a "marvel"; "it is powerful yet humble, dignified yet utterly unpretentious," though it may be "too strange and strong, too frank, for many people" (5). And Jean Martin in the *Nation* (1961) admires McCullers's courage in rising above her early success with "the albatross of reputation hanging around her neck and the thumping signboard of 'genius' staring her in the teeth." *Clock* is "warm, funny, and readable; its point may not quite click, but the writing is quietly superb" (411).

Of the negative reviews, a few were disdainful – notably those by Irving Howe, Whitney Balliett, and Robert O. Bowen. Howe in the *New York Times Book Review* (1961) alleges lack of "inner conviction and imaginative energy"; the result is flat, mechanical, and poorly constructed, merely "an unadorned and scrappy scenario for a not-yet-written novel" (5). Balliett in the *New Yorker* (1961) says, memorably, that "Mrs. McCullers's prose, rumpled and gossipy, gives the peculiar impression of having been slept in" (179). And Bowen, in the *Catholic World* (1961) applies Fiedlerian labels in saying the novel is "Southern Gothic of an almost purely Partisan Review-New Yorker-Guggenheim Foundation bias" that follows a trite recipe: "a dash of sympathy for homosexuals, a bit of the macabre, some basting with lavatory-wall vulgarisms and a garnish of pseudo-liberal canards on race and religion" (186). Louis D. Rubin, Jr., in *Sewanee Review* (1962) calls it "a confusing book" whose "failure is exemplified in the failure of Sherman Pew as a character; sometimes he is a symbol, sometimes a human being, but never both at the same time" (509).

Gore Vidal, McCullers's admirer, but not friend, marvels that twenty-one years have elapsed since the publication of *Hunter,* when "McCullers was *the* young writer. She was an American legend from the beginning" (1962a, 178). Recalling the fashion-magazine publicity responsible for her celebrity, Vidal admits that "McCullers's dreaming androgynous face in its ikon elegance subtly confounded the chic of the lingerie ads all about her. For unlike other 'legends,' her talent was as real as her face. Though she was progenitress to much 'southern writing' (one can name a dozen writers who would not exist in the way they do if she had not written in the way she did), she had a manner all her own. Her prose was chaste and severe, and realistic in its working out of narrative. I suspect that of all the southern writers, she is the most apt to endure, though her vision is by no means as large or encompassing as that, say, of Faulkner, whom she has the grace to resemble not at all" (179).

In *Clock* "Carson McCullers acknowledges the public world for the first time in her work. Though her response is uneasy and uncertain, it is good to note that she writes as well as ever, with all the old clarity and fine tension. But the book is odd, and it is so because what has always been the most private of responses has been rudely startled and bemused by the world outside. The changing South. The Supreme Court Decision. Integration. The aviator as new man. All these things crop up unexpectedly in her narrative. One cannot say she handles these things badly; it is just that they do not quite fit her story" (182). Judge Clane's raging recitation of the Gettysburg Address strikes Vidal as off-the-mark. "Are we to take that as the South's last gasp as a new order begins? If so, I don't believe it . . . . But even this near failure of McCullers is marvelous to read, and her genius for prose remains one of the few satisfying achievements of our second-rate culture" (183). This from a fellow writer who disdained to occupy the same room with her.

Beneath Vidal's none-too-precise distinction between private and public, then and now, lies an important observation about the difference between *Clock* and *Hunter,* the novel which surely competes for the distinction of having acknowledged a public world. It is in fact largely the same world. Sherman Pew is Benedict Mady Copeland, younger and with more self-irony. The difference is at base stylistic. Public events, public injustices hover everywhere on the periphery of the first novel, verifying and validating the obsessions and emotional turmoil out of which Singer's satellites seek release in love and understanding. In the last novel, public events more centrally motivate the plot as well as the characters. We remember Judge Clane's public response to desegregation as climactic. Comparable incidents in *Hunter* – Jake's public display of Copeland; Copeland's plan to march on Washington; the race riot; a rent strike – are powerful, but not central.

Nick Aaron Ford's review essay for *Phylon* on novels by and about Negroes (1962) offers the perspective of a leading black scholar for whom the public purposes and motives of *Clock* are welcome. This novel by a white woman from Georgia, he says, is "the most significant novel of the year concerning race relations. It manages to be deeply moral without preachment, raising questions of right and wrong in Negro-white relations that cannot be lightly dismissed by thoughtful readers" (130–31). Ford notes more directly than some early critics Jester's "spark of man-love for Sherman which continues to grow (but never bursts into flame) throughout the story" (131). Ford's review focuses on Sherman's festering knowledge of racism in the Judge and the community, which leads him to "assert his own belief in equality" by renting a house in a white neighborhood and dying a martyr in its "bombed wreckage."

Ford also acknowledges "some shortcomings" in the novel: "a note of fantasy in the unrealistic meeting between Jester and Sherman and their behavior toward one another thereafter. Although they are both seventeen and highly intelligent, their conversation is reminiscent of *Alice in Wonderland.* No two intelligent teen-age boys in Georgia could possibly talk to one another in that fashion. For another thing, the episode of Sherman's believing that Marian Anderson was his mother and his writ-

ing her a letter to that effect is unbelievable. Finally, there is no justifica-
tion for Mrs. McCullers's use of the term 'nigger' at times when she is not
representing the speech of the characters" (132–33). The gist of Ford's
objections has to do with the portrayal of the black teenager as fey and
mincing, a portrait that he seems to believe unrealistic and a detraction
from McCullers's otherwise sensitive treatment of race.

The first extended discussion of the novel occurred within a year of its
publication. Donald Emerson (1962) sees *Clock* as consistent with McCullers's earlier work: "Conflict with 'the sense of moral isolation' is the root
experience of the people in all her work, and defeat is its inevitable outcome" (15). However, McCullers in this novel "attempts to add another
dimension by making her characters stand for the whole South. It is a
mistake. The private and the symbolic roles are not fused; the individual
and the representative do not merge" (16). The symbolic roles Emerson
presumes were intended are staples of southern liberalism: J. T. Malone is
"the conscience of the South"; Judge Clane is "the embodiment of the Old
South"; Jester Clane is "one of the 'men of good will' who may redeem
their society"; and Sherman Pew "is the rebellious Negro" (17). Among
the problems Emerson sees in the conflict between the symbolic burden
and the characters' individual psychologies is a contradiction he finds in
how Judge Clane is to be regarded. If he symbolizes the Old South, he is
"a grotesque"; if he is "a pitiable old man whose curse through life has
been a combination of sentimentality and invincible stupidity in all human
relations, the burden of his symbolic role is too great" (17). Likewise, Emerson faults the symbolic assignment of Sherman Pew as an "Outsider"
and not "the representative of a social class" (17). McCullers is
"sensitively penetrating when she deals with the inner life but fumbling
and uncertain when she attempts a social paradigm" (17–18). "Like
Baudelaire, who could see 'the hour of Eternity' in the handless clock of
his mistress' eyes, Jester in the terrified eyes of Sammy Lank finds the vision which ends his odyssey of passion, friendship, love, and revenge, and
it denies relevance to the uneasy symbolism which has been tacked onto
his experience" (18). Or it could as easily be that Emerson fails to make a
connection McCullers finds implicit: that social violence is a product of
the same selfish disorder – the desire for power over another (an
Other) – that spawns violence between the lover and the beloved.

In a New Critical exegesis of the ambiguity of McCullers's title, Emerson says it refers to Malone's "watching his time run out on a clock without hands. But when . . . Judge Clane bursts into the sickroom with news
of the decision, the reader catches the suggestion that the Court's 'all deliberate speed' is also to be measured by a clock without hands. Behind

this scene and the other references to the clock there is the implied warning 'It is later than you think,' the legend which Baudelaire is supposed to have affixed to his own handless clock in the anecdote which possibly suggested [the] title" (16). Emerson also suggests that the Judge's desire to turn back the clock is met by the question suggested in the title: "But how does one regulate a clock without hands?" (28).

Walter Allen (1964) says *Clock* is McCullers's "most obviously 'Southern' novel . . . . Owing to the greater degree of surface realism, the characters can scarcely be regarded as freaks in the old sense; they are more broadly humorous. The novel is an investigation of Southern guilt, the guilt being represented in all its ambiguity by the octogenarian politician Judge Fox Clane. The Judge is a very considerable comic figure, but pathetic also, caught in a web of evasion and rationalization in which goodwill to the Negro is one strand. Without that, there could be no guilt" (136). Allen sees no disturbing disjunction between Clane's role and that of J. T. Malone. "Malone is the clock without hands. He is utterly alone. Because of Malone, the novel exists in a dimension additional to those that condition realistic fiction generally. And for all the brilliance of the portrayal of the Judge and, even more so, of Sherman, with his fantasy-world of self-aggrandizement, it is to Malone and his fate – the ultimate human fate – that the mind first returns when remembering the novel" (137).

In an essay which acknowledges the extent to which discourse about the isolated self in literature is influenced by similar concerns in postwar popular culture, as articulated by such writers as David Riesman, Erich Fromm, Arthur Jersild, and Vance Packard, Regina Pomerantz (1964) finds that a thematic protest against "self-betrayal" links such contemporary novelists as McCullers and Salinger with the generation of Hemingway, Fitzgerald, and Sinclair Lewis. McCullers's J. T. Malone is a man mired in routine, an "other directed member of a lonely crowd" like Babbitt or Holden's numerous phonies. Only a diagnosis of leukemia reveals to him his self-betrayal. Thereafter "he finds deeply buried within himself the respect and dignity he had forgotten he had ever had. When the mob meets in the back room of his drugstore to plan their diseased and vicious terrorist act, Malone quietly refuses to join them" (27).

In his book-length critical biography of McCullers, Oliver Evans (1965a) writes, "The completion of *Clock Without Hands* . . . cannot be regarded as anything other than a moral triumph" (170). He views it as evidence of her "widening of interest and perspective." Malone, "though he knows he must die[,] . . . does not know when, and is thus like a man watching a clock without hands." With "a flash of self-knowledge born of the realization of his approaching death, he sees that he has never really lived" (171). Jester and Sherman also are in search of identity. "Jester's inherent liberalism is strengthened by the knowledge that racial injustice has been partly to blame for the tragedy of his father's life, and he resolves to become a lawyer himself and take up the battle where his father left off: his life thus achieves moral direction. Sherman is not so fortunate; he is to find his identity in martyrdom" (172). Previously, McCullers

> was concerned with the loneliness that results from a lack of rapport with other individuals; in *Clock Without Hands* she is concerned with the loneliness that results from a lack of rapport with the self. The search for self is the theme . . . and in its insistence upon the necessity for moral engagement and upon the importance of moral choice it is impossible not to recognize the impact of existential doctrine in the manner of Sartre (that is to say, anti-religious): indeed, the "existential crisis" – the achievement of identity through engagement and choice – is at the very centre of the narrative. (The book that Malone chooses to read in the hospital is Kierkegaard's *Sickness Unto Death,* and the sentence in it which most impresses him is: "The greatest danger, that of losing one's own self, may pass off as if it were nothing; every other loss, that of an arm, a leg, five dollars, a wife, etc., is sure to be noticed"). (172–73)

"And of all Mrs McCullers's books, this is the one that calls most urgently for specific reform . . . . The author seems to be saying that it is boys like [Jester Clane], educated and possessing a sense of fairness, upon whom the South must depend eventually for its moral salvation. In this respect at least *Clock Without Hands* is the most positive of Mrs McCullers's works" (177). Jester's grandfather pathetically and ignominiously "symbolizes the collapse of the old order in the South" (178). "Taken all in all, old Judge Clane, with his turnip greens and his classical allusions, is, with the exception of Mick Kelly and Frankie Addams, Mrs McCullers's most thoroughly realized character to date. Only superficially is he a caricature, and he manages to be ludicrous, pathetic, and contemptible all at the same time." However, it is not to the novel's advantage that he is so memorable: "though he dominates the book, [the Judge] is relevant in only a mechanical way to the central allegory. One is grateful for having met him, but the design of the novel requires that he play a relatively minor part. The protagonist ought to be Malone . . . . [The novel's] interest lies in [the characters'] moral progression, and in the Judge's case there is no progression, only deterioration. The author has allowed herself to be carried away in the process of creating a character who, for all his lifelikeness, is minor to her essential purpose" (180).

Evans concludes, "When, as in *The Ballad of the Sad Café,* the medium is uniformly abstract, the result is high art. When, as in *The Member of the Wedding,* the medium is an almost perfect compromise or adjustment between the abstract and the concrete, the symbolic and the realistic, the result is, again, high art. On the other hand, when the medium is uncertain, when realism struggles with allegory, and the concrete alternates and is made to compete with the abstract, the result is a hybrid. *The Heart Is a Lonely Hunter* is such a hybrid; so also . . . is *Clock Without Hands.* And both are among the most interesting American novels of the last quarter century" (187).

The pamphlet-length treatments of McCullers's career that appeared in 1969 had little good to say of the novel. Dale Edmonds finds it "a well intended embarrassment" (30), and Lawrence Graver calls it "an unhappy reminder of a talent no longer at full strength" (43). Edmonds targets improbable characterization: Jester Clane, for example, "is another character fashioned from the thinnest pasteboard. He harbors a ludicrous homosexual passion for Sherman Pew. In an unintentionally laughable sexual encounter, when Jester visits his first prostitute, he closes his eyes and keeps in mind 'a dark face and blue flickering eyes'" (30). Graver is equally critical of "lifeless and improbable characters" (45), laying blame on an obscure and sometimes absurd symbolic intention. In trying "to link the existential crisis of a man doomed by cancer to the sociological crisis of the South, poisoned by racial strife," McCullers works "against her natural grain, [and] the novel is deficient both in psychological intuition and cultural analysis" (42).

Lewis A. Lawson (1969) traces the path of the introduction of Kierkegaard's philosophy in the United States through the 1940s and 1950s, including the advocacy of W. H. Auden in his collection of *The Living Thoughts of Kierkegaard* (1952), an important connection with McCullers that goes unremarked. Lawson finds the influence of Kierkegaard reflected in novels by Richard Wright and Ralph Ellison and then in a constellation of works in the late 1950s and early 1960s, including J. D. Salinger's *Seymour, An Introduction* (1959), William Styron's *Set This House on Fire* (1960), John Updike's *Rabbit, Run* (1961), Walker Percy's *The Moviegoer* (1961), and McCullers's *Clock Without Hands.* McCullers's

> theme here is still the one to which she was always attracted, the isolation of the human heart, for she emphasizes that J. T. Malone, one of the chief characters (who is appropriately named), is suffering not only from a deadly disease but also from a deadly disease called life. Malone is said to have picked out the Kierkegaardian study [*The Sickness Unto Death*] from a hospital library cart, and certain passages from it occupy his con-

sciousness from time to time thereafter. But still the use of Kierkegaard seems extraneous and intrusive, for Malone does not need Kierkegaard's unique point of view to persuade him of the rightness of his final action, and thus the inclusion of the Kierkegaardian material simply weakens an already unsatisfactory novel. (123)

Although Lawson does not connect McCullers's existential preoccupations to the European philosophical movement influenced by Kierkegaard, the article is valuable for reminding us of the extent of *Clock's* ties to cultural motifs — angst, "leap of faith," "sickness unto death," the faces of despair — traceable to Kierkegaard.

Alice Hamilton (1970) calls *Clock* "the story of four 'adolescent' people who face death in different ways" (227). The novel "confirms some of Mrs. McCullers' earlier ideas. Men still love others for what is at that moment the dream in their own hearts. Their self is objectified in their choice of a beloved. But people in *Clock Without Hands* grow in moral stature . . . . When it ends, Malone and Jester have found pity and remorse. The old Judge doesn't know what he has said in quoting Lincoln's speech on freedom — but he has said it. Only Sherman Pew, who 'lived it up' rather than lived, died making 'senseless pounding on the piano, the senseless laughter' of some one who has lost belief in compassionate care" (228). Hamilton suggests the influence of Auden: "Probably Mrs. McCullers was remembering W. H. Auden's 'As I Walked Out One Evening' when she wrote this passage [when Malone hears the clamour of city clocks]. Her long acquaintance with Auden, his publication of selections of Kierkegaard, and the cynical voice of the city clock in the Auden poem, are too striking a combination of circumstances to be disregarded" (229n).

Floyd C. Watkins (1970) assails liberal white southern novelists for a peculiar brand of bigotry in stereotyping human relationships in the service of their political motives. In a survey of thirty-four novels written after *Brown* v. *Board of Education,* Watkins says, "Even well-known novels like Carson McCullers' *Clock Without Hands,* William Faulkner's *The Reivers,* and Harper Lee's *To Kill a Mockingbird* invent false worlds, and their racism has been widely admired" (14). In *Clock* "both the white murderer and his Negro victim are caricatures. The Negro is as loving and cultured and intelligent as the white is cruel and ignorant and stupid" (21). Sherman "has almost superhuman and clairvoyant intelligence" (25). "Some Negroes are hot-headed and passionate, but seldom is any Negro unkind or evil in cold, calculated premeditation. Thus even the Negro's crime can become symbolic of the white man's evil rather than of the Negro's. Sherman . . . acts not in anger but out of a deep-seated need to escape isolation and inadequacy. He hangs his employer's friendly dog . . . . Sherman's pitiful state is caused by the neglect of white men. He is lonely also because Southern white society unjustly executed his father for murder, and Sherman's own employer passed the sentence" (29). White southern lawmen and politicians are typically reviled. "Judge Fox Clane . . . is one of the most contemptible political figures in all these novels. He has almost all the flaws that he possibly could have" (55). "His flaws stress and emphasize the error of his violent segregationist views . . . . The South has its demagogues, but such extreme cases as this live only in the mind of a Southern white novelist" (56). Watkins concludes, "Great Southern characters of the recent past have degenerated into sentimentalized figures sketched for racist aims rather than designed as great literature . . . . Type characters are good and bad according to simple black and white racial and moral categories . . . . The death of art in the recent Southern novel perhaps was not caused by the subject of race, but the art of fiction has certainly died in novels about race since the Supreme Court decision of 1954" (64–65). Watkins also treats novels by Shirley Ann Grau, Walker Percy, Reynolds Price, Lillian Smith, Elizabeth Spencer, and Robert Penn Warren.

A lengthy and insightful essay review in 1966 (reprinted in translation, 1972) by Inna M. Levidova, head bibliographer at Moscow's Library of Foreign Literatures, brings a welcome perspective to the question of McCullers's private and public visions in the novel. Summarizing the career, which was near its end when a translation of *Clock* was published in the U.S.S.R. in 1966, in an edition of 115,000 copies, Levidova says that McCullers "occupies a special place" among contemporary Southern writers, several of whom "are already known to the Russian reader." However, "unlike the other Southerners, she is a reflective artist, quiet, strictly limiting herself to her definite themes and repeating motifs. But this is not rarefied 'chamber' literature; within the bounds of her artistic and real-life experiences she 'digs' deeply, she has a steady eye and an uncompromising intellect" (89). The situations of her characters – the dying Malone, the orphaned teenagers, the foolish judge – "are organic for McCullers: human loneliness, lost and despairing love . . . . There is, however, something totally new (though not alien to the rest of the writer's work): for the first time the political, civic theme becomes the basis of the action, its dramatic mainspring. There is nothing unexpected in this. McCullers is an artist who has rare sensitivity to human suffering and debasement of its worth" (93).

Levidova focuses acutely on the young men of the novel. "Sherman is drawn very curiously. In no way is he a stereotype of the 'good Negro,' to whom white liberals from the time of Harriet Beecher Stowe have turned.

And not at all the stylizedly primitive, sensual creature drifting through many of the books of writers of the 'Southern school.' Sherman has characteristics of that American youth of the fifties which J. D. Salinger captured so perspicaciously. But in the 'blue-eyed Negro' this confusion of feelings and cautious mistrust of the reason which is piercing through his shell is naturally burdened by something which he is fated to bear from birth and which multiplies tenfold his innate arrogant rebelliousness – the burden of race discrimination" (94). Jester is reminiscent of Mick Kelly and other girls in McCullers's fiction. He is "a youth with a man's problems. His nature is seemingly frail, vulnerable, reflective, but its core is strong and healthy and his mind works in the right direction. The writer has big hopes for Jester and is confident about his future: he will follow not his grandfather but his father, a progressive lawyer who perished tragically in the thirties during an unequal clash with the laws of the racist South" (94).

The novel is "conceived to be capacious, and one keeps expecting this conception to be overgrown with thick rustling foliage, to take on the depth and an epic quality which win one over in *The Heart Is a Lonely Hunter*. But here the nakedness of the social conflicts, the sometimes almost sketchy brevity, the point by point report on the psychological life of the heroes create the impression of something externally 'rounded off' and internally incomplete" (94). This contrast between the organic and the imposed explains as well as anyone has the source of what is deficient about the novel. "Her book is talented no matter how severely one judges it – every figure has its successful aspects and the intuitive illuminations in which her work is so rich. The Malone line of the novel is given with especial interest, subtlety, wholeness. In his process of 'spiritual assimilation' of the idea of death and his late arrival at a reevaluation of the values of his interrupted life, one cannot but catch echoes of Tolstoi's 'The Death of Ivan Ilych' – and of course Tolstoi and Dostoevsky played a great role in the formation of the writer's individuality" (95). Levidova takes issue with the translation of the novel and acknowledges difficulty in translating the distinctive tone, spirit, and rhythm of McCullers's style.

Delma Eugene Presley (1974) contends that *Clock* is both a "technical failure" and a "failure of artistic nerve." The novel's flaws offer "a poignant example of the consequences of Mrs. McCullers' perception of her native region. This novel, she said, concerned 'the South regenerate,' and 'the South finding its conscience at 11:59.' Again she treats the theme of the adolescent's quest for identity in Sherman Pew . . . and in Jester Clane . . . . [who] go through the motions of inner struggle [while] . . . J. T. Malone . . . faces the larger problem posed by his impending death.

The ending of the novel asserts hope for man when enemies dare look into the eyes of each other. No one can deny that these characters and their situations are the stuff of serious fiction. However, *Clock Without Hands* does not qualify as serious fiction. The characters' manifold, at times inconsequential, ambiguities rob their destinies of potential meaning. For example, when Jester Clane refuses to kill the Klansman Sammy Lank, he does so out of moral weakness which may be related to his previous homosexual attraction to the black victim of Lank" (29).

Presley argues that McCullers's alienation from the South mars her fiction. "The early novels and stories were written by a pessimistic young woman who, like her adolescent protagonists, longed to transcend the environment of her frustrated childhood. The last novel came from a less sober, more optimistic McCullers who claimed there was something worth saving in her South. But in *Clock Without Hands* she was unable to identify exactly what she had in mind. If her early familiarity with the South bred contempt, then her exile's unfamiliarity with it bred something worse than contempt – vacuity" (32).

McCullers, he goes on to say, "experienced the South quite differently" from the Agrarian poets and novelists "whose parents and/or grandparents were aristocrats of the Southern mind." From a different class, McCullers "did not inherit a sense of tradition, and the record she left indicates she did not attempt to embrace any tradition" (32). "One cannot know what might have happened to Carson McCullers had she remained in the land of her birth, or had she attempted to absorb the heritage, say, William Faulkner absorbed. Possibly she would have wrestled with the demon of self-destruction not a few landlocked Southern intellectuals have experienced. Out of the agony might have emerged creation of a different kind" (32). Presley's chauvinism is multidimensional, embracing allegiances to class and gender as well as region. His is one of the most substantial and important attacks launched against McCullers on the basis of biographical as well as literary evidence. The characterization of the later McCullers as "less sober" than the earlier and better writer is telling. Less noticeable on the surface is the fairly blatant hostility toward her that is linked to his sympathy for Reeves McCullers, the subject of an essay by Presley the previous year (1973). In that essay it is the ongoing love/hate relationship with Reeves that fuels her creativity; its absence after his death dooms her later fiction. So strongly does Presley advocate the victimization of Reeves McCullers that even in the 1974 article he refers to the man's "alleged suicide" (29) and suggests that *Reflections in a Golden Eye* is "an adaptation of Reeves's unpublished manuscript entitled 'Army

Post'" (28). The claim for McCullers's having appropriated her husband's story is not credible.

Charlene Kerne Clark (1975a), in assessing McCullers's place in the tradition of southern literary humor, says, "She presents us with two of the most effective examples of [the] comic aspect of death in *Clock Without Hands,* a novel which in many ways adheres more closely to the prototype of the Southern novel than any of her other works" (162–63). Citing Judge Clane's disbelief in Malone's blood disease, given that Malone "has some of the best blood in this state," Clark says, "In this type of 'juxtaposition of the immense with the trivial,' particularly in the face of impending death, Mrs. McCullers reaches her forte. A similar situation occurs at the conclusion of the novel . . . . Confronted with death, Sherman, like Faulkner's Bundren family, exhibits a greater concern for the material than the spiritual. Even at the cost of his life, he refuses to forsake his newly acquired possessions – his 'bought-on-time baby grand piano, bought-on-time genuine antique sofa and two chairs,' the 'bedroom suit, with the pink sheets and boudoir pillows,' and the 'four brand new Hart, Schaffner & Marx suits'" (163).

Margaret B. McDowell (1980) claims that McCullers "gambled audaciously in her attempt to bring together, often with deliberately abrupt transitions, the realistic portrayal of a historical political situation and symbolic fantasy; to bring together repeatedly a violent tragedy and a sequence of broadly satiric comedy; to bring together flat stereotypical figures like the Judge and a deeply understood character like J. T. Malone; and to pursue throughout an entire novel two sets of largely unrelated themes – those involving the individual's facing of death and those involving racial conflict and abuse of political and legal power" (98). McDowell convincingly demonstrates the conscious risk-taking and calculated dissonance within the work and makes a persuasive contribution to the "new reading, interpretation, and evaluation" she believes *Clock* deserves (98).

Locating the novel in McCullers's preoccupation with illness, dying, failure, and depression, McDowell takes careful note of the extent of the novel's concern with death. "In it, a half dozen deaths occur in a little over a year in 1953 and 1954 in the town of Milan, Georgia, where five other people had died in a short period eighteen years before. The earlier deaths inform McCullers' vision and intensify the brooding, somber effect generated in the novel. Two women die in childbirth, and two people slowly succumb to cancer. Violent deaths in both periods reflect racial conflict: a black man murders a white and is executed; a retarded black adolescent dies when a policeman carelessly strikes him; a black youth hangs the pet dog of a white youth and he himself is later killed when his house is bombed by racists" (96).

Judge Clane "attempts to ignore the course of history and the passage of time," thereby following a clock without hands. He "plans continually to outwit death," weeps for the orphans of Dickens but is insensitive to the two in his own household, plots the revival of Confederate currency, and waxes nostalgic for his departed wife and the Old South. "Jester's name is . . . an ironic one for a child born into a household where so much grief prevailed" (99). "Jester remains unbelievably patient – perhaps masochistic – in his attempts to secure Pew's friendship, in spite of the continual insults heaped upon him" (100), like hanging his dog! Jester relinquishes his plan to avenge Sherman's death, realizing "in a sudden revelation that his vengeful passion derives from the same bitter feelings which motivate a mob when its members engage in lynchings . . . . He begins to understand that his zeal to avenge the death of Sherman Pew may be no different from the Judge's bigotry" (101). In the final chapter Malone dies, taking a long, indifferent view of the Judge's rage over "the death of the South, because the white race has lost incontrovertible power over the black race" (102).

"Basic as Malone's death is to the thematic line . . . his presence throughout the novel contributes significantly to its aesthetic effects and structural design. He, rather than Judge Clane, provides the strong emotional center in the novel. His inevitable progress toward an unspecified moment of death, like the changing of the seasons, provides the author with a definite, but somewhat flexible, measure of the passing of time. Because Malone witnesses, or comments upon, most of the situations and characters in the novel – as well as the momentous events which occurred eighteen years earlier – he provides the work with a degree of unity. As a middle-aged man, he becomes a pivotal figure between the outmoded political and social views of the elderly Judge Clane and Jester Clane and Sherman Pew. A relatively inarticulate person, Malone continually supplements with his silent musings the voice of the narrator and extends the range of the authorial comment by thus indicating his own point of view" (111).

If Malone is pivotal, other structurally important characters work in parallel. Jester "parallels Sherman Pew as a youth of similar age, as a person who bows to the Judge's authority and who is responsible to the Judge for financial support, while rejecting his views. Jester Clane's dream is to perform a solo flight in his plane, and he attains the dream; Sherman Pew's dream is to play his grand piano in his own house, and he also attains his dream. The two are paired in the tragic circumstances that surrounded the year of their birth and in their independent but almost simultaneous discovery of these long-kept secrets" (111). Jester is unsuccessful in preventing the death of Sherman; his father did not prevent the death of Sherman's father.

Critics of Judge Clane as a caricature wrong McCullers's control of her materials and design. "Had he been less clearly a caricature, . . . the political satire would have become too insistent and portentous, and thereby detracted from McCullers' probing of the mysteries of death. The farcical comedy – most broadly contrived in the absurd 'murder' of the Judge, who simply refuses to notice that he has been 'killed' by Sherman Pew's injecting water instead of insulin in his veins for three days – would not have registered so incisively had the Judge's humanity been more fully established. Pew must finally shrug his shoulders on the fourth day and admit that the Judge and what he symbolizes is too strong for an assassination attempt" (112).

The Supreme Court decree of equal education is "mediated through the senile babbling of a man who will try to live as if it were still 'four score and seven years ago.' McCullers refuses at every point . . . to countenance an easy hope for better conditions in the future or to glorify the legendary past" (114). "McCullers, to a greater degree than in her earlier novels, focused in this last book upon the economic, political, and ideological aspects of the South as it was undergoing, or else resisting, change. Although she experimented with techniques of political satire, the exploiting of stereotype for ironic effect, and a stylized comedy of manners, her greatest talent remained where it had always been – in her dramatization of internal conflict in her characters. Racial antagonism, political controversy, class differences, and the barriers between generations are all issues explored in this novel, primarily as realities which magnify loneliness, isolation, and internal conflict" (115).

Clifton Snider (1982) describes the novel's congeniality to Jungian interpretation and its exemplification of the stages of dying outlined by Elisabeth Kubler-Ross, though the novel preceded publication of Kubler-Ross's *On Death and Dying* (1969). The stages of dying treated, largely through Malone but also incidentally through Judge Clane and Sherman Pew, are (1) "denial, common to most terminally ill patients"; (2) "anger, rage, envy, and resentment"; (3) "bargaining [as] an attempt 'to postpone the inevitable happening'"; (4) depression; and (5) inevitable acceptance. "On the unconscious level, Malone has achieved what Jung calls individuation, the integration of the self. In his decision to rise above violence against Sherman Pew, he has conquered his own shadow – the beast within. His wife, from whom he had been estranged for most of his mar riage in spite of the fact they had continued to live together, is symbolic of the contrasexual, the anima; and in loving her again he has achieved as much of a union with the anima as he can" (45).

In a keenly particularized discussion of language in the novel, Lynn Veach Sadler (1988) suggests that *Clock* is "about the blurring of such distinctions as Black and White in a common identity that appreciates language as a *human* institution and about the role language plays in reconciling us with our humanity" (49). "Clane, Jester, and Pew are linked by their attraction to language, and this trait separates them from Malone, a generally silent man. His reconciliation is largely traditional as he realizes the miracles of nature and moves with its rhythms" (49).

Among Sadler's other observations about the significance of language is this comment on the ending: "The great authorial joke on the Judge . . . is his inability to speak his protest against integration on the radio; he can only recite the Gettysburg Address." Ironically, "the seasons do tell time and far more gently than the 'clock without hands' . . . that drives Malone; the noon whistle of the mill; the noon hour that permits the Judge his first toddy; or the city clock . . . . " Furthermore, "Jester's experiences also constantly demand new understandings of words, their relativity, and their quick silverness." Sherman's "penchant for the aphoristic is keener than the Judge's – and Sherman's aphorism . . . is true. The victim of Judge Clane's manipulation of words, he finally exposes the ultimate danger of their *under*valuing: 'Knowing nothing about what the Judge was discussing, Sherman responded to rhetoric, repetition and rhythm, to the language of passionate demagoguery, senseless and high flown . . . '" (50–51). "McCullers exposes the Judge through his relationships to language. He can apply beautiful light imagery . . . and, ironically, sees Johnny's losing the Jones case as a failure of rhetoric and style: simple truth plus the verbal sin of getting tongue-tied" (51). "Golden-tongued with Southern oratory Judge Clane can be, nonetheless, and we appreciate, for example, if not his ignorance of and crimes against Latin, his 'push come to shovel' . . . and his sense of having had 'not only to raise but to rear' Jester . . . . We know how Verily hates his standard Sunday dinner joke, a play on her name and on scripture . . . . Or cliche serves a verbal rigidity that is a lie before it is formed: 'White is white and black is black – and never the two shall meet if I can prevent it.' . . . Sherman Pew is neither one or the other" (52). "Like Malone, he has come to rely on the words of books, but his appreciation for *Diet Without Despair* parodies the fixation of J. T. on *Sickness Unto Death.*" Jester and Sherman are special examples of play with language. "Both boys are impressed by such words as 'stygian,['] and Sherman coins ('epizootical,' . . .) easily. Not to be outdone, Jester salutes the 'nocturnal evening'" (52). The Judge bans the *Kin-sey Report* but reads it behind the cover of *The Decline and Fall of the Roman Empire*. McCullers's "appreciation for the interplay between literal and figural is displayed throughout in the references to time; for the web language weaves in her images of light and jewels; and for the interchangeability of art forms, in her reliance on music, both as itself and as analogy. She is also mistress of the authorial purple passage, as in her beautiful intrusion into Jester's plane ride . . . . McCullers and her favored characters see pink mules and delight in language that shares them" (53). Her point seems to be that language leads the characters toward a reconciliation not with death but with life.

Donna Bauerly (1988) suggests that "one of the major influences on McCullers' perception of love was . . . Denis de Rougement," author of *Love in the Western World* and resident in the famous February House in Brooklyn Heights. De Rougement's use of the concepts of Eros and agape echo in McCullers's pronouncements about the lover and the beloved. But, for her, "Eros becomes an image of the isolating individual self-concern that causes unhappiness" (72). "All of McCullers' fiction centers around this flight from narcissism and search for authentic love" (73). In *Hunter* "McCullers traces a strange personal growth in Biff, who moves from the confining love of marriage to a kind of universal and androgynous love, a love for all humanity . . . . [His] final vision allows him a momentary glimpse of the true love of Agape, of fellowship" (73). Bauerly reads Jester Clane as the protagonist of *Clock Without Hands* and says his "journey from the Love of Eros to the Love of Agape is set against a backdrop of the struggles of two other major characters – J. T. Malone . . . and Sherman Pew" (75).

Virginia Spencer Carr (1990) traces McCullers's work on the novel in embryo, a story called "The Pestle," to her stay at Yaddo in 1942, nearly twenty years before its completion, and to the influence of W. H. Auden's enthusiasm for Kierkegaard, urged on McCullers during their joint residence at February House. Reading the novel as an exploration of existential choice, Carr says that *Clock* "exemplifies her faith in the ultimate victory of *agape*" (114). Carr says McCullers's scathing portrait of the First Baptist Church of Milan, Georgia, and its inept pastor may be evidence of her dissatisfaction with religion as practiced but not evidence of a lack of Christian faith. Gleaning from the passage memorized from *Sickness Unto Death* knowledge of his loss of self and, consequently, a heightened sense of his "livingness," Malone "resembles Captain Penderton, who 'suddenly began to live' during his wild ride on Firebird when he was sure that he would die . . . . Of all McCullers's despairing characters, only Captain

Penderton rivals Malone in his profound sense of moral aloneness. So, too, does life take on a new awareness for Malone" (117–18). "To McCullers, Malone's real sickness is not leukemia, but existential despair" (118). He is confronted by two existential choices: the temptation to take his own life and the refusal to take the life of Sherman Pew. He answers affirmatively to both, though the first is a false choice, as his overdose of sleeping pills brings sleep but not death. The second, genuine choice brings "Malone's ultimate epiphany . . . in his awareness that he is dying, finally, and his former revulsions give way to a strange lightness and exaltation" (119).

Sherman Pew, like *Hunter's* Dr. Copeland, "does not 'fit in' with his race, yet vibrates with every injustice his people have suffered" (120). Carr also likens him to Honey Brown in *Member*. In a perhaps too generous view of the matter, Carr says that Jester's homoerotic passion for Sherman distills itself into "an abiding love, a trust-filled friendship, that poses no sexual threat to either of them" (122). Jester acquires purpose and perspective from his experience of agape. Carr concludes, "Despite the novel's being more often than not remembered as the unfortunate end to a brilliant writing career, it remains today an inspiring manifestation of the author's own existential will to live and to write a notable work despite great adversity" (125).

Such a "notable work" is ripe for reassessment, particularly through analyses sensitive to the interaction of race, class, and gender. New insights into the social construction of masculinity, now arising from feminist theories of gender and sexuality, might profitably be used to understand the tragicomic pairing of Sherman Pew and Jester Clane or the gendered politics of race hatred and class prejudice, rooted in proofs of male potency or territoriality. Furthermore, the Brechtian dissonance between horror and comedy needs to be more precisely traced in McCullers's work generally, and specifically in this novel. The jarring relationship between levels of outrage, comic and tragic, has not yet been functionally explored. Is McCullers striving here (and in *Square Root, Ballad,* and *Reflections* particularly) for the postmortem effects now associated with the black comedy of Joseph Heller, John Hawkes, John Barth, Kurt Vonnegut, Thomas Pynchon, and the postmodern? The refusal to read the novel as viable on two levels may be evidence of a lack of critical agility in the era into which it was released. Or it may stem from the fact that the novels that would be recognized as paradigmatic of this absurdist strain were still a few years in the future, and the methods in place for reading McCullers, the wunderkind, were too well set, too institutionalized to permit recognition of the heightened "Sense of the Awful" she evokes in *Clock Without Hands*.

8: Stories, Essays, and Poems

MCCULLERS'S CONTRIBUTIONS TO short fiction are perhaps best represented not by the story but by the novella. It was in fact with the publication of her most successful novella, *The Ballad of the Sad Café*, that her six most distinguished stories were collected in 1951. "Wunderkind," "The Jockey," "Madame Zilensky and the King of Finland," "The Sojourner," "A Domestic Dilemma," and "A Tree. A Rock. A Cloud." as well as two others ("Correspondence" and "Art and Mr. Mahoney") had appeared singly in such magazines as *Mademoiselle, Harper's Bazaar,* and the *New Yorker* before the first collected edition. "The Haunted Boy" was added in a 1955 edition. A posthumous collection, *The Mortgaged Heart* (1971), edited by McCullers's sister, Margarita G. Smith, included fourteen stories as well as fifteen essays, five poems, and McCullers's outline of "The Mute" *(The Heart Is a Lonely Hunter)*. Five stories – "Court in the West Eighties," "Poldi," "The Orphanage," "The Aliens," and "Untitled Piece" – had their initial publication here; three others – "Breath from the Sky," "Instant of the Hour After," and "Like That" – were sold to *Redbook* for publication immediately preceding publication of *The Mortgaged Heart.* Other previously published but uncollected stories included are "Sucker" and "Who Has Seen the Wind?" All nineteen stories first appeared together in 1987 in *Collected Stories,* introduced by Virginia Spencer Carr. That volume also reprinted *The Member of the Wedding* and *The Ballad of the Sad Café.* One story, "The March," published by *Redbook* in 1967, was omitted by both posthumous collections.

The two collections represent substantial events in the course of McCullers's reputation. Individual stories had earlier achieved a certain prominence by virtue of awards ("The Jockey," 1942; "A Tree. A Rock. A Cloud," 1944; and "The Sojourner," 1951, included in the *O. Henry Memorial Award Prize Stories* volumes); television adaptation ("The Sojourner," adapted for Omnibus Theater as "The Invisible Wall" in 1953); and fortuitous anthologizing (such as the inclusion of "A Domestic Dilemma" in Cleanth Brooks and Robert Penn Warren's influential textbook *Understanding Fiction,* 2nd ed., 1959; or "Who Has Seen the Wind?" in *40 Best Stories from Mademoiselle,* 1960). However, critical attention to other individual stories and, of course, to the stories as a whole was entirely a consequence of the posthumous collections.

Response to *The Mortgaged Heart* was mixed, with favorable reviews focusing on the value of the stories for an understanding of the novels and negative reviews discounting the literary significance of many of the essays and several early stories. The image of McCullers as a wunderkind was duly and reasonably revived by many reviewers who commented on the quality of the apprentice stories, several of which were written while McCullers was a teenager. The cover art draws attention precisely to this fact. Photographed in 1938, a youthful, willowy McCullers wades ankle-deep in a sparkling stream; her hair falls long and loose over one shoulder; her left hand lifts her summer dress slightly, as if to protect it from the water. The impression is totally feminine and totally uncharacteristic – a marked contrast to the white-shirted tomboy waif who appears on early dust jackets and in celebrity photographs. Reviewers said that the collection "reveals the early emergence of McCullers' talent and growth as an artist"; she is "one of the most gifted but underrated authors of the 20th century" *(Choice* 1972, 61). The stories show "glimpses of her genius for characterization, her ability to shadow forth a vague sense of disaster, her power to fuse the poles of anguish and farce" (Howes 1971, B7). Paul Theroux, writing for the London *Times,* observes that the collection constitutes "a kind of literary biography" which reveals "the style and perception developing and expressing a unique sensibility" (1972, 10). Other reviewers protested that the volume shows McCullers to her disadvantage (Avant 1972, 73) and that its value is that of "a memento for collectors" (Clemons 1971, 7). Critical commentary in the United States often compared *The Mortgaged Heart* with a collection of stories by Flannery O'Connor, finding O'Connor the superior stylist but McCullers the creator of more compelling characters and situations.

The English reviews typically paired *The Mortgaged Heart* with an edition of *The Shorter Novels and Stories* of McCullers, both issued in 1972 by Barrie and Jenkins of London. The reviewer for the *New Statesman and Nation* appears to continue that magazine's customary condescension toward McCullers in suggesting that the journalistic essays "would have been better forgotten" and that the title is "awful." However, there is much to praise in the early stories, which "display cool and lucid detail wonderfully fused with the psychological current of narrative." Together the two volumes show "how magnificently she perfected and complicated the earlier pattern" (Dunn 1972, 756). *The Guardian* remarks on the autobiographical details supplied by Margarita Smith's introduction, written four years after McCullers's death and painfully allusive to McCullers's final infirmities, saying, "There is material here for a legend, and the work is probably just sufficient to sustain it" (Nye 1972, 24). Nadine Gordimer in the *London Magazine* makes the appearance of *The Mortgaged Heart* the occasion for a full discussion of McCullers's career. Gordimer observes, "If Carson McCullers was one of the very few great talents to come out of America since the war — and every critic bobs an obeisance to that — her early writings must be of the deepest interest" (1972, 134). Although "not an outstanding short story writer," McCullers left in the early stories important evidence of her development. "In them one can follow, fascinated, the private apprenticeship of a writer — without guild, without master, an apprenticeship to oneself, standing by all the while with one eye screwed up in assessment" (135). The result was the formidable craft of the novelist: "She is the high priestess of adolescence: not just the physical adolescence of some of her best characters, but of a kind of second adolescence, an ambivalent state of spiritual possibility, a state of growth outside the optimum of bones and arteries in which she sees the maimed as having a head start" (136).

The publication of *The Mortgaged Heart* elicited two other omnibus review essays. One certifies the collection as "excellent for classroom instruction" (Kelly 1982, 68); the second is a measured tribute by younger-generation southern fiction writer David Madden, for whom "Carson McCullers was the Goddess Muse of my creative adolescence" (1972, 161). The compatibility of McCullers's fiction with the educational interests of adolescents has been both a boon and a stigma. Her influence on contemporary writers, apart from isolated tributes such as Madden's, has been insufficiently studied. Madden's verdict on *The Mortgaged Heart* is, however, vicious in its outsized contempt for a handful of essays and articles that constitute only forty pages of the collection. He calls them "textbook examples of shallow, cliché-ridden, stereotyped women's magazine trivia whose dubious fascination is that a fine writer hacked them out." Madden's admiration for the bulk of the stories, essays, and poems belies his initial judgment that the collection presents "the mediocre side" of McCullers and "enables us to see the writer's virtues ineffectively employed in her early work and her early faults put to good use in her later work" (137–38).

The posthumous collection appeared too late to gain McCullers a place in the comprehensive scholarly treatments of the American short story that began to appear in the 1950s and 1960s. She receives brief mention in such books by Ray B. West (1952) and William Peden (1964). However, two scholarly articles respond to *The Mortgaged Heart* directly. Irving H. Buchen (1974) takes "The Flowering Dream: Notes on Writing" as his text for a Freudian discussion of McCullers's aesthetics. Robert S. Phillips (1978) focuses on the thematics of spiritual isolation treated in

"The Flowering Dream" as a key to the stories as well as the novels, with
the difference that the stories treat the theme "with less sensationalism . . .
and often with true distinction" (73). The stories "are all less likely to be
labeled 'Gothic' or 'grotesque' when compared to her novels. For whatever reason, there is less physical abnormality in the stories. Instead of
mutes and dwarfs, what we generally encounter here are people isolated
by circumstance rather than physical appearance or malady. Instead of
freaks we find an inner freaking-out" (66). This essay owes as much to the
publication of Virginia Spencer Carr's biography (1975) as to *The Mortgaged Heart,* though it uses Carr's revelations lamely, as in suggesting that
McCullers's choice of a boy's point of view in such stories as "Sucker"
and "The Haunted Boy" "may have roots deeper than mere considerations of technique" – i.e., may be an expression of homosexuality. One
wonders what Buchen might have done with his analysis had he had the
benefit of the biography.

The appearance of *Collected Stories* on the twentieth anniversary of
McCullers's death, sixteen years after *The Mortgaged Heart* and twelve
years after Carr's *The Lonely Hunter,* elicited a more fundamentally focused
response. The volume contains only fiction (the stories and two short
novels) and thereby avoids the distraction presented by the journalistic
pieces in the earlier collection. Virginia Spencer Carr's introduction,
moreover, invites the biographical reading often given to the stories in this
incarnation. Although *Collected Stories* drew the standard dismissive labels – "limited," "monotonous" subject matter and treatment (Desmond
1988, 458) – two of the most important reviews suggest that the collection
should liberate McCullers from outmoded categories. Michiko Kakutani
of the *New York Times* observes that most of the stories do not partake of
McCullers's "penchant for gothic melodrama"; they do, however, strike a
contemporary reader as "old-fashioned," owing to the "knowing authorial
voice" that they share. "While admiring the author's rich storytelling gifts,
we're also reminded why her better known works are so frequently
taught in high school English courses: They're well-crafted parables, easy
to decipher and easy to comprehend" (1987, C20). Katherine Dieckmann's *Village Voice* review replies in part to Kakutani with the acknowl-
edgment that "the words *Carson McCullers* and *high school* go hand in hand.
That's where she's read, in low-priced paperbacks with embarrassingly
soulful cover art, and that's where she's abandoned – adults rarely return
to assigned texts once they can choose their own booklists." Dieckmann
urges readers to "return to McCullers, and you'll be shocked at what you
never knew then, that she knew, that you know now." McCullers practices a minimalist prose style charged with "complicated emotions that

know no age and no restricted reader." The review acknowledges as well
the role of McCullers's personal history – "frequent illnesses, suicide attempts, problems with sexual identity, and her miserable marriage to
Reeves McCullers" – in creating "an air of gloomy eccentricity, which
distracts from her true achievement: the production of taut, ringing prose,
economic and precise." *Collected Stories* "shows off the full range of McCullers's sympathies, which extend far beyond the misshapen outcasts she's
famous for," and "may finally win [for its author] the grown-up status she
deserves" (1987, 58).

Prior to the publication of the two collections, the only substantial
treatments of the short fiction focused on a single story. Oliver Evans's
chapter (1965a) on "A Tree. A Rock. A Cloud." is the best early example.
This extended discussion is unique in book-length treatments of McCullers before 1980. Margaret B. McDowell's Twayne study of that year and
Carr's *Understanding Carson McCullers* (1990) adduce notable general patterns among the stories that deserve comment before concentrating on
trends in the interpretation of individual stories.

Most prominent among the patterns are assertions of the stories' connection with or differences from the novels. "Instead of being approached
as discrete works of art, worthy of evaluation on their own terms, too often [the stories] tend to be utilized primarily as source material" (Petry
1988, 31). Calling the stories "her least impressive work," Mark Schorer
observes that "many . . . abandon that southern setting that is most congenial to her talent and, apparently, necessary to its fullest expression"
(1963, 84). More often, emphasis on the distinctions between stories and
novels typically devolves into the contrast noted by Phillips (1978) of pain
externalized more (in novels) or less (in stories). This distinction appears
in Madden's review of *The Mortgaged Heart* and Carr's introduction to
Collected Stores as abnormal (novels) vs. normal (stories) behavior and condition: the "early stories reveal a much more normal family – comfortably
middle-class – than the novels suggest" (Madden 1972, 143); and characters in the stories "have none of the physical grotesqueries that mark her
longer works" (Carr 1987b, ix). Carr notes as well that half of the stories
are set outside the South, a departure from the consistent southern settings of the novels. "In the novels McCullers strove for grand moments;
in the stories, for quiet occasions which nevertheless are vital occasions"
(Phillips 1978, 68). If, as William Peden claims, "the depiction of the mentally ill and the emotionally maimed became one of the major directions
taken by the American short story since 1940" (1964, 88), McCullers's
stories of alcoholic debility and childhood emotional wounds are in step
with their times.

More often critics have noted the formative importance of the stories. Characters, situations, narrative techniques, and sometimes actual passages originate in stories and emerge more memorably in the novels (Madden 1972). Prototypes of John Singer in *The Heart Is a Lonely Hunter* have been discovered in "Court in the West Eighties," "The Aliens," and "Untitled Piece" (Carr 1990). "Untitled Piece" is in fact less a freestanding story than an early draft of portions of that novel (Smith 1971). Mr. Brook of "Madame Zilensky and the King of Finland" is, improbably, linked to Biff Brannon (Carr 1990). Early versions of Mick Kelly can be seen in "Like That" (Carr 1990) and "Correspondence" (Edmonds 1972; McDowell 1980). Henky Evans in the latter story also prefigures Frankie Addams of *The Member of the Wedding* (Edmonds 1972; Carr 1990), as does Frances in "Wunderkind" (Evans 1965a). The relationships in "Sucker" constitute a same-sex version of Mick's treatment of Bubber (McDowell 1980; Carr 1990) and Frankie's treatment of John Henry (McDowell 1980). Bitsy Barlow in "The Jockey" presages Cousin Lymon in *The Ballad of the Sad Café* (Carr 1990).

Autobiographical elements of the stories have been usefully noted. "Correspondence" derives from McCullers's pique over her husband's failure to answer her letters from Yaddo in summer 1941 (Carr 1990). The case for McCullers's beloved piano teacher, Mary Tucker, as a model for the betrayal reflected in "Sucker" and "Like That" (Carr 1990) is less persuasive. "Wunderkind," however, by McCullers's own testimony, grew out of their pupil-teacher relationship.

Characteristic themes have been effectively demonstrated. One of the most typical is that of the incomplete or "fragmented family" (Carr 1990, 142) in such stories as "The Aliens," "A Domestic Dilemma," or "The Sojourner." As in the novels, mothers are either absent from the stories or portrayed as abnormal. Fathers are distant but, for the most part, favorably portrayed (Carr 1990). Spiritual isolation lies behind the tropes of characters hungry for communication, as in "Sucker" and "Correspondence," or tense to the point of explosion, as in "The Haunted Boy," "Like That," and "Poldi" (Madden 1972). Like the novels, the stories contain a preponderance of artist figures, as in "Wunderkind," "The Sojourner," and "Madame Zilensky and the King of Finland" (Buchen 1974).

Although the critical attention to individual stories has run counter to the order of their composition, stories from the 1940s and 1950s having been published and therefore recognized well before stories from the 1930s, approaching them in chronological order has the advantage of making easier and more obvious the connections among them. The earli-

est of the collected stories, "Sucker" lay buried among McCullers's manu-
scripts until discovered by dissertation researcher Simeon Mozart Smith,
Jr. (1964). It was published by the *Saturday Evening Post* in September 1963
with a note from McCullers that she had written it when she was seventeen. In embryonic form, "Sucker" reveals the pattern of fascination and
rejection experienced by each of McCullers's lovers and "duplicated most
precisely" in *The Ballad of the Sad Café* (Evans 1965a, 25). Sucker adores
his older cousin Pete, who responds magnanimously to the boy when his
own relationship with Maybelle is thriving. Rejected by Maybelle, Pete
rejects Sucker, who, spurned, rejects Pete. "At first 'Sucker' seems to be
the story of the narrator, Pete, and the pull between *agape* (Pete and
Sucker) and *eros* (Pete and Maybelle). But by the time of the story's climax, the awful scene in which Pete tells Sucker he doesn't care for him
one bit, we realize the story bears the correct title after all. It *is* Sucker's
story, the story of an outsider who tries to fit in. In one epiphany he is
made to realize he never will, and thus he freaks out and becomes a hard-
ened rebel" (Phillips 1978, 66).

A first-person narrative from Pete's point of view, the story shows
McCullers's attempt "to imitate the spontaneous language of the child or
the adolescent [which] results in looseness of organization, relatively un-
connected expressions of emotion, and the inclusion of irrelevant detail"
(McDowell 1980, 120). With its parallel first-person story, "Like That,"
"Sucker" constitutes a stage in McCullers's development of artistic control
over her material, which McDowell identifies with the shift to omniscient
viewpoint (121). Carr calls this apprentice work a story of a child's "fall
from innocence" (1990, 132).

McCullers, through an agent, unsuccessfully circulated "Sucker" and
"Court in the West Eighties" in 1939. First published in *The Mortgaged
Heart,* "Court in the West Eighties" is a "fairly successful story told in the
first person by a young woman who resembles McCullers" (Madden
1972, 141–42). The narrator's belief that the redheaded man visible in the
apartment across the court is as troubled as she is by the conflicts observed in and between other apartments is an example of "the self-
generated illusion" that characterizes McCullers's "hero-witness relationships" in the novels and later stories (150). To Robert Phillips the supposed hero figure is "a demiurge, looking on unfeelingly while a young
jobless couple . . . slowly starve. McCullers injects a potent symbol into
the story in the form of a balloon man – that is, a man made of balloons,
bearing a silly grin and hanging perpetually from one apartment window.
He is an effigy mocking mankind and man's helplessness. In the world of
McCullers's imagination we are all dangling, hanged men" (1978, 69).

Written for Sylvia Chatfield Bates's course at New York University and published thirty-five years later in *The Mortgaged Heart,* "Poldi" appears to be a companion piece to "Court in the West Eighties." It is "a thin, superficial third person story told from the point of view of a young man in love with [the title character]," a female cellist (Madden 1972, 142). Showing "the McCullers love formula at work," the story portrays the hopeless attachment of the young man to Poldi and her infatuation with "a pianist named Kurt, whom she has seen only three times in her life" (Phillips 1978, 69).

"Breath from the Sky," also an early story published first in 1971 in *Redbook* and *The Mortgaged Heart,* is singular in McCullers's fiction for examining the interaction between a mother and daughter, in this case on the eve of the daughter's transfer to a sanitarium for the treatment of tuberculosis. Constance, named perhaps for her sustained suffering, helplessly watches the imposed normalcy of her mother's attention to younger siblings, her brother, Howard, and sister, Mick. Constance is one of McCullers's spiritual orphans, "orphaned from her family not by parental death, but by her own invalidism. Both her shorn hair and the cut flowers are symbolic of the sapping of her strength, the nipping of the bloom of her youth" (Phillips 1978, 67). Describing the story as a realistic portrayal of a dying child, McDowell says that the frank "depiction of the ugliness of her disease, and the petulance, weariness, and self-loathing of the patient sweep aside any trace of sentimentality" (1980, 118). Seeing empathy rather than revulsion in the mother's barely perceptible shudder as she turns from Constance, Carr interprets the work as a "thinly disguised" and not unsympathetic portrait of McCullers's mother. "Ultimately, the story is as much the mother's as it is the ailing daughter's" (1990, 139–40).

"The Orphanage," a sketch first published in *The Mortgaged Heart,* recounts circumstances by which the image of a fetus in formaldehyde became associated in the narrator's memory with children in the local orphanage. The girl is shown the fetus, a lab specimen from pharmacy school, by older children and told it was an orphan. Visits to the orphanage with her grandmother fix the troubling association yet suggest a camaraderie among the residents that excludes the girl. Carr points out the similarity between this tale of exclusion and the anecdote that begins the essay "The Flowering Dream," a story from McCullers's childhood of feeling left out of a children's party taking place behind the walls of a convent. "The Orphanage" is a "prosaic slice-of-life that has no plot or character development (and very little movement)"; yet it is prototypical of McCullers's familiar theme of the excluded child (Carr 1990, 138).

Published in *Redbook* and then in *The Mortgaged Heart* in 1971, "Instant of the Hour After" was submitted as a class assignment to Sylvia Bates, who returned it with the comment, "I like this the least of anything you have done" (qtd. Smith 1971, 62). There is little to like or admire of characters or incident. After an evening of drunken chess and conversation with a male friend, husband and wife prepare for bed, he with slurred insults and bullying, she with ire and pity for his condition. The earliest of three domestic stories about alcoholism (including "A Domestic Dilemma" and "Who Has Seen the Wind?"), "Instant of the Hour After" can hardly be read without reference to the alcoholic strife of Carson and Reeves McCullers. Written when McCullers was nineteen years old, before her marriage but after she and Reeves had begun to live together, the story has seemed a prophecy of their relationship, especially after the revelations of Carr's biography, published only four years after the story's posthumous appearance. Apart from admiring the arresting image of the husband and wife as monkeys trapped in a bottle, "skeetering" crazily up and down the sides without a word to each other, critics have had little to say about the story's quality or importance.

Whit Burnett's *Story* magazine purchased "Like That" in 1936, along with "Wunderkind," but withheld "Like That" from publication. Discovered in the magazine's archives at Princeton University, "Like That" first appeared in *Redbook* and *The Mortgaged Heart*. Told in first person by a girl who watches the effects of her older sister's experience of first menstruation and later, presumably, first sexual intercourse, the story is a companion piece to "Sucker." Rebellion in this instance takes the form of "resist[ing] rather than embrac[ing] maturation" (Phillips 1978, 67).

Submitted to *Story* at the urging of Sylvia Bates, "Wunderkind" is McCullers's first published work of fiction, appearing in December 1936 under her name at that time, Carson Smith. An example of McCullers's own precocity, the story has been praised for the technical dexterity of its point of view and its thematic richness. McDowell calls it "a maze of paradoxes" developed with "precision and sensitivity" (1980, 121, 123). Most critics have acknowledged, as did McCullers, the autobiographical origins of the story. Written in response to the loss of Mary Tucker, her piano teacher, through a move from Georgia to California, the plot of "Wunderkind" allows McCullers, superficially if not emotionally, to reverse the loss. In this version, the would-be prodigy abandons her teacher, though it might easily be argued that the girl's teacher has already withdrawn his approval from her. Frances is a solitary figure in a landscape populated by superior males. Except for Bilderbach's silent wife, Frances finds herself without allies and out of favor with those on whose good opinion she has depended, the teachers Bilderbach and Lafkowitz and her erstwhile peer, Heime Israelsky. Interpretations diverge on two major points: the role of Heime and the meaning of the ending.

To Richard M. Cook, Heime is a member of what "had become for [Frances] an exotic second family," an "exclusive, rarefied paradise" from which her realization that she is ordinary, merely, and no wunderkind, has expelled her (1975, 7). To McDowell, Heime is unproblematical, "a mere distraction," but the ending admits of two readings. It may signal maturity in "her facing of herself as a human being who struggles and still fails," or it may constitute a devastating realization "that she earlier had lost irretrievably her life as an ordinary child, a life marked by noise, confusion, and laughter – and until now, she did not know that the loss of such experience mattered at all" (1980, 122).

Carr says, "Through her teacher, Frances becomes aware not only of her own musical ineptitude, but also of her evolving sexuality" (1990, 134). The relationship between the two – female sexuality and failed talent – was explored in detail earlier by Constance M. Perry (1986). To demonstrate the links among "Wunderkind," *The Heart Is a Lonely Hunter,* and their creator's perception of abandonment by Mary Tucker, Perry patiently traces the development in each plot of the "conflict between a young person's developing talent and her emerging sexuality" in a culture which regards girls and women as inferior to boys and men (39). "Wunderkind" serves as "McCullers's first trial of the theme [that] adolescence brings a paralyzing knowledge of inadequacy to the exceptional girl and bars her passage into the world of art" (37). McCullers's adolescent attachment to Mary Tucker was complicated by homoerotic feelings for her. Such feelings intensified McCullers's sense of betrayal when Tucker announced her impending move. Perry believes "Wunderkind" encodes the association of love and art, desire and loss in Frances's fear and inability to perform the Beethoven sonata with the passion expected by the patriarchs – Bilderbach, Lafkowitz, and the composer himself, the father of twenty children. "Male sexuality becomes associated with musical ability"; Frances cannot "risk exposure of her inadequate femininity," and so, like the adolescent McCullers, "the character Frances quits her lessons" (39). Only Heime, her double, can make "a happy transition from his *Wunderkind* adolescence to adult masculinity . . . . Her realization that she cannot match Heime's success so alienates her mind from her body that she can no longer command herself to play . . . . Frances's ability and desire to be a musician collapse when she realizes that her gender probably thwarts her chance for success like Heime's in the world of art" (39).

Another view of the role of sexuality in the story is offered by Alice Hall Petry (1988), who reads it as "a remarkable rendering of an adolescent's turmoil over her growing awareness of her sexual passion for her music teacher . . . [which is complicated] by her tendency to regard him as a father figure" (31). Quoting passages that, if "read out of context, one would assume . . . a failed sexual encounter, not a piano lesson" (35), Petry argues that the story is "subtle but quite insistent" in "blurring . . . the pedagogical, paternal and amorous dimensions of Bilderbach" (33). The change that has occurred in Frances, she suggests, a change Frances cannot detect in Heime, is associated with menstruation. When she runs from Bilderbach's apartment into the street filled with "other children," Frances temporarily regresses into "an asexual, prelapsarian world to which she can never return, no matter how hard she runs. After all, a 'wunderkind,' by literal definition, is a 'kind' − a *child*. It was an appropriate label for a twelve-year-old, but at fifteen Frances is occupying the tenuous world of the adolescent. As she has been outgrowing her status as a child, she is simultaneously being pressured into adulthood − and with that transformation comes the awareness (even if it cannot yet be articulated) that she has been responding to Bilderbach on a physical level" (36). The ending marks a failed "rite de passage" (37), motivated perhaps by McCullers's personal crisis of sexual identity.

"The Aliens" first appeared in *The Mortgaged Heart*. It is "a static, rather pointless sketch," told in third person from the point of view of Felix Kerr, "a fifty-year-old Jewish man going to live in the South" (Madden 1972, 142). The character is widely recognized as a prototype of John Singer in *The Heart Is a Lonely Hunter*.

"Untitled Piece" also appeared first in *The Mortgaged Heart*. In it Andrew Leander, now age twenty, recalls two earlier periods in his life − the attempt to build a glider plane at age thirteen with his younger sister and sexual intercourse at age seventeen with the family's cook, Vitalis. Calling Andrew "a male Frankie," whose "one act of union and love has forced his separation and fear," Phillips characterizes his lovemaking with Vitalis as "unpremeditated miscegenation" (1978, 68). David Madden links this "static memory piece" with other stories of childhood or adolescence that seem to concern "a girl much like McCullers, who has a sister and a brother like her own" (1972, 141). Included in this grouping are "Orphanage," from the point of view of McCullers as a child; "Breath from the Sky," from the point of view of McCullers as an adolescent; and "Like That," in which "McCullers seems to be trying to look at herself as an adolescent tormented by love through the eyes of her little sister, Margarita" (141). However, he is surely wrong in believing that McCullers experiments with her brother's point of view in "Untitled Piece"; the twenty year old returning home, though given male identity and experiences, is more likely McCullers herself, whose sense of being a misfit in her small town in Georgia arose in part from feelings of sexual transgression. More revealing, perhaps, is the alliance of alcohol and creativity in her portrait of Andrew: "He was drunk and there was power in him to shape things" *(Collected Stories* 1987, 103).

Published in the *New Yorker* in August 1941, "The Jockey" is the first story to appear under the name of Carson McCullers, then the acclaimed young author of *The Heart Is a Lonely Hunter* and *Reflections in a Golden Eye*. Written in residence at Yaddo, a short distance from the Saratoga racetrack milieu in which it is set, the story stages a confrontation between the title character Bitsy Barlow and his trio of putative superiors, who sit over a lavish dinner. Barlow releases his distress for the crippling of another jockey, his "particular friend," in contempt for their ease and self-indulgence. His parting epithet – "Libertines[!]" – is both an indictment and a curse. The story "excels by virtue of its sustained tension between strong emotion and its repression" (McDowell 1980, 124). Barlow is a model of precision and control: "Impulse has no place in his world"; his "final moment" is marked by "extreme restraint" (125). Although his "diminished physical stature" might suggest Anacleto of *Reflections* or Cousin Lymon of *Ballad,* Barlow's conscious dignity thwarts the comparison: "Certainly he would refuse to allow himself to be seen as freakish or childlike" (126). McDowell suggests but does not demonstrate that the story is an example of McCullers's satirical humor. For Carr, "The Jockey" is "another poignant story of loss," and Barlow resembles the hunchback dwarf McCullers was to create for *Ballad* (1990, 153–54). Neither critic alludes to the story's suggestion that Barlow acts out of homosexual revenge for the crippled Irish boy, his lover.

McCullers's second *New Yorker* story, "Madame Zilensky and the King of Finland" appeared in December 1941. The story concerns an accomplished composer who brings to a teaching post at Ryder College no luggage, no metronome, only three pale sons and a ready supply of sustaining illusions. Her colleague, Mr. Brook, on realizing the falsehood of one of her stories – namely, that Finland is a democracy and has no king with whom she could have conversed – confronts her with the lie. But, seeing the devastation his skepticism can inflict, he joins once more in the illusion. "Madame Zilensky's need for illusions in order to exist is greater than her unmasker's need for truth" (Phillips 1978, 72). No one has commented on the fact that she is a refugee, probably; or rootless, a wanderer, another sojourner. The closest approach is Carr's idea that fantasy allows Madame Zilensky to escape "an awareness of her fragmentation in a disordered world" (1990, 147). How would readers on the verge of war, less than two weeks after the Japanese attack on Pearl Harbor, have responded to these characters and events? It is a testament to the power of orthodoxy and its underlying assumptions about the function of literature and criticism that such a detail has gone unnoticed in the dozens of pages written about this story.

The tone of the story has been of particular interest to critics. McDowell calls it "mildly satirical," an example of McCullers's skill in combining "humor and pathos"; the relationship between Mr. Brooks and Madame Zilensky is explored with "delicacy and sardonic mockery" (1980, 126). Explanations of the ending, in which Brook, having capitulated to the necessity of Madame Zilensky's fantasies, sees an old dog running backward, focus on the importance of musical counterpoint to the story. McDowell says, "The intricate elaboration of the contrasts within each of the two characters, the contrasts established between the two people, and the similarity of their desire to transcend a dull reality contribute to the involuted and convoluted comic effects generated in this story . . . . This story is McCullers' most thoughtful comedy" (1980, 128).

Carr valuably connects this story with "Poldi," in which another male character acquiesces in a woman's fantasy. Her interpretation, however, is less satisfactory and, ultimately, wrongheaded. "Just as the metronome provides a mechanical tempo for her performance and teaching of music, so, too, do her lies and fantasies impose an illusory order upon her personal life" (1990, 147). The metronome may in fact be a symbol of imposed order, but its importance in the story stems solely from its absence. Though she frequently remarks on its loss, Madame Zilensky does nothing to replace it, and Mr. Brook never acts on his offer to supply her with a substitute.

Carr seems as well to believe that the ending is sad rather than comic. She may reflect in this interpretation the view of Adelaide H. Frazier (1988) that Brook is one of McCullers's doomed lovers, enthralled by an "unreasonable love" to an unlikely object. "No, this love is as grotesque an emotion as Mme. Zilensky is the zany focus of it" (78). Madame Zilensky's missing metronome represents "some arbitrary order she might once have known and have been able to impose upon herself" (77). Order is Brook's raison d'être. "The logic of reason is no consideration for her; for Mr. Brook, it is all" (77). According to the formula Frazier derives from her study of this story and three others, Brook will be consigned by his love to an inward, isolated existence, though we may wonder, if so, how such a condition would differ from the solitary life he has customarily led.

That the old dog runs backward is taken as a sign of Brook's disrupted world. His "unreasonable love" is "a love both remorseful and incomprehensible" (78).

The *New Yorker* published a third story by McCullers in February 1942. "Correspondence" is McCullers's only published experiment with epistolary form. It consists of four letters from thirteen-year-old Henky Evans to the unresponsive Manoel Garcia, whose name she has chosen from a list of South American pen pals. The letters follow a familiar McCullers trajectory: enthusiastic self-disclosure followed by presumed rejection and anger. The amusing treatment of this pattern shows McCullers's "gift for light comedy" and demonstrates that her "short fiction is more varied in tone than is generally supposed" (Edmonds 1972, 90). In expanding his earlier brief treatment of the story, Dale Edmonds describes Henky Evans as a transitional figure, "a 'way station' between Mick Kelly and Frankie Addams, revealing the development of Mrs. McCullers's ability to create convincing characters" (1969; 1972, 91–92). Pointing to the "exuberance and concomitant pathos of adolescence that keep breaking through Henky's studied attempts to sound sophisticated," Edmonds claims her superiority to "the somber and . . . not very believable" Mick Kelly and credits her with responsibility "for the success of Frankie Addams" (92). The story is "no stunning achievement, but it is a unified and effective minor work of short fiction" (92). McDowell reads the story as Henky's self-serving search for a "spiritual twin," "a mirror-image of herself in another hemisphere," and points to "the essential narcissism of human beings, the longing for reciprocity in any expression of interest or affection and the ironic combination of gain and loss as one grows up" (1980, 124).

"A Tree. A Rock. A Cloud." appeared in *Harper's Bazaar* in November 1942. Frank Baldanza and Oliver Evans provided the first extended treatment of the story, in which an itinerant man, fond of his beer, confides his science of love to a newspaper delivery boy. The café setting and the boy's innocence and unworldliness remind Baldanza (1958) of Hemingway's "The Killers." In the first of several hair-thin disagreements about the story, Evans avers that it more nearly resembles "The Snows of Kilimanjaro" in its assertion that "life without love is meaningless and amounts to a death in life" (1965a, 90). Both men agree that McCullers expresses through the wanderer a Platonic or Neoplatonic philosophy of love learned in gradations, upward through trees, rocks, and clouds toward people in general and ultimately a woman, or another specific human being, in particular. For Evans, the science of love has a closer analog in the Neoplatonic view of Coleridge's ancient mariner, who has the same compulsion as McCullers's wanderer to enlighten others about a "chain of love which connects all objects in the natural universe," the individual with the universal (92). For Evans, Zen rather than Platonism is nearer the mark. McCullers's "saintly tramp" is a precursor of Beat heroes like Dean Moriarty (96).

Later criticism raised what has become the central question about the story: whether, in fact, McCullers endorses the itinerant's philosophy. In elaborating parallels between the story and Coleridge's "Rime of the Ancient Mariner," Mary Dell Fletcher finds that McCullers's tramp "is emotionally unstable and has only a distorted vision of love" (1975, 124). Although occasionally overzealous in asserting the congruities of story and poem – as in insisting that the tramp, like the ancient mariner, has for his sins undergone "physical and spiritual torture in order to achieve an understanding of divine love" (124) – Fletcher is more astute in observing differences between them.

> Both Coleridge and McCullers use the archetypal Cain figure, and both treat a universal theme, but the manner in which the two narratives end points up more than just differences in two artists conceiving a resolution. Between the publication of the two works came the main thrust of both Darwin's and Freud's theories with all the attendant ramifications. At the turn of the eighteenth century, then, Coleridge could write of isolation and still end on a note of hope – the old man has attained spiritual awareness and has communicated something of this experience to the wedding guest – and others, perhaps. By the 1930's, however, Carson McCullers was writing of an age characterized by sensual gratification and restlessness. Her old man, as the little newsboy comments, has done a lot of traveling. But it is his spiritual voyage and fulfillment that McCullers wishes to portray to a society epitomized by the coarse laughter in the all-night café, and she must perforce leave her old grotesque, who in his own way has discovered another dimension, trying to explain the nature of love to a world that is embarrassed by such emotions and which feels far safer in negating them. (125)

McDowell argues that the story is an attempt to duplicate in fiction the theme of "The Twisted Trinity," a poem written and published in 1941 (see below). The poem concerns the belief that, "for any individual, love transforms the perception of the self, nature, and God" (1980, 130). For the story, "McCullers reverses cause and effect, so that it is the close identification with nature which enables the protagonist once again to attempt love and to gain insight thereby into the transcendent aspects of sexual experience" (130). However, the success of such a science is dubious, given the fact that the wanderer tells his story then leaves, with no further attention to the boy he has announced he loves. "The encounter provides no indication that the tramp has learned to love, to see the need for commitment to another person, or to inspire love" (131).

Carr says that the lover in McCullers's fiction "was always vulnerable unless he loved someone – or some thing – from whom he expected nothing in return . . . . The tramp's sterile formula has led him to love things that cannot love back – first, a goldfish, then a tree, a rock, a cloud . . . . Despite his declaration [to the boy], the tramp knows that he can walk out alone into the predawn silence and never see his so-called 'beloved' again. Loving a woman is the 'last step' to his science, he tells the boy. 'I go cautious. And I am not quite ready yet . . . . ' The reader feels intuitively that the dissolute tramp will never be ready for the final step. He will not risk again his vulnerability to *eros*" (Carr 1990, 129).

"Art and Mr. Mahoney" appeared in *Mademoiselle* in February 1949. It is less a story than an expanded anecdote about what must be a nearly universal source of anxiety, applauding in the wrong place during a concert. In so doing, Mr. Mahoney humiliates his wife but later confirms himself in his right to applaud what pleases him, when it pleases him. Madden calls it "a very short cruel satire, based on a trite, shallow notion"; it "serves only to show another side of McCullers' mind and to demonstrate how poorly a first-rate talent can sometimes function" (1972, 142). McDowell remarks that music once again provides background and motive for the action and that the story displays McCullers's "keen sense for detail in phrase and manners": "Although the sketch makes its point as a satire upon ceremonious manners, its chief interest lies in its exposing the pretenses of provincially minded, so-called promoters of culture" – the wife in this case (1980, 128–29).

"The Sojourner" was first published in *Mademoiselle* in May 1950. Its selection for an O. Henry Award was not unanimous, according to Herschel Brickell, editor of the anthology of prizewinners. His own admiration of the story won out over the objection that it showed McCullers writing in an uncharacteristically "slick, popular vein" (1951, xv). Other anthologizers have seen the story as prototypical: "'The Sojourner' combines several of Mrs. McCullers' favorite subjects – children, music and the passage of time. A sense of sadness and waste is suffused throughout the story. This effect is achieved by the author's precise diction and meticulous selection of details" (Carson 1970, 207).

It is the story of John Ferris's return to the South for his father's funeral and journey back to Paris via New York, where his former wife and her husband and son give him an impromptu thirty-eighth birthday party. Exposure to families and reminders of time elapsing cause him to profess more devotion to his French lover and her son than he has previously felt. Phillips says Ferris discovers "his own emotional poverty": "Physically he is an expatriate from America; emotionally he is an expatriate from the human heart," whose chances of changing are doubtful (1978, 71). McDowell observes that Ferris's experiences "suggest to him that a sojourner who seeks the fullness of life by refusing to give up any of his freedom may, in actuality, miss the fullness of life" (1980, 134). "Ferris remains the type of the twentieth-century intellectual who is hedonistic, self-centered, and unable to learn from experience. One concludes that Ferris as sojourner may settle down to a committed love for Jeannine and Valentin, but that the roots he puts down may not be deep. He is so consistently treated with a touch of the satiric and the sardonic that one suspects that he will, in some sense, remain . . . . a sojourner in this life, who evades its challenges and difficulties and so never achieves its rewards" (135).

Adelaide H. Frazier fits "The Sojourner" into her thesis that McCullers writes variations on the theme of destructive love, each manifesting the protagonist's fate: to hoard the unrequited love inside. In this case, Ferris reaches out to the child Valentin desperate "to use his love as a barrier against time." But love, as he has experienced it, is protean. "The changing focus of Ferris' love finally assures that he will sojourn forever. He is doomed to house the exquisite pain within himself. No relationship can respond to this uncertain lover who will doubtless continue moving in endless search" (1988, 79). Noting "its origins, like so many of McCullers's other stories, in her troubled life with her husband," Carr calls it a "subtle and mature story of unrequited love" (1990, 149).

"A Domestic Dilemma" appeared in the magazine section of the *New York Post* in September 1951. Slightly more than twenty years later it was the subject of a critical dustup between James W. Grinnell and Laurence Perrine. At stake was the ethical character of Martin Meadows, the story's father, husband, and protagonist, confronted with the alcoholism of his wife, Emily. Grinnell's maverick reading condemns Martin's motives: he is less interested in "curing his wife's illness" than in "keeping it secret." Martin's dilemma is the confusion of his public and private feelings. He "loved her privately as he did at the end of the story with the lights out. Publicly she threatened his self-image; so outwardly he hated her. The real irony of Martin and Emily's dilemma was that his concern for what others thought rendered him unable to show his love, the love which she needed in order to be well. At the same time, it precluded happiness, public or private, for both of them" (1972, 271).

Seeking to restore the accepted reading, Perrine accuses Grinnell of "egregiously distort[ing] the shape and meaning" of the story. Citing Martin's "tenderness and solicitude" to his children as well as his wife, and suggesting that McCullers would not have named him Martin Meadows if she wanted readers to see him as cold or mechanical, Perrine concludes, "McCullers shows us that love is no simple emotion. It can embrace fear, anger, indignation, disgust, tenderness, impatience, amusement, hate, sorrow, and desire – simultaneously or successively within a very brief span of time. It is a complex of conflicting emotions. This theme demands a central character who is capable of feeling genuinely this complex of emotions. It would be impossible with a protagonist motivated primarily by concern for his own self-image" (1974, 102–3).

Martin's dilemma as McCullers phrases it arises from "the immense complexity of love." That complexity has been effectively read as the combination of love and pity that characterizes other McCullers pairs – Singer and Antonapoulos, Alison and Anacleto, for example (Evans 1965a, 71). McDowell considers this story superior to the other tales of drunken discord – "Instant of the Hour After" and "Who Has Seen the Wind?" – largely because of its depth of characterization. Approaching her characters patiently, McCullers builds gradually toward Martin's recognition of his complex feelings for Emily. "Martin sees himself and Emily caught together in bonds of suffering that are stronger than those of love, but those of love still survive." McDowell is one of the first critics to focus sympathetically on Emily, maintaining that Emily is complexly portrayed. "The emphasis is only initially on Emily's drunkenness . . . . She also suffers from the disharmony of the family situation. Her isolation, her homesickness for the South, and the guilt, anger, and love which she feels toward her children make her a considerable character, who finds a destructive release for unbearable tensions in her bouts of drinking. An irony exists in Martin's moments of great tenderness for his wife, experienced intermittently with his loathing for what she has become" (1980, 133). "Love in this tale is a dominant and incomprehensible force, too complex to be separated from hatred, pity, memory, hope, or despair" (134).

Published by both *Mademoiselle* and *Botteghe Oscure* in 1955, less than a year after the death of McCullers's mother, "The Haunted Boy" depicts "the psychic tension of a child torn between pity for – and anger against – a parent and also between his need to appear mature and his need to express his fear" (McDowell 1980, 119). More an adolescent than a child, the protagonist, Hugh, experiences profound anxiety when, returning home from school, he fails to find his mother downstairs.

Haunted by his memory of once finding her bleeding from a suicide attempt, Hugh reacts with anger and guilt when she arrives elated with the purchase of a new dress. "The story is marred by a pat ending, but Hugh's fear is made extraordinarily real. One does not soon forget his terror at the simple act of opening the upstairs bathroom door" (Phillips 1978, 68). Identifying Hugh's emotions with the cycle of fear and hatred that attends betrayal in McCullers's fiction, Carr reads the story as his successful "emergence from moral isolation into self-knowledge" and notes that it "reflects the ambivalence of McCullers's own feelings toward her mother" (1990, 151–52).

"Who Has Seen the Wind?" appeared in September 1956 in *Mademoiselle,* whose editors, in reprinting it four years later, praised its "brooding and poetic concern with time passing" (Abels and Smith 1960, 234). To Nadine Gordimer it "seems a breathless getting-down, sometimes expanding into the writer's full power, sometimes degenerating into hasty condensation, of what was meant to be a longer work" (1972, 135). And it is. Apparently begun as a draft of the play *The Square Root of Wonderful,* it was rewritten as a story with different character names and altered circumstances, but the plot remains similar. Debilitated by writer's block and alcohol, Ken Harris is further shamed by feelings of inferiority to his more successful wife, Marian. Enraged that she will not indulge him in drink or sex, he comes close to stabbing her before retreating in despair. When he looks for her again, she is gone. At sunrise he stumbles outside in "the frozen radiance of morning," incoherently seeking Marian or, perhaps, suicide. Vestiges of its ties to the drama can be seen in its organization by scenes. Moreover, according to McDowell, "Like the torment of the abusive and suicidal Phillip Lovejoy in [the] play, Ken's situation probably also reflects that of Reeves McCullers and, to some extent, that of Carson herself as a writer whose drinking seemed necessary to sustain her human relationships and even her writing, but which also interfered with them" (1980, 132). Carr notes that the story was written exactly twenty years after "Instant of the Hour After" and that the characters are exactly twenty years older (1990, 159). Both Carr and McDowell see suicide as the inevitable end to the story, but perhaps such a reading is preconditioned by the suicide of Reeves McCullers in 1953.

"The March" is the last story published during McCullers's lifetime. Published in *Redbook* in March 1967 and never collected, "The March" is the first of a trilogy for which McCullers had planned two additional stories, "The Man Upstairs" and "Hush Little Baby." In this final work, McCullers reinforces her concern with the violence and heroism of desegregation efforts depicted in *Clock Without Hands* and, in fact, returns in this story of a Freedom March to themes and incidents suggested in her first novel, *The Heart Is a Lonely Hunter,* nearly three decades earlier.

McCullers's magazine essays published between 1940 and 1963 and collected in *The Mortgaged Heart* have, individually, received little attention, although her reflections on the war years and on Christmas holidays have been dismissed as unworthy (Madden 1972). Substantial notice has been paid only to the seven essays on writers and writing: "The Russian Realists and Southern Literature," *Decision,* 1941; "Isak Dinesen: *Winter's Tales,*" *New Republic,* 1943; "How I Began to Write," *Mademoiselle,* 1948; "Loneliness ... An American Malady," *New York Herald Tribune* magazine, 1949; "The Vision Shared," *Theatre Arts,* 1950; "The Flowering Dream: Notes on Writing," *Esquire,* 1959; and "Isak Dinesen: In Praise of Radiance," *Saturday Review,* 1963.

Nadine Gordimer was among the first to find this section, particularly "The Flowering Dream," preeminent. It constitutes

> her statement of her credo as a writer, and for this alone Margarita Smith's book justifies publication. These notes throw not the easy flash-bulb of tuppenny-ha'penny gossip psychology but the mysterious gleam of the private and individual life-focus on puzzling aspects of her work. Those androgynous characters, the boy-girl Frankies and Micks, the overt homosexuals like wretched little Lily-Mae, and Captain Penderton of *Reflections in a Golden Eye,* and those – how to describe them? – almost polymorphous characters, half human of both sexes, half gentle mythical beast, the hunchback ... and the deaf mute – are they best explained when she writes: "One cannot explain accusations of morbidity .... Nature is not abnormal, only lifelessness is abnormal ... a deaf and dumb man is a symbol of infirmity, and he loves a person who is incapable of receiving his love ... a homosexual is also a symbol of handicap and impotence." Or is the preoccupation with the emotionally and socially alienated and the creation of beings who are at once neither man nor woman but both, an attempt, as with Virginia Woolf's *Orlando,* to bring together all that is human and therefore, by Terence's definition cannot be alien? Is the strange fellowship of these hopeless and unconsummated loves nearest to what is, for this writer, the highest kind of love? (1972, 136)

"The Russian Realists and Southern Literature" presented, at a surprisingly early stage of her career, a rationale for her use of Gothic effects, suggesting "that the grotesque can serve the purposes of a more exact moral and psychological realism in art. By abjuring moral judgment and exaggerating rather than resolving contradictions in human experience, the writer ... could reveal the hidden abnormalities in 'normal' life. Russian writers had been doing this for some time, and as she noted, it was a technique prevalent in the best of recent Southern literature, especially in the fiction of William Faulkner" (Cook 1975, 102–3).

In statements such as "Communication is the only access to love" and the writer is "a conscious dreamer," "The Flowering Dream" reveals "how her aesthetics and her themes are inseparable," according to David Madden (1972, 155). The most compelling discussion of "The Flowering Dream" is Irving Buchen's demonstration that "McCullers' artistic theory is so entangled in her religious quest that the exploration of her aesthetics may be of a piece with that of her metaphysics" (1974, 530). The anecdote which begins the essay, McCullers's account of childhood feelings of exclusion when passing a convent where a party was in progress behind a wall that kept her out, epitomizes "the relationship between the dream and the child": "The gap between the child and the adult reenacts the gap between the unconscious and conscious, between poetry and prose, and above all between what Mick Kelly refuses, because of her dreams, to settle for and what Biff Brannon and many others already have settled for." The prevalence of "the archetypal experience of incompletion" in McCullers's works arises from this. "In her novels the ideal of a Catholic heaven is parcelled out to a Carnegie Hall reserved for Jewish musicians, to the warm ghettoes of the wise blacks, to a honeymoon set amidst never-glimpsed snow, to the citadel of John Singer's silence" (536–37). "The touchstone of both McCullers' artistic theory and work is thus rooted in the child's exclusion from paradise because he is not one of the elect – a Catholic in the original experience, a Jewish musician as an adolescent, a normal heterosexual as an adult.... The permanent drama then for McCullers is that of incompletion" (537).

The bulk of McCullers's poetry remains in manuscript. Her only published collection of poems is *Sweet as a Pickle and Clean as a Pig*, twenty-two poems for children, issued in U.S. and English editions in 1964 and 1965, respectively, illustrated by Rolf Gérard. It was published as well in the December 1964 *Redbook*. *The Mortgaged Heart* reprints five more sober poems published during her lifetime, most of them in the late 1940s and early 1950s: "The Mortgaged Heart," "When We Are Lost," "The Dual Angel," "Stone Is Not Stone," and "Saraband."

David Madden (1972) says, "McCullers began writing poetry after she was already well-established as a writer of fiction; the poetic qualities in her prose have less in common with the poetry of her time than with the poetry of confession and of the emotive imagination being written today. There are traces of Hart Crane in 'Saraband' and of Gene Derwood in 'The Dual Angel.' Like Crane and Derwood, McCullers deals in paradoxes, parallels, ironies, philosophical questionings, and abstractions . . . .

'The Dual Angel: A Meditation on Origin and Choice' is . . . reminiscent of Meredith's 'Lucifer in Star-Light'" (140).

A partial chapter in McDowell's Twayne book (1980) constitutes the most substantial treatment of the poems. "Stone Is Not Stone" began as a shorter and slightly more optimistic poem entitled "The Twisted Trinity," written and published in 1941 in Klaus Mann's *Decision* magazine and set to music by David Diamond. McDowell, who sees "The Twisted Trinity" as germinal to the story "A Tree. A Rock. A Cloud.," says of it, "In 'The Twisted Trinity' the speaker avers that formerly her life had been spiritually integrated, and she had then perceived a clear relationship among self, nature, and God – an 'instant symmetry.' Now a new presence – that of a lover – has not only disturbed this harmony, but has deepened it, in providing a new dimension and mystery to experience. No longer is stone only stone, nor a face a 'finished face,' but stone and face acquire an infinitude of significance which they had never before possessed. Though a later version of this poem, published as 'Stone Is Not Stone' (1947), is less positive and suggests the adverse effects of the lover's absence, it retains the central idea that love has changed the total perception of the speaker" (130).

"The Dual Angel: A Meditation on Origin and Choice" is a cycle of five poems constituting McCullers's "most ambitious work of poetry" (McDowell 1980, 135). The question that inspired Milton also inspires this cycle: why would all-powerful God create a sinful world? McCullers "fails to sustain the heightened imaginative thrust that would have given the cycle of poems a consistent epical quality, not because of any lack of control of prosody or skill in versification, but because she attempts to use the same technique of alternating the formal with the colloquial in diction and phrasing, which she had so successfully mastered in a different medium . . . . The heightened philosophical poem demands more unity and consistency than her kind of fiction did" (136).

The "most significant of McCullers' poems in its craftsmanship may be 'The Mortgaged Heart.' The single theme developed in it is the 'mortgage' which the beloved still holds, even after death, upon the heart of the lover, and the positive effect upon the mourner of the continued and demanding presence of the dead lover. Because the mourner remains inspired by his closeness to the dead, he finds a sense of direction, a pattern for renewed living, a sharpened sensitivity to the beauty of the world about him, and an increased sense of obligation to work to satisfy its needs. Thus, in any genuine sense, mourning is not a negative state but leads toward life instead of away from it and, in fact, doubles one's sense of being fully alive" (140).

9: Prospects

IF THE TERRITORY ahead can be gauged by the landmarks of the past, it should be fair to say that Carson McCullers's protean novels, stories, poems, and plays will withstand new developments in criticism at century's end. We already have a sense of what the future may look like in three recent articles, all by women and all on McCullers's first and still most famous novel, *The Heart Is a Lonely Hunter*. One resurrects race as a central concern of the novel; another finds in the Singer-Christ the social, even textual construction of godhead; and the third takes a postfeminist stance on the venerable concept of the androgyne.

Laurie Champion (1991) gives the first consistent attention to the pattern of Christ imagery as it concerns the novel's black characters. McCullers's concern with racism is thorough and prophetic. Copeland plans to lead a march on Washington to avenge Willie's mutilation in prison. Champion's reading is not an obvious one. She sets against the Christ-like portrayal of Singer the concept of a black Christ-figure. "Doctor Copeland's statement to Portia that 'the Negro race of its own accord climbs up on the cross every Friday' embodies the Christian myth to symbolize the ultimate persecution of the Negro race . . . . Critics often refer to McCullers's portrayal of individual isolation as the reflection of 'spiritual loneliness.' Examinations of themes involving spiritual loneliness often lead to interpretations based on Christianity. These critical assessments . . . repeatedly refer to Singer as the symbolic Christ figure, and they are correct as far as the central theme is concerned; however, Willie symbolically assumes Singer's role as Christ in the anti-racist social theme. Jake tells Singer, 'Jesus would be framed and in jail if he was living today' . . . , and through her portrayal of Willie, McCullers metaphorically executes Jake's commentary" (50). Willie is crucified by white prison guards. "One need not delve too deeply to see the similarities between the crucifixion of Willie and the crucifixion of Christ. First of all, Willie's suffering is not the result of his own crime. He remains innocent but is nonetheless crucified. There are two other boys who hang 'on crosses' in the room with him. They suffer for 'three nights and three days.' More importantly, his body position represents the position of Christ on the cross, only he is situated upside down, a position which intensifies the severity of suffering . . . . Willie's crucifixion, however, is not redemptive. His symbolic death, unlike Christ's, does not offer salvation to his people" (51). In portraying both a black and a white Christ, McCullers allows "the subordinate social theme [to intertwine] with the principal motif in order to intensify both . . . ideas. She depicts the black Christ as persecuted more severely than the white Christ; nevertheless, they are both crucified and that is the sonorous point. Spiritual loneliness and human isolation 'crucify' all members of society" (51–52).

In an essay published, like Champion's, in the *Southern Literary Journal,* Jan Whitt (1992) analyzes the Christ imagery associated with Singer. "McCullers created an allegory in which numerous characters seek to work out their own salvation by relaying their individual fears to John Singer. Singer, a deaf mute, becomes a paralyzed Christ figure, so restricted by the expectations of others that he is fictionalized by them" (26). McCullers's portrayal of "Singer and his disciples" moves the story beyond the simple invocation of Christian myth. McCullers demonstrates "the frailty of language, the ultimate failure of self-expression. As McCullers writes in an essay, 'Communication is the only access to love – to love, to conscience, to nature, to God, and to the dream.' But, for all the peace and hope the characters of her first novel experience, each might as well be a mute. As in modern life, McCullers' fictional universe contains too much need, too few listeners" (34). "Rather than his pointing the way to God through a Gethsemane moment, isolation damns Singer. His song is never heard. McCullers has written an allegory of an individual's search for self, and those internal glimpses remain rare and incomplete . . . . Her characters do not carry a pack labelled 'Sin' on their backs, but Singer easily may be cast as an allegorical Everyman. The pain of the characters is as internal as it is destructive, and their cries for deliverance go unheard" (35).

L. Taetzsch (1992) explores "the linked opposing trajectories of Mick Kelly and Biff Brannon. These trajectories start at opposite poles and cross somewhere in the deadly time-space of the novel. Mick Kelly begins in androgyny with high energy, enlightenment, and artistic transcendence. At the end of the novel she has become trapped in the flesh of a sexual being, heading toward confusion, exhaustion, and the loss of artistic drive. Biff Brannon, on the other hand, begins in the morass of his sexual past and moves upward toward androgyny with its concomitant artistic awareness" (192). In consciously choosing androgyny, Biff "plays a double role in the novel. He helps us interpret the other characters' actions, and is transformed himself into artistic, enlightened androgyny" (193). In the opposite crossing trajectories, Biff's intuitive sympathy with children increases and Mick's decreases, as her behavior toward Bubber shows. At her lowest point, "Mick has accepted her cultural role as woman – wearing silk stockings no matter how impractical; wasting her small salary on dangling earrings and a silver bangle bracelet; smiling all day so that 'she had to frown a long time to get her face natural again'" (195–96). She has also lost the music in her mind and access to her inside room. At the same time,

> Biff has moved on to a higher state in which he loves people rather than a particular person: "Who would he be loving now? No one person. Anybody who came in out of the street to sit for an hour and have a drink. But no one person." . . . He has passed the need for connection to an individual, transcending it with love for humanity. The expansion of Biff's spirit culminates in an epiphanic experience comparable to Mick's rapturous union with Beethoven . . . . What Biff sees is the human condition – the struggle of hope and valor against dark forces beyond knowing or control. For a split second (it is a position impossible to maintain) he stands at the intersection of dialectical opposites "between irony and faith." Freed from the constraints of sexual identity, Biff is finally able to see. He has moved to the end of his trajectory, into enlightenment . . . . Mick's trajectory begins on the rooftop and travels downward to a low point at the end of the novel . . . . We leave Mick angry and frustrated, and can only imagine a life for her similar to her sisters' and mother's. Biff's epiphany at the end of the novel, however, signifies his rise to androgynous artistic vision and to enlightenment. While Mick and Biff have not touched in human warmth or contact, their trajectories have crossed and are now complete. (196)

The revival of androgyny as a model, after its disfavor among feminists in the 1980s, may be impelled by the discovery of bi-, ambi-, uni- and non-sexual freedoms among postmodern youth and the cultural avatars that cater to them. The blurring of gender boundaries, the deconstruction of sex roles in contemporary high style may revive this dimension of McCullers's portraits, as a positive force. In addition to re-visioned androgyny, we will no doubt find McCullers's life and work amenable to a variety of critical filters, some already present, some inchoate. We need, for example, to pay heed to the mathematical precision with which she attempted to pinpoint happiness, pain, desperation, and love in such late works as the poems and *The Square Root of Wonderful*. McCullers died in a year of race riots, war protests, and preparations for a lunar landing, a year of high technology and starving Biafrans. The upheavals she had imagined when she was not yet twenty years old – labor agitation, leftist insurgency, black power marches on Washington, and youth rebellion against stifling conformity – were the stuff of an ordinary news day thirty years later. The military-industrial complex then collaborating to drop warheads and chemical fire on Vietnam had come within range of her satire as early as 1940. She had taken the measure of its leaders, the insipid men like Langdon, the tautly sadistic men like Penderton; its pimping power brokers like Cousin Lymon; the zealots for whatever cause, the Jake Blounts and Judge Clanes; the ignorant and brutal men for hire like Marvin Macy and Sammy Lank; and others, too – the cold philosophers; the failing artists; the overgrown bully girls who want so hard the wanting is painful, who dream so big that their dreams would consume the globe, and who want, most of all, not to claim the weakness society has marked off for them; girls who want to be free and heedless without being sexual, who want ice cream in the burning summer, who want music that completes itself in them; the black women who want their men to survive, who want love without pain, who want the world to make good sense, who want reckless white children to grow up soon; and all the lonely, ineffectual fathers, Addams, Kelly, Malone, Singer the surrogate, the weak men of routine, the jewelers and pestle wielders. The writer who could imagine all this and animate it on the page, along with hopeless grotesques, countless monkeys, exploited children: why would such a woman be considered limited or narrow? Why would literary history remark her as southern-peculiar?

Perhaps all worthwhile artists have this protean quality that it is the function of literary fashion to obscure. When the formalists looked, they saw a poet, complexly managing themes of classical simplicity and grandeur. When the mythicists looked, they saw a mythmaker, one who was not content to recycle the old but could touch the deep sources that made myth new: Amelia's liquor, the stallion Firebird; the naked Elgee Williams; the flying dwarf; the powerful woman; the foppish blue-eyed Negro youth; the beery tramp. When the feminists looked, they saw a feminist. When the southerners looked, they saw a southerner. When the Freudians looked, they found in that "limited" terrain a soil that is rich, though not always wholesome, like the beautiful poisonous lilies of the swamp and the cold crystal liquor that will make your blood run hot with clarity. Only a few have noticed McCullers's decadence and her naturalism. She is a naturalist, of course, but not of the old school, where cynicism came easily. She is rather a post-Einsteinian naturalist willing to acknowledge relativity of time and space; willing to hold equal and opposite forces in tension and not be overpowered. What are all of those clocks doing in her work? Surely there are better answers than those we have found.

The territory ahead will be fascinating to explore. Throw away the old maps; find a scuppernong arbor and "commence critic." Read her as she was read in wartime. Read her for portents of what was to come. Read her as enmeshed in the private dramas of the gifted and the cursed.

Read her against her favored Russian texts. Read her with your calcula-
tor handy, in respect for the affinity of mathematics and music. Like Poe's
fabled Dupin, she may prove both a mathematician and a poet. Despite
our deepest impressions of her as a one-note writer, as a southern
woman, as an invalid, as a primitive, the undereducated product of southern schooling, despite those stereotypical images of her, she was a seis-
mograph completely sensitive to the direction of social change, a medium
for registering slight reverberations of cultural shift. We should not be
surprised that someone mired in the gritty, messy grotesque should also
have a penchant for the coolly precise rationality of ticking clocks and lunar orbits; nor should we gainsay her power to turn her roiling frustrations in love into a calculus of pain, a brilliant, jarring, absurdist vision,
like Biff Brannon's, of human frailty and valor. There is much left to be
done.

Works Consulted

Works by Carson McCullers

1936. "Wunderkind." *Story* 9 (Dec.): 61–73.

1940. *The Heart Is a Lonely Hunter.* Boston: Houghton Mifflin.

1940. *Reflections in a Golden Eye.* Harper's Bazaar 74 (Oct.): 60–61, 131–43; (Nov.): 56, 120–39.

1941. "Brooklyn Is My Neighborhood." *Vogue* 97 (Mar.): 62–63, 138.

1941. "The Jockey." *New Yorker* 17 (23 Aug.): 15–16.

1941. "Madame Zilensky and the King of Finland. *New Yorker* 17 (20 Dec.): 15–18.

1941. *Reflections in a Golden Eye.* Boston: Houghton Mifflin.

1941. "The Russian Realists and Southern Literature." *Decision* 2 (July): 15–19.

1941. "The Twisted Trinity." *Decision* 2 (Nov.-Dec.): 30.

1942. "Correspondence." *New Yorker* 18 (7 Feb.): 36–39.

1942. *Reflections in a Golden Eye.* London: Cresset.

1942. "A Tree. A Rock. A Cloud." *Harper's Bazaar* 76 (Nov.): 50, 96–99.

1943. *The Ballad of the Sad Café.* Harper's Bazaar 77 (Aug.): 72–75, 140–61.

1943. *The Heart Is a Lonely Hunter.* London: Cresset.

1946. *The Member of the Wedding.* [Part I.] Harper's Bazaar 80 (Jan.): 94–96, 101, 128–38, 144–48.

1946. *The Member of the Wedding.* Boston: Houghton Mifflin.

1946. *The Member of the Wedding.* London: Cresset.

1948. "The Mortgaged Heart." *New Directions* 10: 509.

1948. "When We Are Lost." *New Directions* 10: 509.

1949. "Art and Mr. Mahoney." *Mademoiselle* 28 (Feb.): 120, 184–86.

1950. *Reflections in a Golden Eye.* Introduction by Tennessee Williams. New Classics Series. New York: New Directions.

1950. "The Sojourner." *Mademoiselle* 31 (May): 90, 160–66.

1950. "The Vision Shared." *Theatre Arts* 34 (Apr.): 23–30.

1951. "A Domestic Dilemma." *New York Post Magazine* (16 Sept.): 10–11M.

1951. *The Member of the Wedding: A Play*. New York: New Directions.

1951. *The Ballad of the Sad Café: The Novels and Stories of Carson McCullers*. Boston: Houghton Mifflin.

1952. *The Ballad of the Sad Café: The Shorter Novels and Stories of Carson McCullers*. London: Cresset.

1952. "The Dual Angel: A Meditation on Origin and Choice." *Botteghe Oscure* 9: 213–18.

1952. "The Dual Angel: A Meditation on Origin and Choice." *Mademoiselle* 35 (July): 54–55, 108.

1953. "The Pestle." *Botteghe Oscure* 11: 226–46.

1953. "The Pestle." *Mademoiselle* 37 (July): 44–45, 114–18.

1955. "The Haunted Boy." *Botteghe Oscure* 16: 264–78.

1955. "The Haunted Boy." *Mademoiselle* 42 (Nov.): 134–35, 152–59.

1956. "Who Has Seen the Wind?" *Mademoiselle* 43 (Sept.): 156–57, 174–88.

1957. "Stone Is Not Stone." *Mademoiselle* 45 (July): 43.

1958. *The Square Root of Wonderful: A Play*. Boston: Houghton Mifflin.

1959. "The Flowering Dream: Notes on Writing." *Esquire* 52 (Dec.): 162–64.

1961. *Clock Without Hands*. Boston: Houghton Mifflin.

1961. *Clock Without Hands*. London: Cresset.

1963. "Sucker." *Saturday Evening Post* 236 (28 Sept.): 69–71.

1964. *Sweet as a Pickle and Clean as a Pig*. Illustrated by Rolf Gérard. Boston: Houghton Mifflin.

1964. "Sweet as a Pickle and Clean as a Pig." *Redbook* 124 (Dec.): 49–56.

1965. *Sweet as a Pickle and Clean as a Pig*. Illustrated by Rolf Gérard. London: Cape.

1967. "The March." *Redbook* 138 (Mar.): 69, 114–23.

1971. "Breath from the Sky." *Redbook* 137 (Oct.): 92, 228–33.

1971. "Instant of the Hour After." *Redbook* 137 (Oct.): 93, 194–96.

1971. "Like That." *Redbook* 137 (Oct.): 91, 166–70.

1971. *The Mortgaged Heart*. Ed. Margarita G. Smith. Boston: Houghton Mifflin.

1972. *The Mortgaged Heart*. Ed. Margarita G. Smith. London: Barrie & Jenkins.

1987. *Collected Stories*. Introduction by Virginia Spencer Carr. Boston: Houghton Mifflin.

Works about Carson McCullers

Fadiman, Clifton. 1940. "Pretty Good for Twenty-Two." *New Yorker* 16 (8 June): 69–70.

Feld, Rose. 1940. "A Remarkable First Novel of Lonely Lives." *New York Times Book Review* 16 June: 6.

"First Novel." 1940. *Time* 35 (10 June): 90.

Gannett, Lewis. 1940. "Books and Things." *Boston Evening Transcript,* 5 June, p. 13.

Littell, Robert. 1940. "Outstanding Novels." *Yale Review* 30 (Autumn): vi-xii.

McDonald, Edward D. 1940. "The Mirroring Stream of Fiction." *Virginia Quarterly Review* 16 (Autumn): 602–14.

P[aterson], I[sabel] M. 1940. "Turns with a Bookworm." *New York Herald Tribune Books,* 23 June, p. 11.

Putzel, Max. 1940. Review of *The Heart Is a Lonely Hunter. Accent* 1 (Autumn): 61–62.

Wright, Richard. 1940. "Inner Landscape." *New Republic* 103 (5 Aug.): 195.

"Book to Forget with Promptness." 1941. *Hartford Courant Magazine,* 23 Feb., p. 7.

Cargill, Oscar. 1941. *Intellectual America: Ideas on the March.* New York: Macmillan.

Creekmore, Hubert. 1941. Review of *Reflections in a Golden Eye. Accent* 2 (Autumn): 61.

Davenport, Basil. 1941. Review of *Reflections in a Golden Eye. Saturday Review* 23 (22 Feb.): 12.

Fadiman, Clifton. 1941. "Books." *New Yorker* 17 (15 Feb.): 66, 68.

Feld, Rose. 1941. Review of *Reflections in a Golden Eye. New York Herald Tribune Books,* 16 Feb., p. 8.

Ferguson, Otis. 1941. "Fiction: Odd and Ordinary." *New Republic* 104 (3 Mar.): 317–18.

Littell, Robert. 1941. "Outstanding Novels." *Yale Review* n.s. 30 (Spring): viii-xiv.

Marsh, Fred T. 1941. "At an Army Post." *New York Times Book Review,* 2 Mar., p. 6.

"Masterpiece at 24." 1941. *Time* 37 (17 Feb.): 96.

Poore, Charles. 1941. "Books of The Times." *New York Times,* 15 Feb., p. 13.

Weeks, Edward. 1941. "First Person Singular." *Atlantic* 167 (Apr.): [viii].

Toynbee, Philip. 1942. "New Novels." *New Statesman and Nation* n.s. 24 (11 July): 27–28.

"In the Deep South." 1943. *Times Literary Supplement,* 27 Mar., p. 153.

Pryce-Jones, Alan. 1943. "New Novels." *London Observer,* 28 Mar., p. 3.

Spring, Howard. 1943. Review of *The Heart Is a Lonely Hunter. London Daily Mail,* 27 Mar., p. 2. Qtd. in Shapiro 1980.

Straus, Ralph. 1943. "Novels of the Week." *London Sunday Times,* 21 Mar., p. 3.

Toynbee, Philip. 1943. "Novels and Stories." *New Statesman and Nation* n.s. 25 (1 May): 292.

Bond, Alice Dixon. 1946. "The Case for Books: Two Widely Different New Novels and a Thrilling Book of Adventure." *Boston Herald,* 10 Apr., p. 17.

Boyle, Kay. 1946. "I Wish I Had Written *The Ballad of the Sad Café* by Carson McCullers." In *I Wish I'd Written That: Selections Chosen by Favorite American Authors.* Ed. Eugene J. Woods. New York: McGraw-Hill. 300–1.

Dangerfield, George. 1946. "An Adolescent's Four Days." *Saturday Review* 29 (30 Mar.): 15.

Dunkel, Wilbur. 1946. "Books of the Week – As Adolescent Sees." *Rochester Democrat and Chronicle,* 17 Mar., p. 7D. Qtd. in Shapiro 1980.

Frank, Joseph. 1946. "Fiction Chronicle." *Sewanee Review* 54 (Summer): 534–39.

Gannett, Lewis. 1946. "Books and Things." *New York Herald Tribune,* 20 Mar., p. 23.

Kapp, Isa. 1946. "One Summer, Three Lives." *New York Times Book Review,* 24 Mar., p. 5.

Match, Richard. 1946. "No Man's Land of Childhood." *New York Herald Tribune Weekly Book Review,* 24 Mar., p. 5.

Review of *The Member of the Wedding.* 1946. *Kirkus* 14 (15 Jan.): 20.

Rosenfeld, Isaac. 1946. "Double Standard." *New Republic* 29 (Apr.): 633–34.

Sturges-Jones, Marion. 1946. "Exploring the Mind of a 12-Year-Old Girl." *Philadelphia Record,* 31 Mar., p. M11. Qtd. in Shapiro 1980.

Trilling, Diana. 1946. "Fiction in Review." *Nation* 162 (6 Apr.): 406–7.

Wilson, Edmund. 1946. "Two Books That Leave You Blank: Carson McCullers, Siegfried Sassoon." *New Yorker* 22 (30 Mar.): 87–88.

King, Robin. 1947. "New Novels." *New Statesman and Nation* n.s. 33 (5 Apr.): 241–42.

Straus, Ralph. 1947. "New Novels." *London Sunday Times,* 9 Mar., p. 3.

Young, Marguerite. 1947. "Metaphysical Fiction." *Kenyon Review* 9 (Winter): 151–55. Reprinted in Bloom 1986.

Murdock, Henry T. 1949. "McCullers' 'Member of the Wedding' Bows at Walnut." *Philadelphia Inquirer,* 23 Dec., p. 20.

Atkinson, Brooks. 1950a. "At the Theatre." *New York Times,* 6 Jan., p. 26.

———. 1950b. "Poetry in a Drama – 'The Member of the Wedding' Remains Constant and Unimpaired," *New York Times,* 17 Sept., II: p. 1.

———. 1950c. "Three People – 'The Member of the Wedding' Superbly Acted by an Excellent Company." *New York Times,* 15 Jan., II: p. 1.

Barnes, Howard. 1950. "The Theaters." *New York Herald Tribune,* 6 Jan., p. 12.

Brown, John Mason. 1950. "Plot Me No Plots." *Saturday Review* 33 (28 Jan.): 27–29.

Chapman, John, ed. 1950a. *The Burns Mantle Best Plays of 1949–1950 and the Year Book of the Drama in America.* New York: Dodd, Mead.

———. 1950b. "'Member of the Wedding' and Its Cast Earn Cheers at the Empire." *New York Daily News,* 6 Jan., p. 55.

Clurman, Harold. 1950a. "'Member of [the] Wedding' Upsets a Theory." *New York Herald Tribune,* 29 Jan.: V, 3.

———. 1950b. "Theatre: From a Member." *New Republic* 122 (30 Jan.): 28–29.

Gabriel, Gilbert W. 1950. "New Plays on Broadway – Wend Your Way Westward to the Empire." *Cue* 19 (14 Jan.): 20.

Garland, Robert. 1950. "'The Member of the Wedding' – Something Special But Not Quite a Play." *New York Journal-American,* 6 Jan., p. 18.

Gibbs, Wolcott. 1950. "The Theatre: Brook and River" *New Yorker* (14 Jan.): 44–45.

Kazin, Alfred. 1950. "We Who Sit in Darkness: The Broadway Audience at the Play." *Commentary* 9 (June): 525–29. See Kazin 1955.

Marshall, Margaret. 1950. "Drama." *Nation* 170 (14 Jan.): 44.

Martin, Linton. 1950. "The Call Boy's Chat – Able Acting Aids Illusion; Theater Half Century Ago." *Philadelphia Inquirer,* 1 Jan., Society Section, p. 13.

Nathan, George Jean. 1950. *The Theatre Book of the Year 1949–1950: A Record and an Interpretation.* New York: Knopf.

"New Play in Manhattan." 1950. *Time* 55 (16 Jan.): 45.

"New Plays." 1950. *Newsweek* 35 (16 Jan.): 74

Theatre Arts 1950. 34 (Mar.): 13.

Watts, Richard, Jr. 1950a. "Two on the Aisle – A Striking New American Play." *New York Post,* 6 Jan., pp. 45, 46.

———. 1950b. "Two on the Aisle – The Stage Has a New Playwright." *New York Post,* 15 Jan., p. M4.

Williams, Tennessee. 1950. "This Book." In McCullers's *Reflections in a Golden Eye*. New Classics Series. New York: New Directions. ix-xxi. Reprinted in Bloom 1986.

Bowen, Elizabeth. 1951. "A Matter of Inspiration." *Saturday Review* 34 (13 Oct.): 27-28, 64-65.

Brickell, Herschel, ed. 1951. "Introduction." *Prize Stories of 1951: The O. Henry Awards*. Garden City, N.Y.: Doubleday. vii-xxvi.

Joost, Nicholas. 1951. "'Was All for Naught?': Robert Penn Warren and New Directions in the Novel." In *Fifty Years of the American Novel: A Christian Appraisal*. Ed. Harold C. Gardiner, S.J. New York: Scribners. 273-91.

Kohler, Dayton. 1951. "Carson McCullers: Variations on a Theme." *College English* 13 (Oct.): 1-8. Printed simultaneously in *English Journal* 40 (Oct.): 415-22.

Evans, Oliver. 1952. "The Theme of Spiritual Isolation in Carson McCullers." *New World Writing* 1 (Apr.): 297-310. Reprinted in *South: Modern Southern Literature in Its Cultural Setting*. Ed. Louis D. Rubin, Jr., and Robert D. Jacobs. Garden City, N.Y.: Doubleday, 1961. 333-48.

Gassner, John. 1952. *Best American Plays, Third Series: 1945-51*. New York: Crown.

Pritchett, V. S. 1952. "Books in General." *New Statesman and Nation* 44 (2 Aug.): 137-38.

West, Ray B., Jr. 1952. *The Short Story in America, 1900-1950*. Chicago: Regnery.

Clurman, Harold. 1953. "Some Preliminary Notes for *The Member of the Wedding*." In *Directing the Play*. Ed. Toby Cole and Helen Krich Chinoy. Indianapolis: Bobbs-Merrill. 311-20.

De Beauvoir, Simone. 1953. *The Second Sex*. Trans. H. M. Parshley. New York: Knopf.

Nathan, George Jean. 1953. *The Theatre in the Fifties*. New York: Knopf.

[Symons, Julian]. 1953. "Human Isolation." *Times Literary Supplement*, 17 July, p. 460. Reprinted as "The Lonely Heart." In *Critical Occasions*. London: Hamish Hamilton, 1966. 106-11.

Van Druten, John. 1953. *Playwright at Work*. New York: Harper.

[Vidal, Gore]. 1953. "Ladders to Heaven: Novelists and Critics." *New World Writing* 4 (Oct.): 303-16. See Vidal 1962b; reprinted in Kostelanetz 1964.

Clurman, Harold. 1954. "The Kind of Theatre We Have." In *Let's Meet the Theatre*. Ed. Dorothy Samachson and Joseph Samachson. New York: Abelard-Schuman. 73-79.

Cowley, Malcolm. 1954. *The Literary Situation*. New York: Viking.

Gassner, John. 1954. *The Theatre in Our Times: A Survey of the Men, Materials and Movements in the Modern Theatre.* New York: Crown. See Gassner 1964.

Rexroth, Kenneth. 1954. "The Younger Generation and Its Books." In *The Arts at Mid-Century.* Ed. Robert Richman. New York: Horizon. 262–68.

Christie, Erling. 1955. "Carson McCullers og Hjertenes Fangenskap." *Vinduet* (Oslo) 9 (1): 55–62.

Fiedler, Leslie A. 1955. *An End to Innocence: Essays on Culture and Politics.* Boston: Beacon.

Kazin, Alfred. 1955. "We Who Sit in Darkness: The Broadway Audience at the Play." *The Inmost Leaf: A Selection of Essays.* New York: Harcourt Brace. 127–35. See Kazin 1950.

Sievers, W. David. 1955. *Freud on Broadway: A History of Psychoanalysis and the American Drama.* New York: Hermitage House.

Aldridge, John. 1956. *In Search of Heresy: American Literature in an Age of Conformity.* New York: McGraw-Hill. See Aldridge 1967. Reprinted Port Washington, N.Y.: Kennikat, 1967.

Gassner, John. 1956. *Form and Idea in Modern Theatre.* New York: Holt, Rinehart & Winston.

Atkinson, Brooks. 1957. "Theatre: 'Square Root.'" *New York Times,* 31 Oct., p. 40.

Bolton, Whitney. 1957. "Stage Review – 'Square Root' Odd, Rambling, Verbose." *New York Morning Telegraph,* 2 Nov., p. 2.

Carpenter, Frederic I. 1957. "The Adolescent in American Fiction." *English Journal* 46 (Sept.): 313–19.

Clurman, Harold. 1957. "Theatre." *Nation* 185 (23 Nov.): 394.

Coleman, Robert. 1957. "'Square Root of Wonderful' Ain't." *New York Mirror,* 1 Nov., pp. 32, 33.

Driver, Tom F. 1957. "'Mixed Grill.'" *Christian Century* 74 (27 Nov.): 1424–25.

Durham, Frank. 1957. "God and No God in *The Heart Is a Lonely Hunter.*" *South Atlantic Quarterly* 56 (Autumn): 494–99.

Gibbs, Patrick. 1957. "First Night – Sensibility and Style – Tragi-Comedy with Southern Setting." *London Daily Telegraph and Morning Post,* 6 Feb., p. 8.

Gibbs, Wolcott. 1957. "The Theatre: Music and Words." *New Yorker* 33 (9 Nov.): 103–5.

Hart, Jane. 1957. "Carson McCullers, Pilgrim of Loneliness." *Georgia Review* 11 (Spring): 53–58.

McClain, John. 1957. "'The Square Root of Wonderful' – Diffuse Doubletalk Adds Up to Big 0." *New York Journal-American,* 31 Oct., p. 22.

[Morrison], Hobe. 1957. Review of *The Square Root of Wonderful*. *Variety*, 6 Nov., p. 72.

Shulman, Milton. 1957. "Salute for a Valiant Failure." *London Evening Standard*, 6 Feb., p. 10.

Trewin, J. C. 1957. "One of the Party." *Illustrated London News*, 16 Feb., p. 10.

Tynan, Kenneth. 1957. "At the Theatre – Mood Indigo." *London Observer*, 10 Feb., p. 11.

Walter, Eugene. 1957. "A Rainy Afternoon with Truman Capote." *Intro Bulletin* 2 (Dec.): 1–2.

Worsley, T. C. 1957. "Growing Up." *New Statesman and Nation* n.s. 53 (16 Feb.): 201–2.

Baldanza, Frank. 1958. "Plato in Dixie." *Georgia Review* 12 (Summer): 151–67.

Childers, Helen White. 1958. "American Novels about Adolescence, 1917–1953." Ph.D. dissertation, Peabody College, Vanderbilt University.

Fiedler, Leslie A. 1958. "The Profanation of the Child." *New Leader* 41 (23 June): 26–29.

Kronenberger, Louis. 1958. "The Season on Broadway." In *The Best Plays of 1957–1958*. New York: Dodd, Mead. 3–38.

Review of *The Square Root of Wonderful*. 1958. *Theatre Arts* 42 (Jan.): 24.

Tinkham, Charles B. 1958. "The Members of the Side Show." *Phylon* 18 (Oct.): 383–90.

Wyatt, Euphemia Van Rensselaer. 1958. "Theatre." *Catholic World* 185 (Jan.): 304–8.

Brooks, Cleanth, and Robert Penn Warren, eds. 1959. *Understanding Fiction*. 2nd ed. New York: Appleton-Century-Crofts.

Gelb, Arthur. 1959. "Script Revision Held Increasing: Lantz, Producer, Sees Need for Extensive Rewriting." *New York Times*, 21 Oct., p. L49.

Hassan, Ihab H. 1959a. "Carson McCullers: The Alchemy of Love and Aesthetics of Pain." *Modern Fiction Studies* 5 (Winter): 311–26. Reprinted in his *Radical Innocence: Studies in the Contemporary American Novel*. Princeton: Princeton University Press, 1961. 205–29. Reprinted in *Recent American Fiction: Some Critical Views*. Ed. Joseph J. Waldmeir. Boston: Houghton Mifflin, 1963. 215–30.

———. 1959b. "The Victim: Images of Evil in Recent American Fiction." *College English* 21 (Dec.): 140–46.

Johnson, James William. 1959. "The Adolescent Hero: A Trend in Modern Fiction." *Twentieth Century Literature* 5 (Apr.): 3–11.

Stewart, Stanley. 1959. "Carson McCullers, 1940–1956: A Selected Checklist." *Bulletin of Bibliography* 22 (Jan.-Apr.): 182–85.

Abels, Cyrilly, and Margarita G. Smith, eds. 1960. *40 Best Stories from 'Mademoiselle': 1935–1960.* New York: Harper.

Dusenbury, Winifred L. 1960. *The Theme of Loneliness in Modern American Drama.* Gainesville: University of Florida Press.

Fiedler, Leslie A. 1960. *Love and Death in the American Novel.* New York: Stein and Day.

Taylor, Horace. 1960. "*The Heart Is a Lonely Hunter:* A Southern Waste Land." In *Studies in American Literature.* Ed. Waldo McNeir and Leo B. Levy. Baton Rouge: Louisiana State University Press. 154–60.

Thorp, Willard. 1960. "Suggs and Sut in Modern Dress: The Latest Chapter in Southern Humor." *Mississippi Quarterly* 13 (Fall): 169–75.

Vickery, John B. 1960. "Carson McCullers: A Map of Love." *Wisconsin Studies in Contemporary Literature* 1 (Winter): 13–24.

Balliett, Whitney. 1961. Review of *Clock Without Hands. New Yorker* 37 (23 Sept.): 179.

Bowen, Robert O. 1961. Review of *Clock Without Hands. Catholic World* 194 (Dec.): 186–88.

Cheney, Frances Neal. 1961. "Loneliness Continues to Intrigue Southern Writer." *Nashville Banner,* 15 Sept., p. 23.

De Mott, Benjamin. 1961/1962. "Fiction Chronicle." *Hudson Review* 14 (Winter): 622–29.

Falk, Signi Lenea. 1961. *Tennessee Williams.* Twayne's United States Authors Series. New York: Twayne.

"Free from the Fetters of Dogma." 1961. *Times Weekly Review* (London), 26 Oct., p. 10.

"From Life into Death." 1961. *Times Literary Supplement,* 20 Oct., p. 749.

Godden, Rumer. 1961. "Death and Life in a Small Southern Town." *New York Herald Tribune Books,* 17 Sept., p. 5.

Gossett, Louise Young. 1961. "Violence in Recent Southern Fiction." Ph.D. dissertation, Duke University.

Gross, John. 1961. "Paul Masters." *New Statesman* n.s. 62 (27 Oct.): 614–15.

Grumbach, Doris. 1961. Review of *Clock Without Hands. America* 105 (23 Sept.): 809.

Hassan, Ihab. 1961. *Radical Innocence: Studies in the Contemporary American Novel.* Princeton: Princeton University Press. See Hassan 1959a.

Hicks, Granville. 1961. "The Subtler Corruptions." *Saturday Review* 44 (23 Sept.): 14–15, 47.

Howe, Irving. 1961. "In the Shadow of Death." *New York Times Book Review*, 17 Sept., p. 5.

Hughes, Catharine. 1961. "A World of Outcasts." *Commonweal* 75 (13 Oct.): 73–75.

Martin, Jean. 1961. "Ways of Telling It." *Nation* 193 (18 Nov.): 411–12.

"The Member of the Funeral." 1961. *Time* 78 (22 Sept.): 118–20.

Miller, Jordan Y. 1961. *American Dramatic Literature: Ten Modern Plays in Historical Perspective.* New York: McGraw-Hill.

O'Brien, Edna. 1961. "The Strange World of Carson McCullers." *Books and Bookmen* 7 (Oct.): 9, 24.

Parker, Dorothy. 1961. *"Clock Without Hands* Belongs in Yesterday's Tower of Ivory." *Esquire* 56 (Dec.): 72–73.

Quigly, Isabel. 1961. "In the Mind." *Manchester Guardian*, 20 Oct., p. 7.

Raven, Simon. 1961. "Two Kinds of Jungle." *Spectator* 6956 (20 Oct.): 551–52.

Rolo, Charles. 1961. "A Southern Drama." *Atlantic* 208 (Oct.): 126–27.

Rubin, Louis D., Jr., and Robert D. Jacobs, eds. 1961. *South: Modern Southern Literature in Its Cultural Setting.* Garden City, N.Y.: Doubleday. Reprints Evans 1952.

Sherman, John K. 1961. "Carson McCullers Tells a Parable of Loneliness." *Minneapolis Sunday Tribune*, 8 Oct., p. E6.

Sullivan, Oona. 1961. Review of *Clock Without Hands. Jubilee* 9 (Nov.): 55–56.

Tischler, Nancy M. 1961. *Tennessee Williams: Rebellious Puritan.* New York: Citadel.

Toynbee, Philip. 1961. "Mellowing in the South." *London Observer*, 15 Oct., p. 29.

Vidal, Gore. 1961. "The World Outside." *New York Reporter* 25 (28 Sept.): 50, 52.

Walker, Gerald. 1961. "Carson McCullers: Still the Lonely Hunter." *Cosmopolitan* 151 (Nov.): 26–27.

Williams, Tennessee. 1961. "The Author." *Saturday Review* 44 (23 Sept.): 14–15.

Barry, Jackson. 1962. "José Quintero: The Director as Image Maker." *Educational Theatre Journal* 14 (Mar.): 15–22.

Emerson, Donald. 1962. "The Ambiguities of *Clock Without Hands.*" *Wisconsin Studies in Contemporary Literature* 3 (Fall): 15–28.

Evans, Oliver. 1962. "The Achievement of Carson McCullers." *English Journal* 51 (May): 301–8. Reprinted in Bloom 1986.

Folk, Barbara Nauer. 1962. "The Sad Sweet Music of Carson McCullers." *Georgia Review* 16 (Summer): 202–9.

Ford, Nick Aaron. 1962. "Search for Identity: A Critical Survey of Significant Belles-Lettres by and about Negroes Published in 1961." *Phylon* 23 (Summer): 128–38.

Hassan, Ihab H. 1962. "The Character of Post-War Fiction in America." *English Journal* 51 (Jan.): 1–8. See Hassan 1963b and 1964a.

Kazin, Alfred. 1962. "The Alone Generation." In his *Contemporaries*. Boston: Little, Brown. 207–17.

Malin, Irving. 1962. *New American Gothic*. Carbondale: Southern Illinois University Press.

Mitchell, Julian. 1962. Review of *Clock Without Hands*. *London Magazine* n.s. 2 (Apr.): 91, 93, 95.

O'Connor, William Van. 1962. *The Grotesque: An American Genre and Other Essays*. Carbondale: Southern Illinois University Press.

Rubin, Louis D., Jr. 1962. "Six Novels and S. Levin." *Sewanee Review* 70 (Summer): 504–14.

Vande Kieft, Ruth M. 1962. *Eudora Welty*. Twayne's United States Authors Series. New York: Twayne.

Vickery, Olga W. 1962. "Jean Stafford and the Ironic Vision." *South Atlantic Quarterly* 61 (Autumn): 484–91.

Vidal, Gore. 1962a. "Carson McCullers's *Clock Without Hands*." In *Rocking the Boat*. Boston: Little, Brown. 178–83. Reprinted in Bloom 1986.

———. 1962b. "Ladders to Heaven: Novelists and Critics of the 1940's." In *Rocking the Boat*. 125–46. See Vidal 1953.

Weales, Gerald. 1962. *American Drama Since World War II*. New York: Harcourt, Brace & World.

Albee, Edward. 1963. "Carson McCullers – The Case of the Curious Magician." *Harper's Bazaar* 96 (Jan.): 98.

Bradbury, John M. 1963. *Renaissance in the South: A Critical History of the Literature, 1920–1960*. Chapel Hill: University of North Carolina Press.

Dodd, Wayne D. 1963. "The Development of Theme through Symbol in the Novels of Carson McCullers." *Georgia Review* 17 (Summer): 206–13.

Eisinger, Chester E. 1963. "Carson McCullers and the Failure of Dialogue." In *Fiction of the Forties*. Chicago: University of Chicago Press. 243–58.

Hassan, Ihab H. 1963a. "Carson McCullers: The Alchemy of Love and Aesthetics of Pain." In *Recent American Fiction: Some Critical Views*. Ed. Joseph J. Waldmeir. Boston: Houghton Mifflin. 215–30. See Hassan 1959a.

———. 1963b. "The Character of Post-War Fiction in America." In *Recent American Fiction*. 27–35. See Hassan 1962.

———. 1963c. "The Way Down and Out: Spiritual Deflection in Recent American Fiction." *Virginia Quarterly Review* 39 (Winter): 81–93.

Lubbers, Klaus. 1963. "The Necessary Order: A Study of Theme and Structure in Carson McCullers' Fiction." *Jahrbuch für Amerikastudien* 8: 187–204. Reprinted in Bloom 1986.

Schaefer, Ted. 1963. "The Man in the Gray Flannery McCuller-Alls." *Saturday Review* 46 (23 Feb.): 6.

Schorer, Mark. 1963. "McCullers and Capote: Basic Patterns." In *The Creative Present: Notes on Contemporary American Fiction*. Ed. Nona Balakian and Charles Simmons. Garden City, N.Y.: Doubleday. 83–107. Reprinted in his *The World We Imagine: Selected Essays*. New York: Farrar, Straus and Giroux, 1968. 274–96.

Waldmeir, Joseph J., ed. 1963. *Recent American Fiction: Some Critical Views*. Boston: Houghton Mifflin. Reprints Hassan 1959a and Hassan 1962.

Allen, Walter. 1964. *The Modern Novel in Britain and the United States*. New York: Dutton.

Beja, Morris. 1964. "It Must Be Important: Negroes in Contemporary American Fiction." *Antioch Review* 24 (Fall): 323–36.

Evans, Oliver. 1964a. "The Case of Carson McCullers." *Georgia Review* 18 (Spring): 40–45.

———. 1964b. "The Pad in Brooklyn Heights." *Nation* 199 (13 July): 15–16.

Felheim, Marvin. 1964. "Eudora Welty and Carson McCullers." *Contemporary American Novelists*. Ed. Harry T. Moore. Carbondale: Southern Illinois University Press. 41–53.

Gassner, John. 1964. "New American Playwrights: Williams, Miller and Others." *On Contemporary Literature*. Ed. Richard Kostelanetz. New York: Avon Books. 48–63. Excerpts Gassner 1954.

Hassan, Ihab H. 1964a. "The Character of Post-War Fiction in America." In *On Contemporary Literature*. Ed. Richard Kostelanetz. New York: Avon Books. 36–47. See Hassan 1962 and 1963b.

———. 1964b. "Laughter in the Dark: The New Voice in American Fiction." *American Scholar* 33 (Autumn): 636–38, 40.

Kostelanetz, Richard, ed. 1964. *On Contemporary Literature*. New York: Avon Books. Reprints Vidal 1953, Hassan 1962; excerpts Gassner 1954.

Peden, William. 1964. *The American Short Story – The Front Line in the National Defense of Literature*. Boston: Houghton Mifflin.

Phillips, Robert S. 1964a. "Carson McCullers: 1956–1964, A Selected Checklist." *Bulletin of Bibliography* 24 (Sept.-Dec.): 113–16.

———. 1964b. "Dinesen's 'Monkey' and McCullers' 'Ballad': A Study in Literary Affinity." *Studies in Short Fiction* 1 (Spring): 184–90.

———. 1964c. "The Gothic Architecture of *The Member of the Wedding.*" *Renascence* 16 (Winter): 59–72.

Pomeranz, Regina. 1964. "Self-Betrayal in Modern American Fiction." *English Record* 14 (Apr.): 21–28.

Smith, Simeon Mozart, Jr. 1964. "Carson McCullers: A Critical Introduction." Ph.D. dissertation, University of Pennsylvania.

Witham, W. Tasker. 1964. *The Adolescent in the American Novel: 1920–1960.* New York: Ungar.

Auchincloss, Louis. 1965. "Carson McCullers." In *Pioneers and Caretakers: A Study of Nine American Women Novelists.* Minneapolis: University of Minnesota Press. 161–69.

Brustein, Robert. 1965. "The Playwright as Impersonator." *Seasons of Discontent: Dramatic Opinions 1959–1965.* New York: Simon and Schuster. 155–58.

Evans, Oliver. 1965a. *Carson McCullers: Her Life and Work.* London: Peter Owen. Reprinted as *The Ballad of Carson McCullers: A Biography.* New York: Coward-McCann, 1966.

———. 1965b. "The Case of the Silent Singer: A Revaluation of *The Heart Is a Lonely Hunter.*" *Georgia Review* 19 (Summer): 188–203.

Gassner, John. 1965. *Directions in Modern Theatre and Drama.* New York: Holt, Rinehart and Winston.

Gossett, Louise Y. 1965. "Dispossessed Love: Carson McCullers." In *Violence in Recent Southern Fiction.* Durham: Duke University Press. 159–77. See Gossett 1961.

Malin, Irving, ed. 1965. "The Gothic Family." In *Psychoanalysis and American Fiction.* New York: Dutton. 255–77.

Montgomery, Marion. 1965. "The Sense of Violation: Notes toward a Definition of 'Southern' Fiction." *Georgia Review* 19 (Fall): 278–87.

Moore, Jack B. 1965. "Carson McCullers: The Heart Is a Timeless Hunter." *Twentieth Century Literature* 11 (July): 76–81.

Evans, Oliver. 1966. See Evans 1965a.

Klein, Marcus. 1966. "The Key Is Loneliness." *The Reporter* 34 (30 June): 43–44.

Phillips, Robert S. 1966. "Painful Love: Carson McCullers' Parable." *Southwest Review* 51 (Winter): 80–86.

Rubin, Louis D., Jr. 1966. *The Faraway Country: Writers of the Modern South.* Seattle: University of Washington Press.

Sullivan, Margaret Sue. 1966. "Carson McCullers, 1927–1947: The Conversion of Experience." Ph.D. dissertation, Duke University.

Symons, Julian. 1966. See Symons 1953.

Aldridge, John W. 1967. *In Search of Heresy: American Literature in an Age of Conformity.* Port Washington, N.Y.: Kennikat. Reprints Aldridge 1956.

Bluefarb, Samuel. 1967. "The Escape Motif in the Modern American Novel: Mark Twain to Carson McCullers." Ph.D. Dissertation, University of New Mexico.

Burgess, Anthony. 1967. *The Novel Now: A Student's Guide to Contemporary Fiction.* London: Faber & Faber. Reprinted in 1971.

Fremont-Smith, Eliot. 1967. "The Heart Stands Out." *New York Times,* 30 Sept., p. 40.

Griffith, Albert J. 1967. "Carson McCullers' Myth of the Sad Café." *Georgia Review* 21 (Spring): 46–56.

Hoffman, Frederick J. 1967. "Eudora Welty and Carson McCullers." In *The Art of Southern Fiction: A Study of Some Modern Novelists.* Carbondale: Southern Illinois University Press. 51–73.

Levine, Paul. 1967. "The Intemperate Zone: The Climate of Contemporary American Fiction." *Massachusetts Review* 8.3 (Summer): 505–23.

Madden, David. 1967. "The Paradox of the Need for Privacy and the Need for Understanding in Carson McCullers' *The Heart Is a Lonely Hunter.*" *Literature and Psychology* 17.2/3: 128–40.

McGill, Ralph. 1967. "Carson McCullers: 1917–1967." *Saturday Review* 21 Oct.: 31.

Rechnitz, Robert Max. 1967. "Perception, Identity, and the Grotesque: A Study of Three Southern Writers." Ph.D. dissertation, University of Colorado. See Rechnitz 1968.

Rubin, Louis D., Jr. 1967. *The Curious Death of the Novel: Essays in American Literature.* Baton Rouge: Louisiana State University Press.

Drake, Robert. 1968. "The Lonely Heart of Carson McCullers." *Christian Century* 85 (10 Jan.): 50–51.

Dwyer, Rebecca. 1968. "McCullers in Baltimore." *Drama Critique* 11 (Winter): 47–48.

Gozzi, Francesco. 1968. "La Narrativa di Carson McCullers." *Studi Americani* (Rome) 14: 339–76.

Hendrick, George. 1968. "'Almost Everyone Wants to Be the Lover': The Fiction of Carson McCullers." *Books Abroad* 42 (Summer): 389–91.

Madden, David, ed. 1968. "Introduction." In *Proletarian Writers of the Thirties.* Carbondale: Southern Illinois University Press. xv-xlii.

Phillips, Louis. 1968. "The Novelist as Playwright: Baldwin, McCullers, and Bellow." In *Modern American Drama: Essays in Criticism.* Ed. William E. Taylor. De Land, Fla.: Everett/Edwards. 145–62.

Rechnitz, Robert M. 1968. "The Failure of Love: The Grotesque in Two Novels by Carson McCullers." *Georgia Review* 22 (Winter): 454–63. See Rechnitz 1967.

Schorer, Mark. 1968. See Schorer 1963.

Sherrill, Rowland A. 1968. "McCullers' *The Heart Is a Lonely Hunter:* The Missing Ego and the Problem of the Norm." *Kentucky Review* 2 (Feb.): 5–17.

Webb, Constance. 1968. *Richard Wright: A Biography.* New York: Putnam's.

Edmonds, Dale. 1969. *Carson McCullers.* Southern Writers Series, 6. Austin: Steck-Vaughn.

Graver, Lawrence. 1969. *Carson McCullers.* University of Minnesota Pamphlets on American Writers, 84. Minneapolis: University of Minnesota Press. Reprinted in *American Writers: A Collection of Literary Biographies.* Ed. Leonard Unger. 4 vols. New York: Scribners, 1974. 2:585–608. Also reprinted in *Seven American Women Writers of the Twentieth Century.* Ed. Maureen Howard. Minneapolis: University of Minnesota Press, 1977. 265–310. Excerpted as "Penumbral Insistence: McCullers's Early Novels" in Bloom 1986. 53–67.

Knowles, A. S., Jr. 1969. "Six Bronze Petals and Two Red: Carson McCullers in the Forties." In *The Forties: Fiction, Poetry, Drama.* Ed. Warren French. De Land, Fla.: Everett/Edwards. 87–98.

Lawson, Lewis A. 1969. "Kierkegaard and the Modern American Novel." In *Essays in Memory of Christine Burleson in Language and Literature by Former Colleagues and Students.* Ed. Thomas G. Burton. Johnson City: Research Advisory Council, East Tennessee State University. 113–25.

Coale, Samuel Chase, V. 1970. "The Role of the South in the Fiction of William Faulkner, Carson McCullers, Flannery O'Connor, and William Styron." Ph.D. dissertation, Brown University.

Hamilton, Alice. 1970. "Loneliness and Alienation: The Life and Work of Carson McCullers." *Dalhousie Review* 50 (Summer): 215–29.

Mathis, Ray. 1970. "*Reflections in a Golden Eye:* Myth Making in American Christianity." *Religion in Life* 39 (Winter): 545–58.

Millichap, Joseph Robert. 1970. "A Critical Reevaluation of Carson McCullers' Fiction." Ph.D. dissertation, University of Notre Dame.

Moore, Janice Townley. 1970. "McCullers' *The Ballad of the Sad Café.*" *Explicator* 29 (Nov.): no. 27.

Stanley, William T. 1970. "Carson McCullers: 1965–1969, A Selected Checklist." *Bulletin of Bibliography* 27 (Oct.-Dec.): 91–93.

Watkins, Floyd C. 1970. *The Death of Art: Black and White in the Recent Southern Novel.* Mercer University. Lamar Memorial Lectures, 13. Athens: University of Georgia Press.

Clemons, Walter. 1971. "A Memento for Collectors." *New York Times Book Review*, 7 Nov., pp. 7, 12.

Howes, Victor. 1971. "Score for a Typewriter – Alone in a Crowd." *Christian Science Monitor*, 11 Nov., p. B7.

Kazin, Alfred. 1971. "Heroines." *New York Review of Books* 16 (11 Feb.): 28–34.

Millichap, Joseph R. 1971. "The Realistic Structure of *The Heart Is a Lonely Hunter.*" *Twentieth Century Literature* 17 (Jan.): 11–17. See Millichap 1970.

Smith, Margarita G., ed. 1971. "Introduction." In McCullers's *The Mortgaged Heart.* Boston: Houghton Mifflin. xi-xix.

Avant, John Alfred. 1972. Review of *The Mortgaged Heart. Library Journal* 97 (1 Jan.): 73.

Balakian, Nona. 1972. "Love – Perverse and Perfect." *New York Times*, 3 Jan., p. 25.

Bluefarb, Sam. 1972. "Jake Blount: Escape as Dead End." In *The Escape Motif in the American Novel: Mark Twain to Richard Wright.* Columbus: Ohio State University Press. 114–32. See Bluefarb 1967.

Clurman, Harold. 1972. *On Directing.* New York: Macmillan.

Dunn, Douglas. 1972. "Down South." *New Statesman and Nation* n.s. 83 (2 Jun.): 756.

Edmonds, Dale. 1972. "'Correspondence': A 'Forgotten' Carson McCullers Short Story." *Studies in Short Fiction* 9 (Winter): 89–92.

Gaillard, Dawson F. 1972. "The Presence of the Narrator in Carson McCullers' 'The Ballad of the Sad Café.'" *Mississippi Quarterly* 25 (Fall): 419–27.

Gordimer, Nadine. 1972. "A Private Apprenticeship." *London Magazine* 12 (Oct.-Nov.): 134–37.

Grinnell, James W. 1972. "Delving 'A Domestic Dilemma.'" *Studies in Short Fiction* 9 (Summer): 270–71.

Levidova, Inna M. 1972. "Carson McCullers and Her Last Book." In *Soviet Criticism of American Literature in the Sixties.* Ed. Carl R. Proffer. Ann Arbor: Ardis. 88–95.

Madden, David. 1972. "Transfixed Among the Self-Inflicted Ruins: Carson McCullers's *The Mortgaged Heart.*" *Southern Literary Journal* 5 (Fall): 137–62.

Nye, Robert. 1972. "The Making of a Legend." *The Guardian*, 10 June, p. 24.

Presley, Delma Eugene. 1972a. "Carson McCullers' Descent to Earth." *Descant* 17 (Fall): 54–60.

———. 1972b. "The Moral Function of Distortion in Southern Grotesque." *South Atlantic Bulletin* 37 (May): 37–46.

Review of *The Mortgaged Heart.* 1972. *Choice* 9 (Mar.): 61.

Theroux, Paul. 1972. "Early Sparks of a Unique Sensibility." *London Times*, 8 June, p. 10.

Toynbee, Philip. 1972. "Full of the Deep South." *London Observer*, 4 June, p. 33.

Buchen, Irving H. 1973. "Carson McCullers: A Case of Convergence." *Bucknell Review* 21 (Spring): 15–28.

Hassan, Ihab. 1973. *Contemporary American Literature, 1945–1972: An Introduction.* New York: Ungar.

Kazin, Alfred. 1973. *Bright Book of Life: American Storytellers from Hemingway to Mailer.* Boston: Little, Brown.

McNally, John. 1973. "The Introspective Narrator in 'The Ballad of the Sad Café.'" *South Atlantic Bulletin* 38 (Nov.): 40–44.

Millichap, Joseph R. 1973. "Carson McCullers' Literary Ballad." *Georgia Review* 27 (Fall): 329–39.

Presley, Delma Eugene. 1973. "The Man Who Married Carson McCullers." *This Issue* 2.2: 13–16.

Voss, Arthur. 1973. *The American Short Story: A Critical Survey.* Norman: University of Oklahoma Press.

Broughton, Panthea Reid. 1974. "Rejection of the Feminine in Carson McCullers' *The Ballad of the Sad Café.*" *Twentieth Century Literature* 20 (Jan.): 34–43.

Buchen, Irving H. 1974. "Divine Collusion: The Art of Carson McCullers." *Dalhousie Review* 54 (Autumn): 529–41.

Graver, Lawrence. 1974. See Graver 1969.

Miles, Rosalind. 1974. *The Fiction of Sex: Themes and Functions of Sex Difference in the Modern Novel.* New York: Barnes & Noble.

Pachmuss, Temira. 1974. "Dostoèvsky, D. H. Lawrence, and Carson McCullers: Influences and Confluences." *Germano-Slavica* 4 (Fall): 59–68. Partially reprinted in Pachmuss 1981.

Perrine, Laurence. 1974. "Restoring 'A Domestic Dilemma.'" *Studies in Short Fiction* 11 (Winter): 101–4.

Presley, Delma Eugene. 1974. "Carson McCullers and the South." *Georgia Review* 28 (Spring): 19–32.

Bonin, Jane F. 1975. *Major Themes in Prize-winning American Drama.* New York: Scarecrow Press.

Carr, Virginia Spencer. 1975. *The Lonely Hunter: A Biography of Carson McCullers.* Garden City, N.Y.: Doubleday.

Clark, Charlene Kerne. 1975a. "Pathos with a Chuckle: The Tragicomic Vision in the Novels of Carson McCullers." *Studies in American Humor* 1 (Jan.):161–66.

––––. 1975b. "Selfhood and the Southern Past: A Reading of Carson McCullers' *Clock Without Hands.*" *Southern Literary Messenger* 1 (Spring): 16–23.

Cook, Richard M. 1975. *Carson McCullers.* Modern Literature Monographs. New York: Ungar. Excerpted in Bloom 1986.

Dedmond, Francis B. 1975. "Doing Her Own Thing: Carson McCullers' Dramatization of 'The Member of the Wedding.'" *South Atlantic Bulletin* 40 (May): 47–52.

Fletcher, Mary Dell. 1975. "Carson McCullers' 'Ancient Mariner.'" *South Central Bulletin* 35 (Winter): 123–25.

Ginsberg, Elaine. 1975. "The Female Initiation Theme in American Fiction." *Studies in American Fiction* 3 (Spring): 27–37.

Hicks, Granville. 1975. "Books." *American Way* 8 (Aug.): 34–35.

Maddocks, Melvin. 1975. "Little Precious." *Time* 106 (21 July): 63–64.

Wikborg, Eleanor. 1975. *Carson McCullers' "The Member of the Wedding": Aspects of Structure and Style.* Gothenburg Studies in English, 31. Göteborg, Sweden: Acta Universitatus Gothoburgensis.

Carlson, Judith Garrett. 1976. "The Dual Vision: Paradoxes, Opposites, and Doubles in the Novels of Carson McCullers." Ph.D. dissertation, Case Western Reserve University.

Cook, Sylvia Jenkins. 1976. *From Tobacco Road to Route 66: The Southern Poor White in Fiction.* Chapel Hill: University of North Carolina Press.

Giannetti, Louis D. 1976. *"The Member of the Wedding." Literature/Film Quarterly* 4 (Winter): 28–38.

Gillespie, Sheena. 1976. "Dialectical Elements in the Fiction of Carson McCullers: A Comparative Critical Study." Ph.D. dissertation, New York University.

Kiernan, Robert F. 1976. *Katherine Anne Porter and Carson McCullers: A Reference Guide.* Boston: G. K. Hall.

Korenman, Joan S. 1976. "Carson McCullers' 'Proletarian Novel.'" *Studies in the Humanities* 5 (Jan.): 8–13.

MacDonald, Edgar E. 1976. "The Symbolic Unity of *The Heart Is a Lonely Hunter.*" In *A Festschrift for Professor Marguerite Roberts, on the Occasion of Her Retirement from Westhampton College, University of Richmond, Virginia.* Ed. Frieda Elaine Penninger. Richmond: University of Richmond. 168–87.

Moers, Ellen. 1976. *Literary Women.* Garden City, N.Y.: Doubleday.

Rose, Alan Henry. 1976. *Demonic Vision: Racial Fantasy and Southern Fiction.* Hamden, Conn.: Archon. 121–22.

Smith, Christopher Michael. 1976. "Self and Society: The Dialectic of Themes and Forms in the Novels of Carson McCullers." Ph.D. dissertation, University of North Carolina at Greensboro.

Sullivan, Walter. 1976. *A Requiem for the Renascence: The State of Fiction in the Modern South.* Athens: University of Georgia Press.

Walker, Sue. B. 1976/1977. "The Link in the Chain Called Love: A New Look at Carson McCullers' Novels." *Mark Twain Journal* 18 (Winter): 8–12.

Wallace, Harry Joseph. 1976. "'Lifelessness Is the Only Abnormality': A Study of Love, Sex, Marriage, and Family in the Novels of Carson McCullers." Ph.D. dissertation, University of Maryland.

Cervantes Leal, Alicia M. 1977. "Las Imagines Musicales en la Obra de McCullers." *Káñina* 1.1 (Jan.-June): 23–30.

Graver, Lawrence. 1977. See Graver 1969.

Gray, Richard. 1977. "Moods and Absences: Carson McCullers." In *The Literature of Memory: Modern Writers of the American South.* Baltimore: Johns Hopkins University Press. 265–73. Reprinted in Bloom 1986.

Howard, Maureen, ed. 1977. Introduction. In *Seven American Women Writers of the Twentieth Century: An Introduction.* Minneapolis: University of Minnesota Press.

Millichap, Joseph R. 1977. "Distorted Matter and Disjunctive Forms: The Grotesque As Modernist Genre." *Arizona Quarterly* 33 (Winter): 339–47.

Rich, Nancy B. 1977. "The 'Ironic Parable of Fascism' in *The Heart Is a Lonely Hunter.*" *Southern Literary Journal* 9 (Spring): 108–23.

Rubin, Louis D., Jr. 1977. "Carson McCullers: The Aesthetic of Pain." *Virginia Quarterly Review* 53 (Spring): 265–83.

Shapiro, Adrian Michael. 1977. "Carson McCullers: A Descriptive Bibliography." Ph.D. dissertation, Indiana University. See Shapiro et al. 1980.

Aldridge, Robert. 1978. "Two Planetary Systems." In *The Modern American Novel and the Movies.* Ungar Film Library. Ed. Gerald Peary and Roger Shatzkin. New York: Ungar. 119–30.

Bolsterli, Margaret. 1978. "'Bound' Characters in Porter, Welty, McCullers: The Prerevolutionary Status of Women in American Fiction." *Bucknell Review* 24 (Spring): 95–105.

Box, Patricia S. 1978. "Androgyny and the Musical Vision: A Study of Two Novels by Carson McCullers." *Southern Quarterly* 16 (Jan.): 117–23.

Phillips, Robert S. 1978. "Freaking Out: The Short Stories of Carson McCullers." *Southwest Review* 63 (Winter): 65–73.

Clark, Charlene Kerne. 1979. "Male-Female Pairs in Carson McCullers' *The Ballad of the Sad Café* and *The Member of the Wedding*." *Notes on Contemporary Literature* 9 (Jan.): 11–12.

Smith, C. Michael. 1979. "'A Voice in a Fugue': Characters and Musical Structure in *The Heart Is a Lonely Hunter*." *Modern Fiction Studies* 25: 258–63.

Spivak, Gayatri Chakravorty. 1979/1980. "Three Feminist Readings: McCullers, Drabble, Habermas." *Union Seminary Quarterly Review* 35.1/2 (Fall/Winter): 15–34.

Westling, Louise. 1979. "The Perils of Adolescence in Flannery O'Connor and Carson McCullers." *Flannery O'Connor Bulletin* 8: 88–98.

Cervantes Leal, Alicia. 1980. "Los elementos grotescos en la narrativa de Carson McCullers." *Káñina: Revista de Artes y Letras de la Universidad de Costa Rica* 4 (July-Dec.): 117–21.

McDowell, Margaret. 1980. *Carson McCullers.* Twayne's United States Authors Series. Boston: Twayne. Excerpted in Bloom 1986.

Raczkowska, Marzenna. 1980. "The Patterns of Love in Carson McCullers' Fiction." *Studia Anglica Posnaniensia* 12: 169–76.

Roberts, Mary. 1980. "Imperfect Androgyny and Imperfect Love in the Works of Carson McCullers." *Studies in Literature* 12: 73–98.

Shapiro, Adrian M., Jackson R. Bryer, and Kathleen Field. 1980. *Carson McCullers: A Descriptive Listing and Annotated Bibliography of Criticism.* New York and London: Garland. See Shapiro 1977.

Westling, Louise. 1980. "Carson McCullers's Tomboys." *Southern Humanities Review* 14: 339–50.

Whittle, Amberys R. 1980. "McCullers' 'The Twelve Mortal Men' and *The Ballad of the Sad Café*." *American Notes and Queries* 18 (June):158–59.

Hammer, Andrea Gale. 1981. "Recitations of the Past: Identity in Novels by Edith Wharton, Ellen Glasgow, and Carson McCullers." Ph.D. dissertation, University of California, Davis.

Huf, Linda. 1981. "Portrait of the Artist as a Young Woman: The Female 'Kunstlerromane' in America." Ph.D. Dissertation, University of Maryland. See Huf 1983.

Olavson, Judith. 1981. *The American Woman Playwright: A View of Criticism and Characterization.* Troy, N.Y.: Whitston.

Pachmuss, Temira. 1981. "Dostoevsky and America's Southern Women Writers: Parallels and Confluences." In *Poetica Slavica: Studies in Honour of Zbigniew Folejewski.* Ed. J. Douglas Clayton and Gunter Schaarschmidt. Ottawa: University of Ottawa Press. 115–26. See Pachmuss 1974.

Scott, Mary Etta. 1981. "An Existential Everyman." *West Virginia University Philological Papers* 27: 82–88.

Gannon, Barbara C. 1982. "McCullers' 'Ballad of the Sad Café.'" *Explicator* 41 (Fall): 59–60.

Havely, Cicely Palser. 1982. "Two Women Novelists: Carson McCullers and Flannery O'Connor." In *The Uses of Fiction: Essays on the Modern Novel in Honour of Arnold Kettle.* Ed. Douglas Jefferson and Graham Martin. Milton Keynes, England: Open University Press. 115–24.

Kelly, Patricia P. 1982. "Recommended: Carson McCullers." *English Journal* 71 (Oct.): 67–68.

Levy, Helen Fiddyment. 1982. "No Hiding Place on Earth: The Female Self in Eight Modern American Women Authors." Ph.D. dissertation, University of Michigan.

Paden, Frances Freeman. 1982. "Autistic Gestures in *The Heart Is a Lonely Hunter.*" *Modern Fiction Studies* 28 (Autumn): 453–63.

Snider, Clifton. 1982. "On Death and Dying: Carson McCullers's *Clock Without Hands.*" *Markham Review* 11 (Spring): 43–46.

Westling, Louise. 1982. "Carson McCullers' Amazon Nightmare." *Modern Fiction Studies* 28 (Autumn): 465–73. Reprinted in Bloom 1986.

Wilcox, Earl J. 1982/1983. "And Then There Were Four: Carson McCullers' Place in Southern Literature." *McNeese Review* 29: 3–12.

Carr, Virginia Spencer, and Joseph R. Millichap. 1983. "Carson McCullers." In *American Women Writers: Bibliographical Essays.* Ed. Maurice Duke, Jackson R. Bryer, and M. Thomas Inge. Westport, Conn.: Greenwood. 297–319.

Haar, Maria. 1983. *The Phenomenon of the Grotesque in Modern Southern Fiction: Some Aspects of Its Form and Function.* Umea Studies in the Humanities 51. Stockholm, Sweden: Acta Universitatis Umensis.

Huf, Linda. 1983. *A Portrait of the Artist as a Young Woman: The Writer as Heroine in American Literature.* New York: Ungar. See Huf 1981.

Snider, Clifton. 1984. "Jungian Theory, Its Literary Application, and a Discussion of *The Member of the Wedding.*" In *Psychological Perspectives on Literature: Freudian Dissidents and Non-Freudians: A Casebook.* Ed. Joseph Natoli. Hamden, Conn.: Archon. 13–42.

Coale, Samuel Chase. 1985. *In Hawthorne's Shadow: American Romance from Melville to Mailer.* Lexington: University Press of Kentucky. See Coale 1970.

Dazey, Mary Ann. 1985. "Two Voices of the Single Narrator in *The Ballad of the Sad Café.*" *Southern Literary Journal* 17 (Spring): 33–40. Reprinted in Bloom 1986.

Kahane, Claire. 1985. "The Gothic Mirror." In *The (M)other Tongue: Essays in Feminist Psychoanalytic Interpretation.* Ed. Shirley Nelson Garner, Claire Kahane, and Madelon Sprengnether. Ithaca: Cornell University Press. 334–51.

Karl, Frederick R. 1985. *American Fictions, 1940–1980: A Comprehensive History and Critical Evaluation.* New York: Harper & Row.

Katsurada, Shigetoshi. 1985. "Carson McCullers' 'Eye.'" *Poetica* 21/22: 156–63.

Kinnebrew, Mary Jane. 1985. "The Importance of Dialect Variation in *The Heart Is a Lonely Hunter* and *The Member of the Wedding.*" *Language and Literature* 10: 75–93.

Matsudaira, Yoko. 1985. "On *Reflections in a Golden Eye.*" *Shoin Literary Review* 19: 69–85.

Millichap, Joseph R. 1985. "Carson McCullers." In *The History of Southern Literature.* Ed. Louis D. Rubin, Jr., et al. Baton Rouge: Louisiana State University Press. 486–88.

Westling, Louise. 1985. *Sacred Groves and Ravaged Gardens: The Fiction of Eudora Welty, Carson McCullers, and Flannery O'Connor.* Athens: University of Georgia Press.

White, Barbara A. 1985. "Loss of Self in Carson McCullers' *The Member of the Wedding.*" In *Growing Up Female: Adolescent Girlhood in American Fiction.* Westport, Conn.: Greenwood. 89–111. See White 1975. Excerpted in Bloom 1986.

Bloom, Harold, ed. 1986. *Carson McCullers.* Modern Critical Views. New York: Chelsea. Reprints Young 1947; Williams 1950; Vidal 1962a; Evans 1962; Lubbers 1963; Gray 1977; Westling 1982; Dazey 1985. Excerpts Cook 1975; McDowell 1980; White 1985.

Dalsimer, Katherine. 1986. *Female Adolescence: Psychoanalytic Reflections on Works of Literature.* New Haven: Yale University Press.

Matsudaira, Yoko. 1986. "Some Transformations in *The Ballad of the Sad Cafe.*" *Shoin Literary Review* 20: 51–66.

Perry, Constance M. 1986. "Carson McCullers and the Female *Wunderkind.*" *Southern Literary Journal* 19 (Fall): 36–45.

Petry, Alice Hall. 1986. "Baby Wilson Redux: McCullers' *The Heart Is a Lonely Hunter.*" *Southern Studies* 25 (Summer): 196–203.

Burdison, Neva Evonne. 1987. "The Making of 'The Member of the Wedding': Novel, Play and Film." Ph.D. dissertation, University of Mississippi.

Carr, Virginia Spencer. 1987a. "Carson McCullers: Novelist Turned Playwright." *Southern Quarterly* 25 (Spring): 37–51.

———. 1987b. "Introduction." In McCullers's *Collected Stories*. Boston: Houghton Mifflin. vii-xv.

Dieckmann, Katherine. 1987. "Loners and Other Strangers: Growing Up with Carson McCullers." *Village Voice* (20 Oct.): 58.

Fuller, Janice. 1987/1988. "The Conventions of Counterpoint and Fugue in *The Heart Is a Lonely Hunter*." *Mississippi Quarterly* 41 (Winter): 55–67.

Kakutani, Michiko. 1987. "Books of the Times." *New York Times*, 14 July, p. C20.

Lynskey, Edward C. 1987. *Library Journal* 112 (Aug.): 143.

Matsudaira, Yoko. 1987. "Continuity and Discontinuity." *Shoin Literary Review* 21: 53–66.

Nagpal, Pratibha. 1987. "The Element of Grotesque in *Reflections in a Golden Eye* and *Ballad of the Sad Café* by Carson McCullers." *Panjab University Research Bulletin* 18 (Oct.): 61–66.

Robertson, Peter L. 1987. "Upfront: Advance Reviews." *Booklist*, 1 June, pp. 1466–67.

"Selected Short Notices." 1987. *Kirkus Reviews* 55 (1 June): 832.

Bauerly, Donna. 1988. "Themes of Eros and Agape in the Major Fiction of Carson McCullers." *Pembroke Magazine* 20: 72–76.

Carlton, Ann. 1988. "Beyond Gothic and Grotesque: A Feminist View of Three Female Characters of Carson McCullers." *Pembroke Magazine* 20: 54–62.

Desmond, John F. 1988. Review of *Collected Stories*. *World Literature Today* 62 (Summer): 458.

Farrelly, Barbara A. 1988. *"The Heart Is a Lonely Hunter:* A Literary Symphony." *Pembroke Magazine* 20: 16–23.

Frazier, Adelaide H. 1988. "Terminal Metaphors for Love." *Pembroke Magazine* 20: 77–81.

Gervin, Mary A. 1988. "McCullers' Frames of Reference in *The Ballad of the Sad Café*." *Pembroke Magazine* 20: 37–42.

Hubert, Linda. 1988. "To Alice Walker: Carson McCullers' Legacy of Love." *Pembroke Magazine* 20: 89–95.

Kestler, Frances. 1988. "Gothic Influence of the Grotesque Characters of *The Lonely Hunter*." *Pembroke Magazine* 20: 30–36.

Kimball, Sue L. 1988. "Reflections on *Reflections*." *Pembroke Magazine* 20: 4–8.

Madden, David. 1988. "Tennessee and Carson: Notes on a Concept for a Play." *Pembroke Magazine* 20: 96–103.

Matsudaira, Yoko. 1988. "Time and Identity." *Shoin Literary Review* 22: 75–88.

Petry, Alice Hall. 1988. "Carson McCullers's Precocious 'Wunderkind.'" *Southern Quarterly* 26 (Spring): 31–39.

Portada, Arleen. 1988. "Sex-Role Rebellion and the Failure of Marriage in the Fiction of Carson McCullers." *Pembroke Magazine* 20: 63–71.

Runte, Annette. 1988. "'Im Kreis des Begehrens': Zur semantischen und narrativen Funktion der Gesichtssymbolik in Carson McCullers Roman *The Heart Is a Lonely Hunter* (1940) und Truman Capotes Roman *Other Voices, Other Rooms* (1948)." *Forum Homosexualität und Literatur* 3: 51–77.

Sadler, Lynn Veach. 1988. "'Fixed in an inlay of mystery': Language and Reconciliation in Carson McCullers' *Clock Without Hands*." *Pembroke Magazine* 20: 49–53.

Slabey, Robert M. 1988. "Clocks without Hands: Rilke and McCullers." *Notes on Contemporary Literature* 18 (Jan.): 3–4.

Sosnoski, Karen. 1988. "Society's Freaks: The Effects of Sexual Stereotyping in Carson McCullers' Fiction." *Pembroke Magazine* 20: 82–88.

Thomas, Leroy. 1988. "Carson McCullers: The Plight of the Lonely Heart." *Pembroke Magazine* 20: 10–15.

Walsh, Margaret. 1988. "Carson McCullers' Anti-Fairy Tale: 'The Ballad of the Sad Café.'" *Pembroke Magazine* 20: 43–48.

Whitt, Mary A. 1988. "The Mutes in McCullers' *The Heart Is a Lonely Hunter*." *Pembroke Magazine* 20: 24–29.

Johstoneaux, Raphael B. 1989. "The Forces of Dehumanization: *Reflections in a Golden Eye*." *Encyclia* 66: 97–104.

Messent, Peter. 1989. "Continuity and Change in the Southern Novella." In *The Modern American Novella*. Ed. A. Robert Lee. London: Vision Press. 113–38.

Miyashita, Masatoshi. 1989. "An Introduction to the American Plot of Self-(Re)Naming." *Language and Culture* 17: 177–94.

Carr, Virginia Spencer. 1990. *Understanding Carson McCullers*. Understanding Contemporary American Literature. Columbia: University of South Carolina Press.

Chamlee, Kenneth D. 1990. "Cafés and Community in Three McCullers Novels." *Studies in American Fiction* 18 (Autumn): 233–40.

McBride, Mary. 1990. "Loneliness and Longing in Selected Plays of Carson McCullers and Tennessee Williams." In *Modern American Drama: The Female Canon*. Ed. June Schlueter. Rutherford, N.J.: Fairleigh Dickinson University Press. 143–50.

Champion, Laurie. 1991. "Black and White Christs in Carson McCullers's *The Heart Is a Lonely Hunter*." *Southern Literary Journal* 24 (Fall): 47–52.

Kissel, Susa S. 1991. "Carson McCullers's 'Wunderkind': A Case Study in Female Adolescence." *Kentucky Philological Review* 6: 15–20.

Taetzsch, L. 1992. "Crossing Trajectories in *The Heart Is a Lonely Hunter*." *New Orleans Review* 19 (Fall-Winter): 192–99.

Whitt, Jan. 1992. "The Loneliest Hunter." *Southern Literary Journal* 24 (Spring): 26–35.

Stafford, Tony J. 1993. "'Gray Eyes Is Glass': Image and Theme in *The Member of the Wedding*." *American Drama* 3 (Fall): 54–66.

Vande Kieft, Ruth M. 1993. "The Love Ethos of Porter, Welty, and McCullers." In *The Female Tradition in Southern Literature*. Ed. Carol S. Manning. Urbana: University of Illinois Press. 235–58.

Other Secondary Works

Fromm, Erich. 1941. *Escape from Freedom*. New York: Rinehart.

Brooks, Cleanth, and Robert Penn Warren, eds. 1943. *Understanding Fiction*. New York: Appleton-Century-Crofts.

Fromm, Erich. 1947. *Man for Himself: An Inquiry into the Psychology of Ethics*. New York: Rinehart.

Schorer, Mark. 1948. "Technique as Discovery." *Hudson Review* 1 (Spring): 67–87.

Wellek, René, and Austin Warren. 1949. *Theory of Literature*. New York: Harcourt, Brace.

Fromm, Erich. 1950. *Psychoanalysis and Religion*. New Haven: Yale University Press.

Riesman, David. 1950. *The Lonely Crowd: A Study of the Changing American Character*. New Haven: Yale University Press.

Schneider, Daniel E. 1950. *The Psychoanalyst and the Artist*. New York: New American Library.

Auden, W. H., ed. 1952. *The Living Thoughts of Kierkegaard*. Living Thoughts Library, 23. New York: McKay.

Riesman, David. 1952. *Faces in the Crowd: Individual Studies in Character and Politics*. New Haven: Yale University Press.

Riesman, David. 1954. *Individualism Reconsidered, and Other Essays*. Glencoe, Ill.: Free Press.

Fromm, Erich. 1955. *The Sane Society*. New York: Rinehart.

Geismar, Maxwell. 1956. "Higher and Higher Criticism." *Nation* 10 Nov. Reprinted in his *American Moderns: From Rebellion to Conformity*. American Century Series. New York: Hill and Wang, 1958. 28–33.

Hoffman, Frederick J. 1957. *Freudianism and the Literary Mind*. 2nd ed. Baton Rouge: Louisiana State University Press.

Lesser, Simon O. 1957. *Fiction and the Unconscious*. Boston: Beacon.

Packard, Vance. 1957. *The Hidden Persuaders*. New York: McKay.

Geismar, Maxwell. 1958. See Geismar 1956.

Packard, Vance. 1959. *The Status Seekers: An Exploration of Class Behavior in America and the Hidden Barriers That Affect You, Your Community, Your Future*. New York: McKay.

Fraiberg, Louis. 1960. *Psychoanalysis and American Literary Criticism*. Detroit: Wayne State University Press.

Ransom, John Crowe, ed. 1968. *The New Criticism*. Norfolk, Conn.: New Directions. Reprinted Westport, Conn.: Greenwood, 1979.

Heilbrun, Carolyn G. 1973. *Toward a Recognition of Androgyny*. New York: Knopf.

Ohmann, Carol, and Richard Ohmann. 1976. "Reviewers, Critics, and *The Catcher in the Rye*." *Critical Inquiry* 3 (Autumn): 15–37.

Schwartz, Lawrence H. 1988. *Creating Faulkner's Reputation: The Politics of Modern Literary Criticism*. Knoxville: University of Tennessee Press.

Touchton, Judith G., and Lynne Davis. 1991. *Fact Book on Women in Higher Education*. New York: Macmillan.

Breines, Wini. 1992. *Young, White, and Miserable: Growing Up Female in the Fifties*. Boston: Beacon.

Index